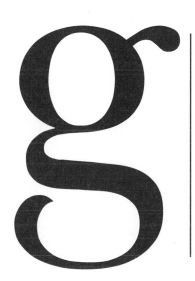

SENTENCE CORRECTION

Verbal Strategy Guide

This essential guide takes the guesswork out of grammar by presenting all the major grammatical principles and minor grammatical points known to be tested on the GMAT.

Do not be caught relying only on your ear; master the rules for correcting every GMAT sentence.

Sentence Correction GMAT Strategy Guide, Third Edition

10-digit International Standard Book Number: 0-9818533-6-6
13-digit International Standard Book Number: 978-0-9818533-6-9

8 GUIDE INSTRUCTIONAL SERIES

Math GMAT Strategy Guides

Number Properties (ISBN: 978-0-9818533-4-5)

Fractions, Decimals, & Percents (ISBN: 978-0-9818533-2-1)

Equations, Inequalities, & VICs (ISBN: 978-0-9818533-1-4)

Word Translations (ISBN: 978-0-9818533-7-6)

Geometry (ISBN: 978-0-9818533-3-8)

Verbal GMAT Strategy Guides

Critical Reasoning (ISBN: 978-0-9818533-0-7)

Reading Comprehension (ISBN: 978-0-9818533-5-2)

Sentence Correction (ISBN: 978-0-9818533-6-9)

ManhattanGMAT
the new standard

September 30th, 2008

Dear Student,

Thank you for picking up one of the Manhattan GMAT Strategy Guides—we hope that this book refreshes your memory of the grammar that you learned a long time ago. Maybe it will even teach you a new thing or two.

As with most accomplishments, there were many people involved in the various iterations of the book that you're holding. First and foremost is Zeke Vanderhoek, the founder of Manhattan GMAT. Zeke was a lone tutor in New York when he started the Company in 2000. Now, eight years later, MGMAT has Instructors and offices nationwide, and the Company contributes to the studies and successes of thousands of students each year.

These 3rd Edition Strategy Guides have been refashioned and honed based upon the continuing experiences of our Instructors and our students. We owe much of these latest editions to the insight provided by our students. On the Company side, we are indebted to many of our Instructors, including but not limited to Josh Braslow, Dan Gonzalez, Mike Kim, Stacey Koprince, Jadran Lee, Ron Purewal, Tate Shafer, Emily Sledge, and of course Chris Ryan, the Company's Lead Instructor and Director of Curriculum Development.

At Manhattan GMAT, we continually aspire to provide the best Instructors and resources possible. We hope that you'll find our dedication manifest in this book. If you have any comments or questions, please e-mail me at andrew.yang@manhattangmat.com. I'll be sure that your comments reach Chris and the rest of the team—and I'll read them too.

Best of luck in preparing for the GMAT!

Sincerely,

Andrew Yang
Chief Executive Officer
Manhattan GMAT

HOW TO ACCESS YOUR ONLINE RESOURCES

Please read this entire page of information, all the way down to the bottom of the page! This page describes WHAT online resources are included with the purchase of this book and HOW to access these resources.

If you are a registered Manhattan GMAT student and have received this book as part of your course materials, you have AUTOMATIC access to ALL of our online resources. This includes all practice exams, question banks, and online updates to this book. To access these resources, follow the instructions in the Welcome Guide provided to you at the start of your program. Do NOT follow the instructions below.

If you have purchased this book, your purchase includes 1 YEAR OF ONLINE ACCESS to the following:

> **6 Computer Adaptive Online Practice Exams**
>
> **Bonus Online Question Bank for *SENTENCE CORRECTION***
>
> **Online Updates to the Content in this Book**

The 6 full-length computer adaptive practice exams included with the purchase of this book are delivered online using Manhattan GMAT's proprietary computer-adaptive test engine. The exams adapt to your ability level by drawing from a bank of more than 1,200 unique questions of varying difficulty levels written by Manhattan GMAT's expert instructors, all of whom have scored in the 99th percentile on the Official GMAT. At the end of each exam you will receive a score, an analysis of your results, and the opportunity to review detailed explanations for each question. You may choose to take the exams timed or untimed.

The Bonus Online Question Bank for *SENTENCE CORRECTION* consists of 25 extra practice questions (with detailed explanations) that test the variety of Sentence Correction concepts and skills covered in this book. These questions provide you with extra practice *beyond* the problem sets contained in this book. You may use our online timer to practice your pacing by setting time limits for each question in the bank.

The content presented in this book is updated periodically to ensure that it reflects the GMAT's most current trends. You may view all updates, including any known errors or changes, upon registering for online access.

Important Note: The 6 computer adaptive online exams included with the purchase of this book are the SAME exams that you receive upon purchasing ANY book in Manhattan GMAT's 8 Book Strategy Series. On the other hand, the Bonus Online Question Bank for *SENTENCE CORRECTION* is a unique resource that you receive ONLY with the purchase of this specific title.

To access the online resources listed above, you will need this book in front of you and you will need to register your information online. This book includes access to the above resources for ONE PERSON ONLY.

To register and start using your online resources, please go online to the following URL:

http://www.manhattangmat.com/access.cfm   (Double check that you have typed this in accurately!)

Your one year of online access begins on the day that you register at the above URL. You only need to register your product ONCE at the above URL. To use your online resources any time AFTER you have completed the registration process, please login to the following URL:

http://www.manhattangmat.com/practicecenter.cfm

Manhattan GMAT Prep
the new standard

TABLE OF CONTENTS

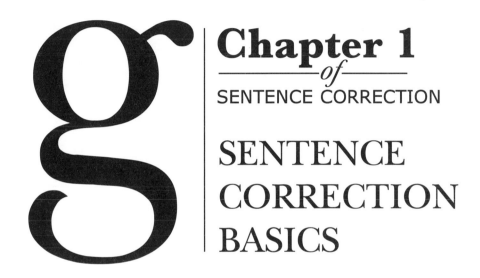

g

Chapter 1
of
SENTENCE CORRECTION

SENTENCE CORRECTION BASICS

In This Chapter . . .

SENTENCE CORRECTION BASICS

Sentence Correction is one of three question types found in the verbal section of the GMAT. Sentence Correction tests mastery of the rules of formal written English. If you master the rules, you can make significant gains in your performance on this question type.

Question Format

The format of a Sentence Correction question is extremely consistent. Read through the sample question below:

> Although William Pereira first gained national recognition for his movie set designs, <u>including those for the 1942 film "Reap the Wild Wind," future generations</u> remember him as the architect of the Transamerica Tower, the Malibu campus of Pepperdine University, and the city of Irvine.
>
> (A) including those for the 1942 film "Reap the Wild Wind," future generations
> (B) like that for the 1942 film "Reap the Wild Wind," future generations will
> (C) like those for the 1942 film "Reap the Wild Wind," future generations
> (D) including that for the 1942 film "Reap the Wild Wind," future generations will
> (E) including those for the 1942 film "Reap the Wild Wind," future generations will

The question consists of a given sentence, part of which is underlined. As in the example above, the underlined segment may be only a small part of the entire sentence. However, the underlined segment may include most or even all of the original sentence. The five answer choices are possible replacements for the underlined segment (if the entire sentence is underlined, each of the answer choices will be a complete sentence). If you look closely at the example above, you may notice something about answer choice **(A)**. In the example above, and in **all Sentence Correction** questions, choice **(A)** is exactly the same as the underlined portion of the sentence above it. The other choices, however, offer different options. The question you are answering in Sentence Correction is always the same: **which of the answer choices, when placed in the given sentence, is the best option of those given, in terms of grammar, meaning and concision** (all of which will be discussed in depth in later chapters). By the way, answer choice **(A)** is not always wrong. The original sentence, **(A)**, is the correct answer just as often as the other answer choices—about 20% of the time.

"Best" Does Not Mean Ideal

It is very important to recognize that Sentence Correction questions ask for the best option of *those given*, not the best option in the *universe*. Indeed, often you will feel—and rightly so—that all the answers, including the correct one, "sound bad." Correct GMAT Sentence Correction answers can sound very formal or awkward, so it is important to keep in mind that **your task is to evaluate the given answer choices, not to create the ideal sentence**. The ideal sentence often is not an option, and the right answer may sound rather wrong. To complicate matters, incorrect answer choices often sound right. Indeed, the GMAT exploits the fact that the English we hear is commonly riddled with grammatical mistakes.

Do not rewrite the sentence in your own words! You must choose the best answer choice from among those available.

Splits and Re-Splits

If you have not already chosen an answer for the sample question, go ahead and do so now:

> Although William Pereira first gained national recognition for his movie set designs, <u>including those for the 1942 film "Reap the Wild Wind," future generations</u> remember him as the architect of the Transamerica Tower, the Malibu campus of Pepperdine University, and the city of Irvine.

(A) including those for the 1942 film "Reap the Wild Wind," future generations
(B) like that for the 1942 film "Reap the Wild Wind," future generations will
(C) like those for the 1942 film "Reap the Wild Wind," future generations
(D) including that for the 1942 film "Reap the Wild Wind," future generations will
(E) including those for the 1942 film "Reap the Wild Wind," future generations will

Usually, the easiest splits to spot are at the beginning or end of the answer choices.

Now, how did you solve this question? Did you read the full sentence and then compare the answer choices by re-reading the sentence with each of the possible answers? That is a very common strategy, but it is one that you cannot afford. In order to complete the entire Verbal section, including the many time-consuming Reading Comprehension and Critical Reading questions, you should take no more than 90 seconds on average to answer a Sentence Correction question. In fact, consider setting your goal to 1 minute per Sentence Correction question.

The key to answering Sentence Correction questions within this time frame is to **split the answer choices** after you have read the given sentence. Follow these steps:

1. Write down "A   B   C   D   E" on your paper (or yellow tablet if you are taking the actual test). It does not matter if you write this horizontally or vertically.

2. Read the sentence, noting any obvious errors as you read.

3. Scan the answer choices vertically—do not read them—looking for differences that split the answer choices. For example, in the sample question above, you can split the answers between those that begin with *including* and those that begin with *like*. Similarly, at the end of the answers, there is a split between those with *will* and those without *will* (essentially a split between the present and the future tense of *remember*). Ideal splits will divide the answer choices into a 2–3 split (two choices with one option, three with the other). Sometimes you will find a three-way split (for example, another problem might have *have lifted*, *lifted* and *have been lifted* among the answer choices). A three-way split is useful as long as you can eliminate at least one of the options. If you identify a split that distinguishes only one answer choice from the others (a 1–4 split) and you eliminate the choice represented by only one answer choice, you will end up eliminating only that one answer. Thus, 1–4 splits are less useful than other kinds of splits, though they should still be considered.

4. Choose a split for which you <u>**know** the grammatical rule and which side of the split is correct</u>. Sometimes you find a split, but you do not know which side is correct. In this case, maybe you did not yet master the relevant rule. Alternatively, the split might be a "red herring split," meaning that both sides of the split are grammatically correct.

5. On your paper, cross out the answer choices that include the incorrect side of the split.

6. Compare the remaining answer choices by **re-splitting**. Continue to find differences in the answers, but make sure you use only the answer choices that remain from your initial split.

7. Continue to split remaining choices until you have one answer left.

Splitting and Re-Splitting is the foundation of the Manhattan GMAT approach to Sentence Correction questions, so it is worth walking through the process with our sample question:

> Although William Pereira first gained national recognition for his movie set designs, <u>including those for the 1942 film "Reap the Wild Wind," future generations</u> remember him as the architect of the Transamerica Tower, the Malibu campus of Pepperdine University, and the city of Irvine.
>
> (A) including those for the 1942 film "Reap the Wild Wind," future generations
> (B) like that for the 1942 film "Reap the Wild Wind," future generations will
> (C) like those for the 1942 film "Reap the Wild Wind," future generations
> (D) including that for the 1942 film "Reap the Wild Wind," future generations will
> (E) including those for the 1942 film "Reap the Wild Wind," future generations will

After reading the sentence and scanning the answer choices, you may notice that the answer choices have a 3–2 split between *including* and *like*. Let us assume that we do not know the rule for this issue (or whether it is a red herring split); another split needs to be found. Fortunately, there is another 3–2 split at the end of the answers: *will remember* versus *remember*. The rule for this split is clear. Since the subject of that verb is *future generations*, any action assigned to those generations, including remembering, must be in the future tense. Therefore, answer choices **(A)** and **(C)** can be eliminated.

Next, as we compare **(B)**, **(D)** and **(E)**, we find a split between *those* and *that*. Since the word *that* or *those* refers to *movie set designs*, a plural noun, it is incorrect to use the singular pronoun *that*. We must use the plural pronoun *those*. Therefore answers **(B)** and **(D)** can be eliminated, leaving us with the correct answer, **(E)**.

In fact, we could have split the answer choices using *including* versus *like*. According to the GMAT, *like* cannot introduce examples (*such as* must be used instead). Since the underlined segment begins with an example of a set that William Pereira designed, answer choices **(B)** and **(C)** can be eliminated. Using *like* alters the meaning of the sentence, suggesting that William Pereira's designs were simply *similar to* the designs for "Reap the Wind."

If it seems daunting to master every rule of the English language tested by the GMAT, it may be comforting to know that, as we saw in the sample question above, most Sentence Correction questions test several different rules at once. Therefore, most answer choices can be eliminated for multiple reasons. During your review, you should master all the rules tested by a particular problem, but on test day, you only need to find one way to the right answer. Moreover, the GMAT tests only a finite number of grammatical principles, all of which are discussed in the following chapters.

Most Sentence Correction problems test multiple issues of grammar and style. During the exam, you need only one path to the right answer.

Reading the Entire Sentence

Using Splits and Re-Splits focuses your attention appropriately on the answer choices, so that you avoid repeatedly (and inefficiently) re-reading the given sentence with each possible answer inserted. However, you must begin by reading the entire sentence. For example, consider this underlined part of a sentence:

<u>and so was unable to go to recess</u>

You cannot decide whether this version is correct until you see the sentence in its entirety:

The students came to school without their mittens <u>and so was unable to go to recess</u>.

If you somehow completely ignore the non-underlined section of the sentence, you cannot know that the use of *was* is incorrect. (The subject of the verb *was* is *students*, a plural noun, so the verb should be *were*.)

The example above is elementary, but as you encounter more Sentence Correction questions, you will see that the relationship between the underlined and non-underlined parts of the sentence is both complex and crucial. Without understanding that relationship, you will miss errors and perhaps choose the wrong answer. Always read the entire sentence, as the GMAT often places important words far from the underlined portion. In fact, after you have made your choice, you should double-check that your answer works in the context of the entire sentence.

Make sure that the answer you choose works in the sentence as a whole.

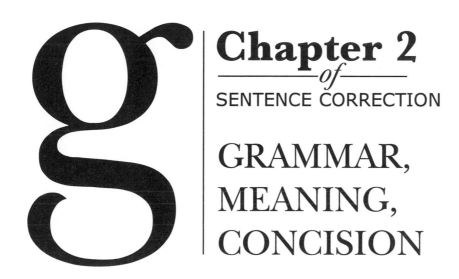

Chapter 2
of
SENTENCE CORRECTION

GRAMMAR,
MEANING,
CONCISION

In This Chapter . . .

GRAMMAR, MEANING, CONCISION

Sentence Correction appears on the GMAT because business schools want to be sure that their admitted applicants grasp the principles of good business writing:

1) **Grammar:** Does the sentence adhere to the rules of Standard Written English?
2) **Meaning:** Is the meaning of the sentence obvious and unambiguous?
3) **Concision:** Is the sentence written as economically as possible?

When evaluating Sentence Correction problems, begin by looking for errors in grammar. After you have found grammar errors, look for meaning issues. Finally, if you have still not singled out an answer, choose the remaining choice that is most concise.

Grammar: Much of the language that one hears in everyday speech actually violates one rule or another. The GMAT tests your ability to distinguish between good and bad grammar, even when the bad grammar seems natural.

Consider this example: *Does everyone have their book?* This may sound fine, but only because you hear similar things all the time. The sentence actually violates the rules of Standard Written English; it should be *Does everyone have his or her book?*

Meaning: Confusing writing is bad writing. If you have to read a sentence more than once to figure out what the author is saying—or if the sentence lends itself to multiple interpretations—it is not a good sentence. Moreover, the sentence must reflect the author's true intent. The correct answer can resolve ambiguity in the original version, but you should not change the meaning that the author intends.

Concision: The GMAT does not like to waste words. If an idea expressed in ten words can be expressed grammatically in eight, the GMAT prefers eight.

> Even though a sentence may *sound* natural, it may not be grammatically correct according to the rules of Standard Written English.

Grammar: A Closer Look

This book will steer you through the major points of Standard Written English on the GMAT. Each chapter will present a major grammatical topic in depth: subject–verb agreement; parallelism; pronouns; modifiers; verb tense, voice, and mood; comparisons; and idioms. You will learn both the overarching principles of each grammatical topic and the nitty-gritty details that will help you differentiate correct grammar from poor grammar. Moreover, you will be given exercises to hone your skills in that topic.

For your reference, a glossary of common grammatical terms appears in the Appendix of this book. Do NOT be overly concerned with the grammatical terms used, as the GMAT will only test your ability to spot issues and mistakes. The terms are simply necessary to explain various grammatical rules. You should focus on being able to apply these rules, not on memorizing terms.

Grammar is the major focus of this book. The rest of this chapter, however, focuses on the other two principles of good writing: Meaning and Concision.

Meaning: A Closer Look

A clear sentence is transparent—the author's intended meaning shines through. On the GMAT, however, either the original sentence or its variations may muddy the waters. One of your tasks is to choose the answer choice that transmits the author's intent as clearly as possible.

Sometimes the original sentence will have a clear, unambiguous meaning. In these cases, your goal is to preserve this original meaning as you correct other issues. Do not alter the author's intent when you make your choice!

At other times, the original sentence will be confusing, and you will need to discern the author's intent. Fortunately, this intent will not be buried too deeply. After all, the correct sentence has to be one of the five choices. Thus, the GMAT tends to make use of "small" errors in meaning that can be easy to overlook.

Most instances of **_meaning errors_** fall into one of three major categories:

> 1) **Choose Your Words**
> 2) **Place Your Words**
> 3) **Match Your Words**

Meaning: Choose Your Words

Did the author pick the right words out of the dictionary? If a word has more than one meaning, is the author using that word correctly, to indicate the right meaning? The GMAT rarely tests you on pure "dictionary knowledge," but very occasionally, it tries to pull a trick on you by switching a particular word and its cousin.

> My decision to drive a hybrid car was motivated by ECONOMIC considerations.
> ECONOMICAL considerations motivated my decision to drive a hybrid car.

The second sentence, which is shorter and punchier, may look preferable. Unfortunately, it is wrong! _Economical_ means "thrifty, efficient." Notice that this meaning is not too distant from what the author intends to say: he or she wants an efficient automobile. But the appropriate phrase is _economic considerations_—that is, <u>monetary</u> considerations.

Consider the following pairs of "cousin" words and expressions, together with their distinct meanings.

> _aggravate_ (worsen) vs. _aggravating_ (irritating)
> _known as_ (named) vs. _known to be_ (acknowledged as)
> _loss of_ (no longer in possession of) vs. _loss in_ (decline in value)
> _mandate_ (command) vs. _have a mandate_ (have authority from voters)
> _native of_ (person from) vs. _native to_ (species that originated in)
> _range of_ (variety of) vs. _ranging_ (varying)
> _rate of_ (speed or frequency of) vs. _rates for_ (prices for)

Manhattan **GMAT** Prep
the new standard

rise (general increase) vs. *raise* (a bet or a salary increase)
such as (for instance) vs. *like* (similar to)
try to do (seek to accomplish) vs. *try doing* (experiment with)

Big changes in meaning can be accomplished with switches of little words. Pay attention to the precise meaning of every word in each answer choice. Certain <u>Helping Verbs</u>, such as *may, will, must,* and *should,* provide another way for the GMAT to test meaning.

These helping verbs express various levels of certainty, obligation, and reality. Simply by swapping these verbs, the GMAT can completely change the meaning of the sentence. Pay attention to these little helping verbs!

Example 1
Certain: The drop in interest rates WILL create better investment opportunities.
Uncertain: The drop in interest rates MAY create better investment opportunities.

Either of these sentences could be correct. However, do not jump from one to the other! Stay with the intent of the original sentence, whether it uses *will* or *may.*

Example 2
Absolutely Necessary: The court ruled that the plaintiff MUST pay full damages.
Morally Obliged: The court ruled that the plaintiff SHOULD pay full damages.

Notice that the second sentence <u>cannot</u> be correct. Why? The word *should* means "moral obligation"—something that a court cannot impose. On the other hand, the use of *must* in the first sentence indicates a legally binding obligation imposed upon the plaintiff. Thus, you should go with *must,* whether the original sentence used *must* or not. Note also that on the GMAT, *should* means "moral obligation," <u>not</u> "likelihood."

Example 3
Actual: If Chris and Jad met, they DISCUSSED mathematics.
Hypothetical: If Chris and Jad met, they WOULD DISCUSS mathematics.

The first sentence could be said by someone who is unsure whether Chris and Jad have actually met: "If this did indeed happen, then that is the consequence." The second sentence, however, predicts the consequences of a hypothetical meeting of the two men: "If this were to happen, then that would be the consequence."

Pay attention to the original sentence's helping verbs—and only change them if the original sentence is obviously nonsensical.

For more on helping verbs, see Chapter 7: Verb Tense, Mood, & Voice.

> Little words, such as helping verbs, are extremely important to the meaning. Do not overlook them!

Meaning: Place Your Words

Beware of words that move from one position to another; the placement of a single word can alter the meaning of a sentence.

> ALL the children are covered in mud.
> The children are ALL covered in mud.

In these sentences, changing the placement of *all* shifts the intent from the <u>number</u> of children covered in mud to the <u>extent</u> to which the children are covered in mud. Consider another set of examples:

> ONLY the council votes on Thursdays.
> The council votes ONLY on Thursdays.

Note that the meaning of the sentence changes as *only* shifts position. In the first sentence, the placement of *only* indicates that the council alone votes on Thursdays (as opposed to the board, perhaps, which votes on Mondays and Fridays). In the second sentence, the placement of *only* indicates that the council does not vote on any day but Thursday.

If a word changes its position in the answer choices, you must consider whether the change has an impact on the meaning of the sentence. Look out especially for short words (such as *only* and *all*) that quantify nouns or otherwise restrict meaning.

At a larger level, you need to pay attention to ***overall word order***. All the words in a sentence could be well-chosen, but the sentence could still be awkward or ambiguous.

> The council granted the right to make legal petitions TO CITY OFFICIALS.

What does the phrase *to city officials* mean? Did the city officials receive the right to make legal petitions? Or did someone else receive the right to make petitions <u>to the officials</u>? Either way, the correct sentence should resolve the ambiguity:

> The council granted CITY OFFICIALS the right to make legal petitions.
> OR
> The right to make legal petitions TO CITY OFFICIALS was granted by the council.

If the sentence is still confusing, check the overall word order for unnecessary inversions. For instance, English normally puts subjects <u>in front of</u> verbs. Try to preserve that order, which is natural to the language.

> Awkward: A referendum is a general public vote through which <u>IS PASSED</u> <u>A LAW OR OTHER PROPOSAL</u>.
> Better: A referendum is a general public vote through which <u>A LAW OR OTHER PROPOSAL</u> <u>IS PASSED</u>.

Sometimes, changing the position of a single word can alter the meaning of an entire sentence.

Meaning: Match Your Words

Sentences contain pairs of words or phrases that must match. For example, the subject and the verb must match. This "matching" concept has grammatical implications (for instance, the subject and the verb must agree in number), but it also has <u>logical</u> implications. In other words, we must remember that the subject and the verb must ***make sense together***!

You might think that this principle is so obvious that it would not be tested. But under exam conditions, you have to remember to check this point. After you find the subject and the verb (a task described in the next chapter), always ask yourself, "Do they make sense together?"

A similar matching principle holds for other grammatical connections (e.g., pronouns and the nouns they refer to). Future chapters will explore each type of connection in turn, but never forget to apply the meaning issue and test the <u>meaning</u> of any potential connection. Connected words must always make sense together.

> Words that are connected in a sentence, such as subjects and verbs or pronouns and antecedents, must always make sense together.

Concision: A Closer Look

Many Sentence Correction problems will involve concision. Often two or three answers are wrong not only because they contain grammatical mistakes, but also because they are wordy. If two choices are both grammatically correct and clear in meaning, but one is more concise than the other, then choose the shorter one.

Wordy:	They HAVE DIFFERENCES over THE WAY IN WHICH the company should MAKE INVESTMENTS in new technologies.
Better:	They DIFFER over HOW the company should INVEST in new technologies.

The first sentence is easily understood, but still poorly written. The phrases *have differences*, *the way in which*, and *make investments* are all wordy. They can be replaced with more concise expressions, as in the second sentence.

Generally, the GMAT frowns upon using a phrase where a single word will do. For example, the phrase *have differences* means the same as the word *differ*, so use the word rather than the phrase.

Remember, however, that Concision is the LAST of the three principles tested on Sentence Correction problems (Grammar, Meaning, *Concision*). Do not simply pick the shortest choice and move on. Quite frequently, the GMAT will force you to pick a <u>longer</u> choice that is grammatically correct and clear in meaning.

Concision: Avoid Redundancy

Another aspect of concision is redundancy. Each word in the correct choice must be necessary to the meaning of the sentence. If a word can be removed without subtracting from the meaning of the sentence, it should be eliminated.

A common redundancy trap on the GMAT is the use of words with the same meaning:

Wordy:	The value of the stock ROSE by a 10% INCREASE.
Better:	The value of the stock INCREASED by 10%.
Or:	The value of the stock ROSE by 10%.

Since *rose* and *increase* both imply growth, only one is needed.

Wordy:	The three prices SUM to a TOTAL of $11.56.
Better:	The three prices SUM to $11.56.
Or:	The three prices TOTAL $11.56.

Since *sum* and *total* convey the same meaning, only one is needed.

Wordy:	BEING EXCITED about her upcoming graduation, Kelsey could barely focus on her final exams.
Better:	EXCITED about her upcoming graduation, Kelsey could barely focus on her final exams.

Here, *being* does not add to the meaning of the sentence, so it should be eliminated. In fact, the word *being* almost always signals redundancy on the GMAT. You should avoid it whenever possible. (Note that the GMAT has recently come up with ways to make *being* right—generally, by making alternative choices grammatically wrong. So do not eliminate *being* purely as a knee-jerk reaction.)

Pay attention to expressions of time. It is easy to sneak two synonymous and redundant time expressions into an answer choice (especially if one expression is in the non-underlined part, or if the two expressions do not look like each other):

PAST:	Previously	Formerly	In the past	Before now
PRESENT:	Now	Currently	Presently	At present
YEARLY:	Annual	Each year	A year (e.g., *three launches a year*)	

Generally, a sentence should include only one such expression. This does not mean that you can never repeat time expressions in a sentence; just be sure that you are doing so for a good reason.

Concision: Specific Patterns of Wordiness (Advanced)

Wordiness is not as fuzzy a concept as you might think. The GMAT has particular ideas about what sorts of phrases are wordier than others. Of course, wordier expressions generally have more words! But if you can recognize these specific patterns, you can make faster and more confident assessments. Always keep in mind that Concision is the third issue to consider in Sentence Correction. The Idiom List in Chapter 9 expands on the examples below.

Here is how to rank parts of speech by "concision power": **drive the V-A-N!**

V-A-N = <u>Verb</u> > <u>Adjective</u> (or Adverb) **> <u>Noun</u>**

An active **<u>Verb</u>** is usually stronger and more concise than an **<u>Adjective</u>** or an action **<u>Noun</u>**.

The preferred form may differ slightly in meaning from the non-preferred form. In general, the preferred form is what the author intended to say anyway, so kill two birds with one stone: make the expression more concise <u>and</u> clarify the meaning.

> If you can express an action as either a verb or a noun, pick the verb. It will be shorter and stronger.

<u>V-A-N Pattern 1: Prefer a Verb to an Action Noun</u>

> Wordy: The townspeople's REVOLUTION WAS AGAINST the king.
> Better: The townspeople REVOLTED AGAINST the king.

An <u>Action Noun</u>, such as *revolution*, is a noun that expresses an action. Try to express actions with verbs (such as *revolt*), rather than with action nouns (such as *revolution*). Generally, a short, simple verb is stronger than a phrase with the relevant action noun and a generic verb, such as *be* or *make*. In the other examples listed below, notice how the nouns create wordy prepositional phrases.

<u>Wordy</u>	<u>Better</u>
They <u>are</u> subject to the <u>applicability</u> of rules.	Rules <u>apply</u> to them.
The <u>cost</u> of storms to the country <u>is</u> billions.	Storms <u>cost</u> the country billions.
Her <u>decision was</u> to go.	She <u>decided</u> to go.
His example <u>was</u> an <u>influence</u> on me.	His example <u>influenced</u> me.
Her example <u>was</u> an <u>inspiration</u> to me.	Her example <u>inspired</u> me.
They <u>made</u> a <u>reference</u> to the strike.	They <u>referred</u> to the strike.
The <u>weight</u> of the apples <u>is</u> a pound.	The apples <u>weigh</u> a pound.

However, note that this pattern is NOT a hard-and-fast rule. For instance, in problem #112 in *The Official Guide, 11th Edition*, the right answer reads *is an acknowledgment of* while two wrong answers read *acknowledge*. Note that these two terms are not equivalent: *His absence from the proceeding may be an acknowledgment of guilt* is fine, but *His absence from the proceeding may acknowledge guilt* is <u>not</u> fine. Objects or things can be an acknowledgment, but only people can actually acknowledge. Moreover, the answers in this problem that include *acknowledge* are clearly wrong for other reasons (which will be covered in later chapters). In many cases, a difference among answer choices involving Concision also hinges on other issues.

<u>V-A-N Pattern 2: Prefer a *That*-Clause (with Verbs) to a Series of Phrases (with Nouns)</u>

Wordy: The hypothesis <u>ABOUT the COMPOSITION OF the universe AS largely dark energy</u> seems strange.

Better: The hypothesis <u>THAT the universe IS largely COMPOSED OF dark energy</u> seems strange.

When you tack a long thought onto a noun, try to put the thought in a *That*-Clause rather than in a long series of prepositional phrases.

A <u>*That*-Clause</u> starts with the word *that* and contains a <u>Working Verb</u>. A working verb is a verb form that, <u>as is</u>, can be the main verb of a sentence by itself. For instance, *is composed* is a working verb, since *The universe is composed of dark energy* is a sentence.

By choosing the *That*-Clause, you are choosing the verb form of the action. This pattern is really a special case of Pattern #1, Prefer a Verb to an Action Noun.

The prepositional phrases are not always much longer than the clause. But even a few prepositional phrases in a row may be hard to grasp without a verb. *<u>About the composition of the universe as largely dark energy</u>* is muddled. So this issue is partly about meaning, too.

"Idea" nouns, such as *hypothesis, idea,* or *suggestion,* lend themselves particularly well to this pattern. Other examples include *belief, evidence, indication,* and *report.* These sorts of nouns are often modified by *That*-Clauses that contain full sentences: *The BELIEF <u>THAT the world is flat</u> is contradicted by EVIDENCE <u>THAT the world is round</u>.*

<u>V-A-N Pattern 3: Prefer a Verb to an Adjective</u>

Wordy: The artist WAS INFLUENTIAL TO the movement.
Better: The artist INFLUENCED the movement.

Try to pick the verb form of the action, rather than an adjective form plus the verb *to be*.

<u>Wordy</u>	<u>Better</u>
This rash <u>is aggravating</u> to the pain.	This rash <u>aggravates</u> the pain.
We <u>are able</u> to go to the store now.	We <u>can</u> go to the store now.
This signal <u>is indicative</u> of a problem.	This signal <u>indicates</u> a problem.
Her example <u>was inspirational</u> to me.	Her example <u>inspired</u> me.
This painting <u>is suggestive</u> of calm.	This painting <u>suggests</u> calm.

Again, remember that this pattern is not a strict rule. Problem #118 in the 11th Edition prefers *are lacking in* over the verb *lack.* (*Lacking* is used as an adjective, just as *aggravating* is an adjective above.) As before, we must note that the two terms are not precisely equivalent: *lacking in* means *deficient in.* You can say *This kettle lacks a whistle* but not *This kettle is lacking in a whistle.* More importantly, the answers that include the suboptimal form *lack* are wrong for other reasons.

The verb is the "engine" of a sentence. By picking a verb over a noun or adjective, you are making the engine stronger.

<u>V-A-N Pattern 4: Prefer an Adjective to a Noun</u>

Wordy: THERE IS AN ABUNDANCE OF funds for school construction.
Better: Funds for school construction ARE ABUNDANT.

To describe a noun or noun phrase (e.g., *funds for school construction*), use an adjective (*abundant*). Avoid the noun derived from that adjective (*abundance*) if you can. And remember to watch out for possible slight changes of meaning. Other examples (also included in the Idiom List):

<u>Wordy</u>
She <u>has the ability</u> to juggle.

She <u>has the capability</u> to juggle.
We <u>have a disinclination</u> to stay.
He is <u>in isolation</u>.

<u>Better</u>
She <u>is able</u> to juggle.
(Note: The best form here is *She can juggle.*)
She <u>is capable</u> of juggling.
We <u>are disinclined</u> to stay.
He is <u>isolated</u>.

<u>V-A-N Pattern 5: Prefer an Adverb to a Prepositional Phrase</u>

Wordy: Oil prices have fallen, but prices at the gasoline pump have not fallen TO A COMPARABLE EXTENT.
Better: Oil prices have fallen, but prices at the gasoline pump have not fallen COMPARABLY.

To modify a verb phrase (e.g., *have not fallen*), use a simple adverb rather than a long prepositional phrase that means the same thing. Since prepositional phrases contain nouns, this is another example of the V-A-N principle.

Notice also that the first example above is suboptimal for another reason. The phrase *fall to* often indicates the <u>level</u> to which something falls, rather than the <u>extent</u>: *Prices have fallen to under a dollar.* As a result, you might misread the first example.

<u>Wordy</u>
to a considerable extent
to a significant degree

<u>Better</u>
considerably
significantly

> Since adjectives are designed to modify nouns, they often do so more concisely than longer phrases.

Two other concision patterns do not fit the V-A-N framework but are worth noting. Both of these patterns involve overuse of the generic verb *to be*. As we have already seen, the verb *to be* can appear in many instances of wordiness. When you search for the most concise answer, run an **"Elimination *BE*"**: get rid of any unnecessary uses of *be*. (Remember that the verb *to be* can take on many other forms: *am, are, been, is, was, were.*)

Concision Pattern 6: Prefer an Adjective to an Adjective Clause with *Be*

> Wordy: Marcos is a professor WHO IS ADMIRABLE.
> Better: Marcos is an ADMIRABLE professor.

> *In some situations, the verb to be is unnecessary. Run an "Elimination BE" to get rid of excess occurrences of be.*

An adjective clause that contains the verb *to be* (in any of its forms) is generally wordier than the adjective by itself. In particular, if the main clause contains *be* as well, try to use the adjective alone. The first example has two occurrences of the word *is*, one of which is unnecessary. The second example has only one *is*, because the adjective *admirable* has been moved in front of the noun *professor*.

This principle works similarly with nouns that identify or describe other nouns:

> Wordy: Joan, WHO IS a FIREFIGHTER, works in Yosemite Park.
> Better: Joan, a FIREFIGHTER, works in Yosemite Park.

Remember that this is a preference, like all concision techniques. Do not use this principle to eliminate choices right away.

Concision Pattern 7: Remove *IT IS... THAT...*

> Wordy: IT IS without fear THAT children should play.
> Better: Children should play without fear.

The first construction is perfectly grammatical and even useful when you want to emphasize some aspect of the situation (such as *without fear*). But the GMAT avoids such constructions in correct answers. You should do the same as you make your choice.

Concision: Don't Make It Too Short (Advanced)

As you cut out unnecessary words, be careful not to cut too much out of the sentence! Avoid creating awkward phrasings or introducing new errors.

The GMAT sometimes tries to trick you with ***false concision***: tempting expressions that are too short for their own good. Some patterns are listed below.

"Too Short" Pattern 1: Keep the Prepositional Phrase if You Need To

Too Short: I talked to the BOSTON SOLDIER.
Better: I talked to the SOLDIER FROM BOSTON.

In many cases, when we have one noun modified by a prepositional phrase, we <u>can</u> turn the phrase into a <u>Noun-Adjective</u> and put it in front of the first noun, thus shortening the whole expression. A Noun-Adjective is a noun that is placed in front of another noun and that functions as an adjective.

Right: A wall <u>OF stone</u>   *OR*   A <u>stone</u> wall
                                                (*stone* is a Noun-Adjective)

This process works the best when the preposition is *of,* the simplest and most common preposition in English. However, **if the preposition is <u>not</u> *of,* then you should avoid collapsing the prepositional phrase.** The phrase *Boston soldier* is hard to understand: it seems to indicate a <u>type</u> of soldier, not a soldier who happens to be from a particular city.

Study the table below. The expressions on the left are certainly comprehensible, but the GMAT regards them as unclear. Notice that places or locations rarely work well as Noun-Adjectives, unless the original prepositional phrase begins with *of.*

Too Short	Better
<u>Aegean Sea</u> salt	salt <u>FROM the Aegean Sea</u>
<u>Ural Mountain</u> ore	ore <u>FROM the Ural Mountains</u>
<u>Danube River</u> access	access <u>TO the Danube River</u>
<u>population</u> changes of honeybees	changes <u>IN the population</u> of honeybees

Moreover, you should not collapse certain *Of*-prepositional phrases into Noun-Adjectives. Whenever you have a **time period, quantity** or other **measurement** as the first word, keep the prepositional phrase with *of.* Never modify a measurement using a Noun-Adjective. Also, you should generally avoid using a possessive (*'s* or *s'*) to modify a measurement. Study the examples in the table on the next page.

Too Short	Better
<u>Memorial Day</u> week OR <u>Memorial Day's</u> week	the week <u>OF Memorial Day</u>
the <u>merger</u> year	the year <u>OF the merger</u>
the <u>oxygen</u> amount	the amount <u>OF oxygen</u>
the <u>honeybee population</u> density OR the <u>honeybee population's</u> density	the density <u>OF the honeybee population</u>

"Too Short" Pattern 2: Keep *That Of* or *Those Of* if You Need To

Too Short: <u>The face</u> I see in ads every day is <u>a famous actor</u>.
Better: <u>The face</u> I see in ads every day is <u>THAT OF a famous actor</u>.

As you trim words, you can wind up creating an illogical sentence if you are not careful. The first sentence above seems nice and short, until you check the meaning. Can a *face* be an *actor*? No. *The face I see…* must be *THE FACE OF a famous actor*. The word *that* stands for *face*, so the second sentence is correct.

Note that the GMAT sometimes inserts an <u>unnecessary</u> *that of* or *those of*, which you <u>do</u> have to remove.

Wordy: <u>The fields</u> I most enjoy studying are <u>THOSE OF physics and chemistry</u>.
Better: <u>The fields</u> I most enjoy studying are <u>physics and chemistry</u>.

Physics and chemistry <u>are</u> in fact *fields* (of study), so you should simply say *The fields… are physics and chemistry.*

"Too Short" Pattern 3: Keep *That* after a Reporting Verb

Too Short: The study INDICATES the problem has vanished.
Better: The study INDICATES THAT the problem has vanished.

A <u>Reporting Verb</u>, such as *indicate, claim, contend,* or *report*, often in fact <u>reports</u> or otherwise includes a thought or belief. This thought can stand alone as a sentence: *The problem has vanished.*

In informal speech, people often put a thought like this directly after the Reporting Verb. But on the GMAT, you should always put a *that* between the Reporting Verb and the thought. If you drop the *that*, you might get confused for a moment as you read: *The study indicates the problem…* . At this stage, the author might be saying that *the study* simply <u>points out</u> *the problem*. To avoid the ambiguity, the GMAT prefers that you keep the *that*. The GMAT insists that the following Reporting Verbs take *that* whenever you follow them with a clause (a thought expressed in its own mini-sentence).

Certain small words and phrases, such as That after a verb or That Of / Those Of, may be essential in the sentence.

Verb	Better
Agree	The criminals AGREED THAT gold would be the scam.
Claim	They CLAIMED THAT gold was growing scarce.
Contend	They CONTENDED THAT the price of gold would rise.
Declare	They DECLARED THAT they had discovered gold.
Find	Investors FOUND THAT they could not get answers.
Indicate	An article INDICATED THAT the mine was worthless.
Reveal	An investigation REVEALED THAT the gold was a mirage.
Rule	The court RULED THAT the criminals were guilty of fraud.
Show	This story SHOWS THAT crime does not pay.

It is likely that the GMAT will insist on *that* after most other Reporting Verbs. Other common Reporting Verbs include *announce, assert, believe, confess, demonstrate, doubt, expect, know, mention, observe, proclaim, reason, repeat, state, think*, and *warn*.

The main exception to this pattern seems to be the verb *say*. Somewhat oddly, the GMAT does not require you to put *that* after the verb *say*:

> Right: The water was so cold that people SAID polar bears would shiver.

The GMAT does not explain why this omission is acceptable, but the reason is probably that there is very little chance of confusion:

> …people SAID polar bears…

You rightly expect a full thought, since you cannot *say polar bears* as you might *say a prayer* (you can *say* the words "polar bears," but you cannot *say* the animals themselves). In a GMAT sentence, the verb *say* will almost certainly be followed by an entire thought, not necessarily introduced with *that*.

In brief, the Concision principle has many applications. The three important points to remember are these:

> (1) **Avoid redundancy**.
> (2) **Avoid wordiness**. Drive the V-A-N and run an Elimination *BE*.
> (3) **Don't make it TOO short**. Avoid changing the meaning for the worse.

As you apply the Concision principle, avoid redundancy and wordiness, but don't make it too short.

Problem Set

A.   Meaning

The underlined portion of each sentence below may contain one or more errors. Each sentence is followed by a **boldface** sample answer choice that changes the meaning of the original sentence. Select (**A**) if the original version is correct, (**B**) if the boldface version is correct, and (**C**) if neither is correct.

If you select (**A**), explain what is wrong with the boldface version. If you select (**B**), explain how the boldface version corrects the original version. (Remember that in Sentence Correction a change of meaning is ONLY justified if the meaning of the original sentence is illogical or unclear.) If you select (**C**), explain why both versions are incorrect. Note: several of these questions refer to rules and distinctions that will be discussed further in upcoming chapters.

1.   No matter how much work it may require, getting an MBA turns out to be a wise investment for most people.
    Even though it requires much work

2.   The driver took the people for a ride who had been waiting.
    the people who had been waiting for a ride

3.   Rising costs to raw materials may impel us to rise prices farther.
    costs of raw materials may impale us to raise prices further

4.   The yellow-toed macaque, which is native to Madagascar, is known as keeping cool by laying down in damp caves during the hottest part of the day.
    is native of Madagascar, is known to keep cool by lying down

5.   She is the most dedicated gardener on the block, every day watering the more than 50 plants in her yard.
    every day watering more than the 50 plants in her yard

6.   Hector remembers San Francisco as it was when he left ten years ago.
    as though he had left ten years ago

7.   Students at Carver High School are encouraged to pursue extracurricular activities like student government, sports, and the arts.
    activities such as student government, sports, and the arts

8.   Martin's routine includes reading the daily newspaper and going to the gym.
    Martin's daily routine includes reading the newspaper

9.   Stacey would have gone to the party if she knew about it.
    if she had known about it

B.   Concision

Rewrite each of the following sentences more concisely. Use the concepts in the chapter (including redundancy, the various V-A-N patterns and the other concision patterns) to justify the changes you make.

10.   After the fact that the test format was changed, scores subsequently dropped by more than a 25% decrease.

11.   Electronic devices can constitute a distraction to a driver.

12.   It is possible that the earthquake may have been causal to the building's collapse.

13.   Many directors have a suspicion of there being an attempt by managers to conceal the extent of losses at the company.

14.   They are in readiness for whatever it is that may happen.

15.   It was with haste that the senator read her speech.

16.   A cake that is tasty will not last for a long amount of time in a room full of children who are hungry.

17.   A bottle of red wine was ordered by Grant, even though Marie had had the expectation that he would be placing an order for a bottle of white wine.

18.   Studies have shown a mentor can be a help in causing an increase to a student's academic performance in schoolwork.

19.   Although most consumers are suspicious of such offers, Colin is desirous of purchasing the two-for-one vacation package.

20.   The team has a determination to gain a victory.

21.   Work on the new railroad is progressing at a rapid rate of speed.

22.   The woman from Miami sat on the bench of wood and ate a soup bowl.

23.   The carbon emissions kilogram weight from cars is higher in summer than that of winter.

24.   The press release claims the France president is older than the United States.

A.   Meaning

1.   **(A).** The original sentence does not say that getting an MBA requires a lot of work. The expression *no matter how much work it may require* simply says that the amount of work (whether large or small) does not matter. The revised version eliminates the word *may*, so that the new sentence <u>does</u> say that an MBA requires a lot of work. This change of meaning is UNJUSTIFIED.

2.   **(C).** In the original sentence, the modifier *who had been waiting* does not clearly modify *the people*. It appears, illogically, to modify the closer noun (*the ride*). The boldface version moves *who had been waiting* next to *the people*, thus making clear that it is *the people* who *had been waiting*. This change of meaning is JUSTIFIED.

However, the boldface version also makes another change of meaning. The words *for a ride* now come right after *waiting*, so it seems that these people had been *waiting for a ride*. This change of meaning is UNJUSTIFIED.

3.   **(C).** The boldface version makes several changes to the meaning of the original sentence. Most of these changes are justified, but one of them is not—so the answer has to be **(C)**.

The switch from *cost to* to *costs of* is JUSTIFIED. *Costs to X* are what X has to pay, whereas *costs of X* are how much somebody must pay to buy X. The latter meaning makes much more sense here, because *raw materials* are being paid for, not doing the paying.

The switch from *impel* to *impale* is UNJUSTIFIED. To *impel* is to *force* someone to do something. To *impale* something is to pierce it with a sharp instrument!

The switch from *rise* to *raise* is JUSTIFIED. *Raise* is a verb that always takes a direct object: <u>*The Fed*</u> (subject) *raised* <u>*the interest rate*</u> (object) *in March*. *Rise* is used only in contexts where there is no direct object: <u>*Interest rates*</u> (subject) *rose in March*. In our sentence, *prices* are a direct object, so the verb must be *raise*.

The switch from *farther* to *further* is JUSTIFIED. *Farther* refers only to distance (*I can throw a javelin farther than you can*) whereas *further* refers to degree of something other than distance (*We need further time and money for this project*).

4.   **(C).** The switch from *is native to* to *is native of* is UNJUSTIFIED. The expression *X is native to Y* is used to say that X (a species) is from Y (a place). The expression *X is a native of Y* tells us that X (an individual) was born in Y (a place). Note that the boldface version is doubly wrong, because it does not even get the latter idiom right—the article *a* is missing before *native*.

The switch from *is known as keeping* to *is known to keep* is JUSTIFIED. The expression *X is known as Y* means that X is commonly referred to by the name Y: *Sean Combs was once known as "Puff Daddy."* The expression *X is known to Y* means that doing Y is a characteristic behavior of X.

The switch from *laying* to *lying* is JUSTIFIED. *Lay* is a verb that always takes a direct object: <u>*I*</u> (subject) *decided to lay* <u>*my coat*</u> (object) *on the sofa*. In contrast, *lie* is a verb that never takes a direct object: *I* (subject) *decided to lie down*.

5.   **(A).** The original version contains the phrase *the more than 50 plants*. Here the words *more than* modify the number *50*. The sentence therefore means that she waters her plants, of which there are more than fifty. In the boldface version, we have the phrase *watering more than the 50 plants*. Here the words

more than are separated from the number *50*, and therefore do not modify that number. The new version tells us that she waters something *more than* (i.e., in addition to) the *plants* – for instance, she might water her gravel walkway or her garden gnomes. This change of meaning is UNJUSTIFIED because there was nothing wrong with the original sentence.

6.   **(A)**. The boldface version makes two UNJUSTIFIED changes to the original version.

The original sentence tells us that Hector actually DID leave San Francisco ten years ago. The revised version tells as that he did NOT leave San Francisco ten years ago: the expression *as though* is used to discuss things that are untrue or did not happen (*You behave as though you were richer than Bill Gates!*).

Another important change in meaning comes because the revised version takes out the words *it* (i.e., San Francisco) *was*, and therefore does not refer directly to the state of affairs in San Francisco ten years ago.

7.   **(B)**. *Such as* is used to introduce examples, whereas *like* is used to make a comparison. The original sentence, which uses *like*, literally means that the students are encouraged to pursue extracurricular activities similar to, but not necessarily including, *student government, sports, and the arts*. This is very unlikely to be what the author really meant, so you should choose the boldface version, which replaces *like* with *such as*.

8.   **(A)**. The original sentence does not say how often Martin goes to the gym, nor even how often he reads the newspaper. (Perhaps he subscribes to a daily newspaper, but saves all the issues until the weekend, when he reads them all at once.) The boldface version, on the other hand, asserts that Martin reads the paper every day and goes to the gym every day. It does not make clear, as the original sentence does, that the newspaper is a daily (as opposed to, for example, a Sunday paper). These changes of meaning are all UNJUSTIFIED.

9.   **(B)**. The original sentence contains the phrase *would have gone*, indicating that (1) Stacey did NOT go, but that (2) she would surely have done so if she had known. The only way (1) and (2) can both be true is if Stacey did NOT know about the party. The phrase *if she knew* is therefore illogical here because it conveys the meaning that perhaps Stacey DID know about the party. The boldface alternative uses the subjunctive mood (*if she had known*), appropriately indicating that Stacey did NOT know about the party.

B.   Concision

10.   **After the test format was changed, scores dropped by more than 25%.**

The fact that is redundant here, as it is in almost any sentence in which it occurs. We do not need both *dropped* and *decrease*, since both words convey the same idea. For the same reason, we do not need both *after* and *subsequently*.

11.   **Electronic devices can distract a driver.**

The verb *distract* is preferable to the phrase *constitute a distraction to*, according to V-A-N pattern 1.

12.   **The earthquake may have caused the building's collapse.**

It is possible that and *may* both express uncertainty, so we can remove one of them without changing the meaning. *Have caused* is preferable to *have been causal to*, according to V-A-N pattern 3.

13. **Many directors suspect that managers are trying to conceal the extent of losses at the company.**

Suspect is better than *have a suspicion*, according to V-A-N pattern 1. *That managers are trying* is better than *of there being an attempt by managers*, according to V-A-N pattern 2.

14. **They are ready for whatever may happen.**

Are ready is preferable to *are in readiness*, according to V-A-N pattern 4. *Whatever may happen* is more concise than *whatever it is that may happen*, according to Concision pattern 7.

15. **The senator read her speech hastily.**

This sentence is better without the *it was…that* construction, according to Concision pattern 7. Moreover, *hastily* is preferable to *with haste*, according to V-A-N pattern 5.

16. **A tasty cake will not last long in a room full of hungry children.**

Tasty cake is preferable to *cake that is tasty*, according to Concision pattern 6. *Last long* is preferable to *last for a long amount of time*, according to V-A-N pattern 5. *Hungry children* is preferable to *children who are hungry*, according to Concision pattern 6.

17. **Grant ordered a bottle of red wine, even though Marie had expected him to order a bottle of white wine.**

The first clause is more concise when placed in the active voice—*Grant ordered a bottle* rather than *a bottle…was ordered…by Grant*.

In the second clause, the verb *expected* is preferable to the phrase *had the expectation*, according to V-A-N pattern 1. For the same reason, the verb *order* is preferable to the phrase *be placing an order for*.

18. **Studies have shown that a mentor can help improve a student's academic performance.**

The verb *help* is preferable to the phrase *be a help*, according to V-A-N pattern 1. *To improve* is more concise than the phrase *in causing an improvement to*, according to V-A-N pattern 1. Lastly, the phrase *in schoolwork* is redundant because we already have the word *academic*. You can write either *help improve* or *help to improve*.

In one respect, however, the original sentence is too short: it is missing the word *that* after the reporting verb *shown* (see "Too Short" pattern 3).

19. **Although most consumers are suspicious of such offers, Colin wants to purchase the two-for-one vacation package.**

The verb *wants* is preferable to *is desirous of*, according to V-A-N pattern 3. Notice, however, that you should NOT change *are suspicious of* to the verb *suspect*, because *consumers suspect such offers* is unidiomatic. (*Suspect* vs. *are suspicious of* is, like *lack* vs. *are lacking in*, one of the rare exceptions to V-A-N pattern 3.)

20. **The team is determined to win.**

Is determined to is preferable to *has a determination to*, according to V-A-N pattern 4. (Here *determined* is an adjective.) The verb *win* is preferable to *gain a victory*, according to V-A-N pattern 1.

Notice that you should not attempt to apply V-A-N pattern 3 to the correct sentence above, because *The team determines to win* changes the meaning of the sentence.

21. **Work on the new railroad is progressing rapidly.**

The noun *rate* is preferable to the modified noun *rate of speed*, because the modifier *of speed* is redundant. (*Rate* means *speed*.) Thus, *at a rapid rate* would be better than the original *at a rapid rate of speed*. Even better, however, is to follow V-A-N pattern 5 and replace the prepositional phrase *at a rapid rate* with the adverb *rapidly*.

22. **The woman from Miami sat on a wooden bench and ate a bowl of soup.**

The adjective *wooden* is preferable to the phrase *of wood*, according to V-A-N pattern 4. Alternatively, you could write *a wood bench*, making *wood* a Noun-Adjective. This change is acceptable, because the original phrase *of wood* simply indicates the material out of which the bench was made, as does the word *wood* placed in front of *bench*.

However, V-A-N pattern 4 does <u>not</u> require us to change *woman from Miami* to *Miami woman*. This is because *Miami*, unlike *wooden*, is a Noun-Adjective, and therefore is governed by "Too Short" pattern 1, which identifies *woman from Miami* as preferable.

Choosing between *bowl of soup* and *soup bowl* is somewhat more complicated. According to "Too Short" pattern 1, both expressions should be equally acceptable. However, you must think about the <u>meaning</u> before you apply one of the concision rules. *Soup bowl* refers to a kind of <u>bowl</u>, whereas *bowl of soup* refers to the <u>soup</u> inside a bowl. It is more logical to say that she ate the soup than that she ate the bowl!

23. **The weight of the carbon emissions from cars is higher in summer than in winter.**

The word *kilogram* before *weight* is redundant, and should therefore be removed. On the other hand, *carbon emissions weight* is too short, because *weight* is a quantity word that should be modified by the phrase *of carbon emissions* (see "Too Short" pattern 1).

The words *that of* in the original sentence need to be removed because they have no clear meaning. The intended comparison is best rendered with the parallel prepositional phrases *in summer* and *in winter*.

24. **The press release claims that the president of France is older than that of the United States.**

The original sentence is too short.

We need the word *that* to introduce a clause after the reporting verb *claims* (see "Too Short" pattern 3).

The president of France is clearer and more idiomatic than *the France president* (see "Too Short" pattern 3). Moreover, the phrase *the president of France* is needed to set up the intended parallelism between *of France* and *of the United States*. You could write *the French president*, but it will not be parallel to the second part of the comparison.

Finally, we need the words *that of* before *the United States*, in order to make clear that the French president is older than the American <u>president</u>, not older than the United States itself. (Without *that of*, the sentence means that the French president was born on or before 1776!)

Sentence Correction

Now that you have completed your study of MEANING & CONCISION, it is time to test your skills on problems that have actually appeared on real GMAT exams over the past several years.

The problem set that follows is composed of past GMAT problems from two books published by GMAC (Graduate Management Admission Council):

The Official Guide for GMAT Review, 11th Edition (pages 638–660)
The Official Guide for GMAT Verbal Review (pages 234–253)

The problems in the set below are primarily focused on MEANING & CONCISION issues. For each of these problems, identify errors in the answer choices relating to meaning and concision. Avoid answer choices that muddy the meaning or alter the original intent. Also avoid unnecessarily wordy or redundant choices.

Meaning & Concision

      11th Edition: 8, 12, 14, 33, 36, 44, 50, 80, 103, 108, 120, 124 , 135
      Verbal Review: 2, 13, 57, 76, 83, 87

Chapter 3
of
SENTENCE CORRECTION

SUBJECT–VERB AGREEMENT

In This Chapter . . .

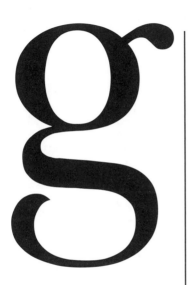

SUBJECT-VERB AGREEMENT

Every sentence must have a <u>Subject</u> and a <u>Verb</u>. The subject is the noun that performs the action expressed by the verb:

> The <u>DOG</u> with the gray ears <u>RUNS</u> out of the house.

The subject is *dog*, and the verb is *runs*. In every sentence, the subject and the verb must make logical sense together. Moreover, the subject and the verb must agree in number.

Subject and Verb Must Both Exist

If a sentence is missing the subject or the verb, the sentence is a <u>Fragment</u>: in other words, it is not a complete sentence! On the GMAT, an answer choice that makes the sentence a fragment is wrong. This error is rather rare, but you need to be ready to recognize it when it occurs. One way the GMAT disguises the error is by dropping the verb:

> Wrong: The electron named in 1894.

Wait a minute, what about *named*? *Named* certainly looks like a verb. But in this context, *named* is NOT a working verb, one that can run a sentence. Of course, we do not mean that the subject (*the electron*) actually <u>named</u> anything. Rather, something or someone else did the naming.

> Right: Stoney NAMED the electron in 1894.

In this sentence, *named* is a working verb. Or we can express the sentence this way:

> Right: The electron WAS NAMED in 1894.

In this sentence, the words *was named* make up the full working verb. Within *was named*, the word *named* is a <u>Past Participle</u>. A Past Participle by itself is not a working verb: *The electron named in 1894* is not a sentence.

A sentence can be a fragment in another way: it could start with a <u>Connecting Word</u> and contain no <u>Main Clause</u> (a clause that could stand alone as a sentence as is, with its own subject and verb):

> Wrong: BECAUSE the dog was never mine.
> Wrong: WHICH will be approved tomorrow.

Because and *which* are connecting words. These are also known as <u>Subordinators</u>, because they turn the clauses they are attached to into <u>Subordinate Clauses</u>, which cannot stand by themselves. To fix this sort of fragment, you either need to attach it to a main clause or drop the connecting word (and if necessary add some words, as in the second case: *The plan will be approved tomorrow*). For more on connecting words, see Chapter 10: Odds & Ends.

> Make sure that the sentence has both a subject and a working verb.

Subject and Verb Must Make Sense Together

Remember the Meaning principle? A correct answer must have a clear meaning. Thus, it must make logical sense.

Wrong: The development of a hydrogen car based on expected performance parameters will be able to travel hundreds of miles without refueling.

At first glance, this sentence may seem okay. But be careful: *The development of a hydrogen car... will be able to travel...*? Something is wrong. It is not the development that *will be able to travel*. We want to say that the hydrogen car *itself will be able to travel*.

If you come across a confusing grammatical term in this book, flip to the Glossary in the back for an explanation.

Right: Once developed, a hydrogen CAR based on expected performance parameters WILL BE able to travel hundreds of miles without refueling.

Make sure that the subject and the verb actually have a sensible meaning together!

Subject and Verb Must Agree In Number

Last but not least, the subject and the verb must agree in number. The number can be singular (one) or plural (more than one).

A singular subject requires a singular verb form: The dog runs out of the house.

A plural subject requires a plural verb form: The dogs run out of the house.

Singular and plural verb forms are second nature to you—you use them so often that there is nothing to memorize. You would never write *the dog run out* or *the dogs runs out*. Therefore, the GMAT often tries to confuse you before you make the subject–verb match.

How? The GMAT hides the subject, so that you are unsure whether the subject is singular or plural! If you do not know the number of the subject, then you will not be able to select the verb form that agrees with it. Consider this example:

The discovery of new medicines (was/were) vital to the company's growth.

What is the subject, *discovery* or *new medicines*? If you ask yourself "What is vital to the company's growth?" you may be able to talk yourself into either choice.

The key to making subjects and verbs agree in GMAT sentences is to find the subject that goes with a particular verb. To find the subject, you must ignore all the words that are not the subject.

Eliminate the Middlemen, and Skip the Warmup

The GMAT hides the subject in a few ways. The most common way by far is to insert words between the subject and the verb. You must learn to eliminate these Middlemen words to reveal the subject.

Furthermore, the GMAT often puts a significant number of words <u>in front of</u> the subject you want. In these cases, you have to "skip the <u>Warmup</u>" that comes before the subject you are looking for.

There are a few common types of middlemen and warmups.

1) <u>Prepositional Phrases</u>
A <u>Prepositional Phrase</u> is a group of words headed by a <u>Preposition</u>.

<u>of</u> mice	<u>for</u> milk	<u>by</u> 1800
<u>in</u> Zambia	<u>with</u> her	<u>at</u> that level
<u>to</u> the store	<u>on</u> their orders	<u>from</u> the office

The prepositions underlined above are among the most common in English. A list of common prepositions is included in the Glossary. Prepositions are followed by nouns or pronouns, which complete the phrase. Prepositional phrases modify or describe other parts of the sentence. Thus, you can generally eliminate them to find the subject.

> Near Galway, the houses on the road to Spiddle is/are gorgeous.
> ~~NEAR Galway~~, the <u>HOUSES</u> ~~ON the road~~ ~~TO Spiddle~~ <u>ARE</u> gorgeous.

In the example above, the subject is *houses* (plural), and the correct verb is *are* (also plural).

2) <u>Subordinate Clauses</u>
We came across subordinate clauses earlier, in the discussion of sentence fragments. These clauses, which begin with connecting words such as *who* or *which*, cannot stand alone as sentences. Instead, they are always attached to a main clause. Like prepositional phrases, many subordinate clauses modify other parts of the sentence, acting as "big adjectives" or "big adverbs." Some subordinate clauses even act as "big nouns."

Either way, since these clauses do not contain the main subject or verb, they are frequently used as middlemen and warmups.

> When the auditors left, the executive who had been interviewed was/were glad.
> ~~When the auditors left~~, the <u>EXECUTIVE</u> ~~WHO had been interviewed~~ <u>WAS</u> glad.

Both the subject *executive* and the verb *was* are singular.

3) <u>Other Modifiers</u>
Other words can also function as <u>Modifiers</u>, which modify or describe other portions of the sentence. Modifiers will be covered in depth in Chapter 6. In the meantime, to find and eliminate other modifiers, look for <u>Present Participles</u> (-*Ing* forms derived from verbs) and <u>Past Participles</u> (-*Ed* and -*En* forms derived from verbs). Commas are another helpful sign, since commas sometimes separate modifiers from the rest of the sentence.

> Limping, the horse once considered one of the favorites was/were taken away.
> ~~LIMPING~~, the <u>HORSE</u> ~~once CONSIDERED one of the favorites~~ <u>WAS</u> taken away.

If you can remove a phrase from the sentence, and the sentence still makes sense, the phrase is likely to be a Middleman or Warmup.

Manhattan **GMAT** Prep

Use Structure to Decide

Consider the following sentence:

> In the waning days of the emperor's life, the conquest of new lands on the borders of the empire was/were considered vital.

To find the subject of the verb *was* or *were considered*, we might be tempted simply to ask ourselves, "What *was* or *were considered vital*?" This method will get rid of obviously inappropriate subjects, such as *the empire* or *the waning days*, but we could fall into a trap: we might think that *new lands* is the subject. However, *new lands* is in a prepositional phrase modifying the noun *conquest*. **A noun in a prepositional phrase cannot be the subject of the sentence**, with limited idiomatic exceptions that we will see later.

Find the subject using arguments based on structure. Do not be misled by "good-looking" nouns in Middlemen.

> Wrong: ~~In the waning days of the emperor's life,~~ the CONQUEST ~~of new lands on the borders of the empire~~ WERE CONSIDERED vital.

We now see that *conquest* (singular) requires the singular verb *was considered*.

> Right: ~~In the waning days of the emperor's life,~~ the CONQUEST ~~of new lands on the borders of the empire~~ WAS CONSIDERED vital.

Do not fall for tempting nouns, such as *new lands*, inserted to distract you! Use the structure of the sentence (for instance, the prepositional phrases) to find the subject.

Now consider this example:

> The tidal forces to which an object falling into a black hole is/are subjected is/are sufficient to tear the object apart.

We have to match up two subject–verb pairs correctly. First, match up the main clause's subject and verb, fixing them if necessary.

> Better: The tidal FORCES ~~to which an object falling into a black hole are subjected~~ ARE sufficient to tear the object apart.

Next, match up the subject and the verb in the subordinate clause, and fix them as well.

> Right: The tidal forces to which an OBJECT ~~falling into a black hole~~ IS SUBJECTED are sufficient to tear the object apart.

Of course, meaning should always guide you as you connect a subject up with its verb. As we have noted, the subject and the verb must always make sense together. At the same time, you should base your final decisions on the structure of the sentence.

And vs. Additive Phrases

The word *and* can unite two or more singular subjects, forming a compound plural subject.

> Joe AND his friends ARE going to the beach.
> Mathematics, history, AND science ARE mandatory high-school subjects.

Notice that these compound subjects take a plural verb form (*are*).

Many other words and phrases besides *and* can "add" to a subject. These words and phrases are called Additive Phrases. Examples include the following:

> along with Polly   in addition to surgery   as well as the mayor
> accompanied by me   together with a tie   including salt and pepper

Unlike *and*, additive phrases do not form compound subjects. Rather, additive phrases function as modifiers and therefore cannot change the number of the subject.

> Joe, as well as his friends, IS going to the beach.
> Mathematics, in addition to history and science, IS a required subject.

The singular subjects (*Joe* and *Mathematics*) remain singular despite the additive phrases (*as well as* and *in addition to*). Therefore, they each require the singular verb form (*is*). Note, incidentally, that *Mathematics* is singular, although it ends in an *-s*; the same thing is true of other school subjects, as well as of some activities (e.g., *aerobics*) and diseases (e.g., *diabetes*).

Only the word *and* can change a singular subject into a plural one. Singular subjects followed by additive phrases remain singular subjects.

An Additive Phrase is just another Middleman.

Or, Either ... Or, & Neither... Nor

Occasionally, a subject may include a phrase such as *or, either... or,* or *neither... nor*. Such phrases links two nouns. If one of the nouns is singular and the other noun is plural, what verb form should be used? The answer is simple: find the noun nearest to the verb, and make sure that the verb agrees in number with this noun.

> Neither the coach nor the players ARE going to the beach.
> Neither the players nor the coach IS going to the beach.

In the first example, the plural subject *players* is nearest to the verb, so the verb takes the plural form *are*. In the second example, the singular subject *coach* is nearest to the verb, so the verb takes the singular form *is*.

(Note that when the words *either* or *neither* are in a sentence alone (without *or* or *nor*), they are considered singular and take only singular verbs.)

Collective Nouns: Almost Always Singular

A <u>Collective Noun</u> is a noun that looks singular (it usually does not end with an -*s*) but can refer to a group of people or objects. Some examples include the following:

    People: agency, army, audience, class, committee, crowd, orchestra, team
    Items: baggage, citrus, equipment, fleet, fruit, furniture

In <u>some</u> rare circumstances, collective nouns can be considered plural (e.g., when you emphasize the individual actors, not their unity). However, on the GMAT, collective nouns are almost always considered <u>singular</u> and therefore require singular verb forms. Note: in British usage, many of these nouns are normally considered plural. Not so on the GMAT!

<u>The crowd</u> in the stands <u>IS cheering</u> loudly as <u>the home team</u> <u>TAKES</u> the field.
<u>Our army</u> of a hundred thousand soldiers <u>IS attacking</u> the enemy.

Each collective noun (*crowd*, *team*, and *army*) takes a singular verb form.

Indefinite Pronouns: Usually Singular

<u>Pronouns</u> are words that replace other nouns or pronouns. An <u>Indefinite Pronoun</u> is not specific about the thing to which it refers. *Anyone* is an example of an indefinite pronoun. The following indefinite pronouns are considered <u>singular</u> and require singular verb forms. Note that all the pronouns that end in -*one*, -*body*, or -*thing* fall into this category.

Anyone, anybody, anything	No one, nobody, nothing
Each, every *(as pronouns)*	Someone, somebody, something
Everyone, everybody, everything	Whatever, whoever
Either, neither *(may require a plural verb if paired with or/nor)*	

There are, however, 5 indefinite pronouns that can be <u>either singular or plural</u> depending on the context of the sentence. You can remember these 5 by the acronym SANAM.

THE SANAM PRONOUNS: **S**ome, **A**ny, **N**one, **A**ll, **M**ore/**M**ost

How can you tell if these pronouns are singular or plural? Look at the *Of*-phrase which usually follows the pronoun. You may recall that you are generally supposed to ignore *Of*-prepositional phrases (since they are misleading middlemen). The SANAM pronouns are <u>exceptions</u> to this rule. You should look at the noun object of the *Of*-phrase to determine the number of the subject.

Some of <u>the money</u> <u>WAS stolen</u> from my wallet. (*money* is singular)
Some of <u>the documents</u> <u>WERE stolen</u> from the bank. (*documents* is plural)

(Technically, *none of* + plural noun can take either a singular or a plural verb form.)

Even though they represent groups, collective nouns are almost always considered singular.

Each and *Every*: Singular Sensations

You have just learned that as the subject of a sentence, *each* or *every* requires a singular verb form. The same is true for any subject preceded by the word *each* or *every*:

Right:	Every dog HAS paws.
Right:	Every dog and cat HAS paws.
Right:	Each of these shirts IS pretty.

You may think that the subjects of the second and third sentences are plural. However, in each case, the subject is preceded by *each* or *every*. Therefore, the subject is considered singular. Note that *each* following a subject has no bearing on the verb form.

> They each ARE great tennis players.

Here, the plural subject *they* requires the plural verb form *are*.

Quantity Words and Phrases

The phrase *THE* number of takes a singular verb, but *A* number of takes a plural verb.

> The number of hardworking students in this class IS quite large.

This sentence follows the normal rule: eliminate the middlemen (*of hardworking students in this class*). The subject is *the number* (singular), which agrees with the singular verb *is*.

> A number of students in this class ARE hard workers.

On the other hand, *a number of* is an idiomatic expression. In modern English, it has become equivalent to *some* or *many*. As a result, we consider *students* the subject.

In many idiomatic expressions that designate quantities or parts, such as *a number of,* the subject of the sentence is in an *Of*-prepositional phrase. These expressions provide the exception to the rule that the subject cannot be in a prepositional phrase. We have seen the SANAM pronouns as examples of this phenomenon. Other examples include fractions and percents:

> Half of the pie IS blueberry, and half of the slices ARE already gone.

The words *majority, minority,* and *plurality* are either singular or plural, depending on their context. If you want to indicate the many individual parts of the totality, use a plural verb. If you want to indicate the totality itself, then use a singular verb form.

> The majority of the students in this class ARE hard workers.
> In the Senate, the majority HAS coalesced into a unified voting block.

Treat quantity phrases in the same way as SANAM pronouns: the noun in the *Of*-prepositional phrase will indicate whether the verb is singular or plural.

When you see an expression such as Part OF a whole, do not throw out the phrase OF a whole. It might not be a Middleman.

Subject Phrases and Clauses: Always Singular

Sometimes the subject of a sentence is an *-Ing* phrase or even a whole clause. This sort of subject is always singular and requires a singular verb form.

> <u>Having good friends</u> <u>IS</u> a wonderful thing.

The subject is the singular phrase *having good friends*, <u>not</u> the plural noun *friends*.

> <u>Whatever they want to do</u> <u>IS</u> fine with me.

The subject is the clause *whatever they want to do*, which is considered singular.

Flip It!

In most English sentences the subject precedes the verb. However, the GMAT occasionally attempts to confuse you by inverting this order and placing the subject after the verb. In sentences in which the subject follows the verb, flip the word order of the sentence so that the subject precedes the verb. This way, you will identify the subject much more readily.

> Wrong: Near those buildings SIT a lonely house, inhabited by squatters.
> Flip it!   A lonely <u>house</u>, inhabited by squatters, <u>SITS</u> near those buildings.
> Right: Near those buildings <u>SITS</u> a lonely <u>house</u>, inhabited by squatters.

In the original sentence, the singular subject *house* follows the verb. The verb form *sit* is mistakenly plural, but your ear may not catch this error because it is near the plural word *buildings*. By flipping the sentence so that the subject *house* precedes the verb, we see that we must use the singular form *sits*.

> Wrong: There IS a young man and an older woman at the bus stop.
> Flip it!   <u>A young man and an older woman</u> <u>ARE</u> at the bus stop.
> Right: There <u>ARE</u> <u>a young man and an older woman</u> at the bus stop.

By flipping the sentence so that the subject precedes the verb, we can see that the subject *a young man and an older woman* is plural. In spoken English, *there is* is often used incorrectly with plural subjects. The subject of a *there is* or *there are* expression follows the verb.

Look for flipped subjects and verbs in subordinate clauses as well:

> Uncertain: *Pong* is a classic game from which have/has descended many current computer pastimes.
> Flip it!   *Pong* is a classic game from which <u>many current computer pastimes</u> <u>HAVE descended</u>.
> Right: *Pong* is a classic game from which <u>HAVE descended</u> <u>many current computer pastimes</u>.

When you look for the subject, do not forget to look <u>after</u> the verb: the subject and the verb could be inverted!

When in Doubt, Think Singular

You may have noticed that confusing subjects are more often singular than plural.

Singular subjects dominate the chart. Thus, if you cannot remember a particular rule for determining the number of a subject, place your bet that the subject is singular!

Singular Subjects	Plural Subjects	It Depends
A singular subject linked to other nouns by an additive phrase	Subjects joined by *and*	Subjects joined by *or* or *nor*
Collective nouns		
Most indefinite pronouns		SANAM pronouns
Subjects preceded by *each* or *every*		
Subjects preceded by *the number of*	Subjects preceded by *a number of*	Other numerical words and phrases
Subject phrases or clauses		

Confusing subjects are more often singular than plural. Therefore, they usually require singular verb forms.

Problem Set

In each of the following sentences, (a) circle the verb and (b) underline the subject. Then (c) determine whether the subject and the verb make sense together, and (d) determine whether the subject agrees in number with the verb. If the subject is singular, the verb form must be singular. If the subject is plural, the verb form must be plural.

If the sentence is a fragment, or if the subject and verb do not make sense together, or if the subject and verb do not agree, (e) rewrite the sentence correcting the mistake. If the sentence is correct as it is, mark it with the word CORRECT.

1.   The traveling salesman was dismayed to learn that neither his sons nor his daughter were interested in moving.

2.   I was so thirsty that either of the two drinks were fine with me.

3.   A venomous snake designated the emblem of the rebellion by the insurgency.

4.   A number of players on the team have improved since last season.

5.   Jack, along with some of his closest friends, is sharing a limo to the prom.

6.   The recent string of burglaries, in addition to poor building maintenance, have inspired the outspoken resident to call a tenants meeting.

7.   There is, according to my doctor, many courses of treatment available to me.

8.   After all the gardening we did, the sun shining on the flowerbeds make a beautiful sight.

9.   The placement of the unusual artwork in the mansion's various rooms was impressive.

10. A new textbook focused on recent advances in artificial intelligence assigned by our instructor.

11. Just around the corner is a bakery and a supermarket.

12. Planting all these seeds is more involved than I thought.

13. Whoever rented these movies has to take them back before midnight.

14. Tired of practicing, the orchestra decide to walk out on their astonished conductor.

15. The proliferation of computer games designed to involve many players at once were first developed before the widespread availability of high-speed Internet connections.

16. The young bride, as well as her husband, were amazed by the generosity of the wedding guests.

17. Neither she nor her parents understands the challenging math problem.

18. A congressional majority is opposed to the current policy.

19. Although progress is still difficult to measure, the researchers have found that the benefit of applying interdisciplinary approaches and of fostering cooperation across multiple teams and divisions outweigh any potential cost.

20. She knows that despite the element of luck, the judgment and the wisdom displayed by each contestant evidently affects the outcome.

Answers labeled CORRECT were already correct.

1. The traveling salesman (was) dismayed to learn that neither his sons nor his daughter (was) interested in moving.

2. I (was) so thirsty that either of the two drinks (was) fine with me.

3. A venomous snake (was designated) the emblem of the rebellion by the insurgency.

4. A number of players on the team (have improved) since last season. CORRECT

5. Jack, along with some of his closest friends, (is sharing) a limo to the prom. CORRECT

6. The recent string of burglaries, in addition to poor building maintenance, (has inspired) the outspoken resident to call a tenants meeting.

7. There (are), according to my doctor, many courses of treatment available to me.

8. After all the gardening we did, the sun shining on the flowerbeds (makes) a beautiful sight.

9. The placement of the unusual artwork in the mansion's various rooms (was) impressive. CORRECT

10. A new textbook focused on recent advances in artificial intelligence (was assigned) by our instructor.

11. Just around the corner (are) a bakery and a supermarket.

12. Planting all these seeds (is) more involved than I thought. CORRECT

13. Whoever rented these movies (has) to take them back before midnight. CORRECT

14. Tired of practicing, the orchestra (decides) to walk out on *its* astonished conductor.

15. Computer games designed to involve many players at once (have proliferated); such games (were) first (developed) before the widespread availability of high-speed Internet connections. (other solutions possible)

16. The young bride, as well as her husband, (was) amazed by the generosity of the wedding guests.

17. Neither she nor her parents (understand) the challenging math problem.

18. A congressional majority (is) opposed to the current policy. CORRECT

19. Although progress (is) still difficult to measure, the researchers (have found) that the benefits of applying interdisciplinary approaches and of fostering cooperation across multiple teams and divisions (outweigh) any potential costs. (or *the benefit outweighs the cost*)

20. She knows that despite the element of luck, the judgment and the wisdom displayed by each contestant evidently (affect) the outcome.

Sentence Correction

Now that you have completed your study of SUBJECT–VERB AGREEMENT, it is time to test your skills on problems that have actually appeared on real GMAT exams over the past several years.

The problem set that follows is composed of past GMAT problems from two books published by GMAC (Graduate Management Admission Council):

The Official Guide for GMAT Review, 11th Edition (pages 39–43 & 638–660)
The Official Guide for GMAT Verbal Review (pages 234–253)

The problems in the set below are primarily focused on SUBJECT–VERB AGREEMENT issues. For each of these problems, identify the subject and verb. If it is difficult to find the subject and verb, use structure to decide.

Make sure that the subject and verb make sense together. Finally, decide whether each is singular or plural, using the techniques in this chapter. Eliminate answer choices in which the subject and verb do not agree.

Note: Problem numbers preceded by "D" refer to questions in the Diagnostic Test chapter of *The Official Guide for GMAT Review, 11th Edition* (pages 39–43).

Subject–Verb Agreement
 11th Edition: 1, 3, 21, 34, 41, 42, 52, 61, 74, 77, 90, 101, 116, 131, 138, D41, D43
 Verbal Review: 8, 16, 24, 34, 35, 44, 59, 77, 104

Chapter 4
of
SENTENCE CORRECTION

PARALLELISM

In This Chapter . . .

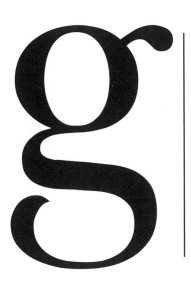

- Parallel Markers
- Parallel Elements
- Lists with *And*
- Idioms with Built-In Parallel Structure
- Superficial Parallelism vs. Actual Parallelism
- Watch Out for Linking Verbs
- Concrete Nouns and Action Nouns (Advanced)
- What Else Is Considered Parallel (Advanced)

PARALLELISM

Arguably, the GMAT's favorite grammar topic is parallelism. According to the principle of parallelism, **comparable sentence parts must be structurally and logically similar**.

> The employees were upset by the company's low pay, poor working conditions, and that they did not have enough outlets for their creativity.

Notice that this example has three comparable parts—the three things that upset the employees. The structure of the first two parts is similar; both parts consist of a <u>Noun Phrase</u> (centered on the nouns *pay* and *conditions*, respectively). However, the third part has a different structure altogether: it is a <u>clause</u> containing a subject, verb, and object. In order to make the sentence parallel, we must change the third item in the list so that its structure is like that of the first two items (a noun phrase):

Right: The employees were upset by the company's low <u>pay</u>, poor working <u>conditions</u>, and <u>shortage</u> of outlets for employees' creativity.

Notice that we do not generally have to make every <u>word</u> parallel in the parallel elements. However, the most important words must be parallel. In this case, the most important words in the three items in the list—*pay*, *conditions*, and *shortage*—are all nouns. As a result, the phrase *the company's* can now modify each of the parallel parts.

the company's low <u>pay</u>
"   poor working <u>conditions</u>
"   <u>shortage</u> of outlets for employees' creativity

Parallel parts of a sentence are always signaled by parallel markers. Learn to spot the markers, and you will find parallelism issues.

Parallel Markers

How do we know that parts of a sentence need to be parallel to each other? Often, we know by spotting <u>Parallel Markers</u>—words that link or contrast items and that force those items to be parallel. Examples of parallel markers include the following:

<u>Markers</u>	<u>Structures</u>	<u>Examples</u>
And	X and Y	<u>Apples</u> AND <u>pears</u>
	X, Y, and Z	<u>Apples</u>, <u>pears</u>, AND <u>bananas</u>
Both/And	Both X and Y	BOTH <u>apples</u> AND <u>pears</u>
Or	X or Y	<u>Apples</u> OR <u>pears</u>
Either/Or	Either X or Y	EITHER <u>apples</u> OR <u>pears</u>
Not/But	Not X but Y	NOT <u>apples</u> BUT <u>pears</u>
Rather Than	X rather than Y	<u>Apples</u> RATHER THAN <u>pears</u>
From/To	From X to Y	FROM <u>apples</u> TO <u>pears</u>

The most important parallel markers are the three common <u>conjunctions</u>: *and, but,* and *or.* Of these, *and* is the most common. However, do not limit yourself to these markers. Any construction that expresses two or more things in the same way requires parallelism.

Parallel Elements

Almost anything in a sentence can be made parallel to a similar <u>Parallel Element</u>.

Elements	Examples
Nouns	Her expression reflected BOTH <u>anger</u> AND <u>relief</u>.
Adjectives	The park was NEITHER <u>accessible</u> NOR <u>affordable</u>.
Verbs	The custodian <u>cleaned</u> the basement AND <u>washed</u> the windows.
Infinitives	We would like NOT ONLY <u>to hear</u> your side of the story BUT ALSO <u>to provide</u> a response.
Participles	The actor left quickly, <u>shunning</u> fans AND <u>ducking</u> into a car.
Prepositional Phrases	It was important to leave the money <u>in the drawer</u> RATHER THAN <u>on the table</u>. (Note: the prepositions do <u>not</u> always have to be the same.)
Subordinate Clauses	They contended <u>that the committee was biased</u> AND <u>that it should be disbanded</u>.

Make sure the two sides of the sentence are both structurally and logically parallel.

Some verbs or forms derived from verbs have more than one word: *was opening, can lose, to increase.* You can often split apart these expressions, so that the first word or words count across all of the elements.

> The division WAS <u>opening</u> offices, <u>hiring</u> staff AND <u>investing</u> in equipment.
> The railroad CAN EITHER <u>lose</u> more money OR <u>solve</u> its problems.
> They wanted TO <u>increase</u> awareness, <u>spark</u> interest, AND <u>motivate</u> purchases.

Parallel clauses should start with the same word.

Wrong:	I want to retire to a place <u>WHERE I can relax</u> AND <u>THAT has low taxes</u>.
Right:	I want to retire to a place <u>WHERE I can relax</u> AND <u>WHERE the taxes are low</u>.

Note that in the example above, the principle of concision yields to the mandate of parallelism. Likewise, do not over-shorten any element. Be sure that each element is complete.

Wrong:	Ralph likes BOTH <u>THOSE WHO are popular</u> AND <u>WHO are not</u>.
Right:	Ralph likes BOTH <u>THOSE WHO are popular</u> AND <u>THOSE WHO are not</u>.

In the first sentence, the second element cannot stand alone: *likes... WHO are not* does not make sense. We have to write *likes... THOSE WHO are not*. (However, we do not have to repeat the word *popular*, which is understood in the second element.)

Lists with *And*

As mentioned above, the word *and* is the most common and important parallel marker. Whenever you see *and* in a GMAT sentence, look for the list and count the items. GMAT sentences have been observed to include as many as four items in a list connected by *and*.

List	Examples
X and Y	Apples **AND** pears
X, Y, and Z	Apples, pears, **AND** bananas
X, Y, Z, and W	Apples, pears, bananas, **AND** peaches

Correct lists obey these templates. No right answer omits *and* in a list just before the last item. Moreover, the GMAT always inserts a comma before the *and* in lists of 3 or 4 items.

If you join 2 <u>main</u> clauses with *and*, put a comma before the *and*.

List of Main Clauses	Example
X, and Y	I like apples, **AND** you like pears.

If the items in a list are long groups of words, such as clauses, that themselves contain lists, you should be careful as you tally items.

Wrong: She argued that the agency acted with disregard for <u>human life</u> AND <u>property</u> AND <u>reckless abandon</u> AND <u>it should therefore be shut down</u>.

The four underlined items, which are all connected by *and* right now, are not all at the same logical level. *Human life* and *property* are parallel to each other, but not to *reckless abandon*. Moreover, none of these items is parallel to the clause *it should therefore be shut down*. To fix the sentence, create a clear hierarchy by repeating words and adding commas where necessary. Also, you should flip lists so that the longest item is last, if possible.

Applying these principles to the example, we get the following.

Right: She argued THAT the agency acted <u>WITH reckless abandon</u> AND <u>WITH disregard</u> for <u>human life</u> AND <u>property</u>, AND <u>THAT it should therefore be shut down</u>.

The lowest level list is *human life AND property*, the object of the same preposition *for*. We have added the preposition *with* before *reckless abandon* to clarify that this noun is parallel to *disregard for human life and property*. Finally, we put *that* before the clause to emphasize that this clause is parallel to the other subordinate clause *that the agency...property*. We also add a comma before the last *and*, creating a pause after the *human life and property* list. You might think that whenever you have just two items in a list, you write *X and Y* without a comma. However, if the first item contains lower-level lists, as the first clause does, you must put in a comma before the *and* that connects the two clauses: *THAT the agency... property, and THAT it...down.*

Never skip past the word *And* in a GMAT sentence. Always figure out which items are in the list.

Idioms with Built-In Parallel Structure

Certain idioms demand parallelism as a result of their structure. The most important idioms demanding parallelism, such as *both X and Y*, have already been described. The chart below lists additional idiomatic structures that require parallelism. These idioms are more fully explored in the Idiom List in Chapter 9.

<table>
<tr><td>X Acts As Y</td><td>Distinguish X From Y</td><td>X is the Same As Y</td></tr>
<tr><td>As X, So Y</td><td>Estimate X To Be Y</td><td>X is good, and So Too is Y</td></tr>
<tr><td>Between X And Y</td><td>X Instead Of Y</td><td>X, Such As Y (example)</td></tr>
<tr><td>Compared To X, Y</td><td>X is Known To Be Y</td><td>Think Of X As Y</td></tr>
<tr><td>Consider X Y</td><td>X is Less Than Y</td><td>X is Thought To Be Y</td></tr>
<tr><td>In Contrast To X, Y</td><td>Make X Y</td><td>View X As Y</td></tr>
<tr><td>Declare X Y</td><td>Mistake X For Y</td><td>Whether X Or Y</td></tr>
<tr><td>X Develops Into Y</td><td>Not Only X(,) But Also Y</td><td>(the comma is optional)</td></tr>
<tr><td>X Differs From Y</td><td>Regard X As Y</td><td></td></tr>
</table>

<aside>Do not be a victim of superficial parallelism!</aside>

Superficial Parallelism vs. Actual Parallelism

You always must figure out which grammatical structures are <u>logically</u> parallel before making them <u>structurally</u> parallel. Be particularly careful with verbs and verbal forms.

> Sal applied himself in his new job, arriving early every day, skipping lunch regularly, AND leaving late every night.

In the sentence above, the *-Ing* participle phrases *arriving early every day, skipping lunch regularly*, and *leaving late every night* are parallel. The main clause, *applied himself in his new job*, is not parallel to these participle phrases. This is CORRECT. The main verb is *applied*, and the *-Ing* phrases provide additional information about how Sal applied himself. It would distort the meaning to change the sentence to this superficially parallel version:

> Wrong: Sal applied himself in his new job, arrived early every day, skipped lunch regularly, AND left late every night.

This version gives all the activities equal emphasis, instead of making the last three activities subordinate to the main activity (*applied himself in his new job*).

Do not assume that <u>all</u> verbs and verbal forms in a sentence must be parallel.

Watch Out for Linking Verbs

A more subtle form of parallelism involves <u>Linking Verbs</u>. Usually, we think of verbs as action words (*walk, dance,* and *jump*), but another class of verbs is called linking verbs. Instead of expressing what a subject <u>does</u>, these verbs express what the subject <u>is</u>, or what condition the subject is in. The most common linking verb is naturally the verb *to be*, but there are other linking verbs as well. Below are two lists. The first contains all the forms of the verb *to be*, while the second contains other common linking verbs:

To Be	Other Linking Verbs	
is	appear	seem
are	become	smell
was	feel	sound
were	grow	stay
am	look	taste
been	remain	turn
be	represent	
being	resemble	

Treat any linking verb as a parallel marker. Make the subject and the object parallel.

Wrong: <u>The bouquet</u> of flowers WAS <u>a giving</u> of love.

The two sides of the linking verb *was* are *the bouquet* and *a giving*. These two sides are not as structurally parallel as possible. In order to achieve true parallelism, we can rewrite the sentence replacing *giving* with the noun *gift*, so that the two sides of the linking verb are as structurally similar as possible.

Right: <u>The bouquet</u> of flowers WAS <u>a gift</u> of love.

You must also ensure that the two sides of the linking verb are parallel in <u>meaning</u>.

Wrong: Upon being nominated, <u>this politician</u> REPRESENTS <u>a step forward</u> in urban-rural relations in this country.

The two sides of the linking verb *represents* are *the politician* and *a step forward*. However, it is awkward to say that a *politician* himself or herself is or represents *a step forward*, which is an occurrence or event. Rather, the <u>event</u> involving the politician—his or her *nomination*—is what we should make parallel to the noun *a step forward*.

Right: <u>The nomination</u> of this politician REPRESENTS <u>a step forward</u> in urban-rural relations in this country.

Note that the verb *to be* does not have to be part of a linking verb phrase. The verb *to be* also forms the progressive tenses (*I am watering the plants*) and the passive voice (*The plants were watered last night*). Do not look for parallelism in these uses of *be*.

When you use a linking verbs, you have to make the subject and the object parallel.

Concrete Nouns and Action Nouns (Advanced)

Not every noun can be made parallel to every other noun. As we saw in the previous section, *the flower bouquet* was not parallel to *a giving of love*, even though *giving* in this context is technically a noun (if an awkward one). We can divide nouns into two categories:

1) <u>Concrete nouns</u> refer to things, people, places, and even time periods or certain events.

> rock, continent, electron, politician, region, holiday, week

2) <u>Action nouns</u> refer to actions, as their name implies. They are often formed from verbs.

> eruption, pollution, nomination, withdrawal, development, change, growth

 To maintain logical parallelism, avoid making concrete nouns and action nouns parallel.

Unfortunately, the distinctions do not end there! *-Ing* forms of verbs can also be used as nouns to indicate actions. *-Ing* verb forms used as nouns are called <u>Gerunds</u>. Gerund phrases are divided into two categories as well:

A) <u>Simple Gerund Phrases</u>

> <u>Drinking the water</u> quenched his thirst. He liked <u>gulping water quickly</u>.

Simple gerund phrases are "Nouns on the Outside, Verbs on the Inside." That is, each underlined phrase acts as a noun:

> <u>Something</u> quenched his thirst. He liked <u>something</u>.

However, <u>inside</u> the actual phrase, the words are arranged as if they follow a verb. *Gulping water quickly* can easily be made part of a working verb phrase: *I AM <u>gulping water quickly</u>*.

B) <u>Complex Gerund Phrases</u>

> <u>THE drinking OF the water</u> quenched his thirst. He liked <u>THE QUICK gulping OF water</u>.

Complex gerund phrases are "Nouns Through and Through." The *-Ing* gerund form is made fully into a noun; in fact, it is often preceded by articles (*a, an,* or *the*) or adjectives (*quick*). The object is put into an *Of*-prepositional phrase (e.g., *the running of marathons*) or placed in front of the *-Ing* form (e.g., *marathon running*). Complex gerund phrases often sound less natural than simple gerund phrases, as in the example above.

Why on earth does this matter? The reason is that the GMAT follows very strict rules of structural parallelism with these gerund forms. **Simple gerund phrases are NEVER PARALLEL to complex gerund phrases**—even though they both are *-Ing* forms of a verb, and both are used as nouns!

Keep concrete nouns and action nouns separate from each other. Do likewise with simple and complex gerunds.

Wrong: I enjoyed <u>drinking the water</u> AND <u>the wine tasting</u>.

Drinking the water is a simple gerund phrase, but *the wine tasting* is a complex gerund phrase.

Right: I enjoyed <u>drinking the water</u> AND <u>tasting the wine</u>.

Of the two types of gerund phrases, **<u>only</u> complex ones can be parallel to action nouns**. In a list of action nouns, a simple gerund phrase might be mistaken for something other than a noun.

Wrong: The rebels demanded the <u>withdrawal</u> of government forces from disputed regions, significant <u>reductions</u> in overall troop levels, <u>raising</u> the rebel flag on holidays, AND a general <u>pardon</u>.

Withdrawal, reductions, and *pardon* are all action nouns. Thus, you should not include the word *raising* by itself (it might be misinterpreted as a modifier). Rather, you should choose *THE raising OF.*

Right: The rebels demanded the <u>withdrawal</u> of government forces from disputed regions, significant <u>reductions</u> in overall troop levels, <u>THE raising</u> OF the rebel flag on holidays, AND a general <u>pardon</u>.

In any list of action nouns, always choose the <u>complex</u> gerund phrase (often with articles and the word *Of*) over the simple gerund phrase!

Also, if an appropriate action noun for a particular verb already exists in English, then avoid creating a complex gerund phrase. Instead, use the pre-existing action noun.

Wrong: The rebels demanded the <u>withdrawal</u> of government forces from disputed regions AND <u>releasing</u> certain political prisoners.

Wrong: The rebels demanded the <u>withdrawal</u> of government forces from disputed regions AND THE <u>releasing</u> OF certain political prisoners.

Right: The rebels demanded the <u>withdrawal</u> of government forces from disputed regions AND THE <u>RELEASE</u> OF certain political prisoners.

Release is a pre-existing action noun (meaning *the act of releasing*), so use this noun. Fortunately, the complex gerund phrase will often sound worse than the pre-existing action noun.

In brief, there are three categories of nouns: (1) Concrete Nouns, (2) Action Nouns and Complex Gerunds, and (3) Simple Gerunds. Do not mix these categories.

This is a complicated issue. Perhaps that is why the GMAT likes to test it. Spend a little time mastering this topic, and your effort will pay off.

> In any list of action nouns, *-Ing* forms should generally be preceded by *The/A/An* and be followed by *Of*, if possible.

What Else Is Considered Parallel (Advanced)

We can outline <u>Parallelism Categories</u> for many other sentence elements as well.

<u>(1) Working Verbs</u>
Only working verbs are parallel to other working verbs.

> The plant BOTH <u>exceeded</u> output targets AND <u>ran</u> more smoothly than ever.

<u>(2) Infinitives</u>
<u>Infinitives</u> are the *TO* form of the verb (e.g., *to be* is the infinitive of *be*). In general, only make infinitives parallel to other infinitives. The *to* can be omitted in the second infinitive (and all subsequent infinitives), unless there is a marker before the first infinitive.

> Wrong: It is critical <u>to suspend</u> activities, <u>to notify</u> investors AND <u>say</u> nothing.
> Right: It is critical <u>to suspend</u> activities, <u>notify</u> investors AND <u>say</u> nothing.
> Right: It is critical <u>to suspend</u> activities, <u>to notify</u> investors AND <u>to say</u> nothing.
> Right: It is critical EITHER <u>to suspend</u> activities OR <u>to notify</u> investors.

<u>(3) Adjectives, Past Participles, and Present Participles (used as adjectives)</u>

> A mastodon carcass, <u>thawed</u> only once AND still <u>fresh</u>, is on display.

Both *thawed* and *fresh* describe *carcass*. *Thawed* is a past participle, whereas *fresh* is an adjective. However, they can be made parallel to each other.

> Only a few feet <u>wide</u> BUT <u>spanning</u> a continent, the railroad changed history.

Both *wide* and *spanning* describe *the railroad*. *Wide* is an adjective, whereas *spanning* is a present participle. However, they can be made parallel to each other.

<u>(4) Clauses</u>
Only clauses starting with the same word should be made parallel. In general, clauses should not be made parallel to anything besides another clause.

> Wrong: A mastodon carcass, <u>thawed</u> only once AND <u>which is still fresh</u>, is on display.
>
> Right: A mastodon carcass, <u>which has been thawed</u> only once AND <u>which is still fresh</u>, is on display.

Keep these categories straight, together with the noun categories.

Common Parallelism Categories

Nouns	Other
(1) Concrete Nouns	(1) Working Verbs
(2) Action Nouns and	(2) Infinitives
Complex Gerunds	(3) Adjectives and Participles
(3) Simple Gerunds	(4) Clauses

For parallelism's sake, separate (1) working verbs, (2) infinitives, (3) adjectives (and similar words), and (4) clauses.

Problem Set

Each of the following sentences contains an error of parallelism in its underlined portion. For each sentence, begin by writing a correct version of the sentence.

Then, using your correct version of the sentence: (1) circle the parallelism markers and (2) place [square brackets] around each set of parallel elements. For an extra challenge, (3) identify the part of speech of each parallel element, if possible.

1. Researchers have found a correlation between regular exercise and earning good grades.

2. Although we were sitting in the bleachers, the baseball game was as exciting to us as the people sitting behind home plate.

3. Many teachers choose to seek employment in the suburbs rather than facing low salaries in the city.

4. Most employers agree that how a candidate dresses for a job interview and even the way he positions himself in his seat leave a lasting impression.

5. A good night's sleep not only gives your body a chance to rest, but energizing you for the following day.

6. The joint business venture will increase employee satisfaction and be improving relations between upper management and staff.

7. The museum displays the work of a wide variety of artists, from those who are world-renowned to who are virtually unknown.

8. We were dismayed to learn that our neighbors were untidy, disagreeable, and they were uninterested to make new friends.

9. The students did poorly on the test more because they had not studied than the material was difficult.

10. The blizzard deposited more than a foot of snow on the train tracks, prompted the transit authority to shut down service temporarily, and causing discontent among commuters who were left stranded for hours.

11.   The experiences we have <u>when children</u> influence our behavior in adulthood.

12.   The band chosen for the annual spring concert appealed to <u>both the student body as well as to the administration</u>.

13.   Dr. King's "Letter from a Birmingham Jail" is <u>a condemning of racial injustice and a calling for</u> nonviolent resistance to that injustice.

14.   Tobacco companies, <u>shaken by a string</u> of legal setbacks in the United States, but which retain strong growth prospects in the developing world, face an uncertain future.

15.   Voters want to elect a president who genuinely cares about health care, the <u>environment, the travails of ordinary men and women, has the experience, wisdom,</u> and strength of character required for the job.

16.   The consultant is looking for a café <u>where they have comfortable chairs</u> and that provides free internet access.

17.   The network security team is responsible for <u>detecting new viruses</u> and the creation of software patches to block those viruses.

18.   He received a medal for <u>sinking an enemy ship</u> and the capture of its crew.

19.   Dr. Crock's claims <u>have been not corroborated</u> by other scientists or published in a prestigious journal but have nonetheless garnered a great deal of attention from the public.

1. Researchers have found a correlation [(between) <u>exercising regularly</u> (and) earning good grades].

Exercising regularly and *earning good grades* are both **gerund phrases**. (More precisely, they are **simple gerund phrases**.)

2. Although we were sitting in the bleachers, the baseball game was [(as) exciting to us (as) to the people sitting behind home plate].

To us and *to the people sitting behind home plate* are both **prepositional phrases**.

3. Many teachers choose to [seek employment in the suburbs (rather than) <u>face low salaries</u> in the city].

(To) seek employment in the suburbs and *(to) face low salaries in the city* are both **infinitive phrases**.

4. Most employers agree that [how a candidate dresses for a job interview (and) even <u>how he positions himself in his seat</u>] leave a lasting impression.

How a candidate dresses for a job interview and *how he positions himself in his seat* are **noun clauses**. [You can tell that they are <u>clauses</u> because each of them contains a subject (*candidate, he*) and a verb (*dresses, positions*). You can tell that they are <u>noun</u> clauses because they do the work of nouns—in this case acting as the subject of a verb (*leave*).]

5. A good night's sleep [(not only) gives your body a chance to rest (, but) also <u>energizes</u> you for the following day].

Gives your body a chance to rest and *energizes you for the following day* are **working verb phrases**.

6. The joint business venture will [increase employee satisfaction (and) improve relations between upper management and staff].

(Will) increase employee satisfaction and *(will) improve relations between upper management and staff* are **working verb phrases**.

7. The museum displays the work of a wide variety of artists, [(from) those who are world-<u>renowned</u> (to) <u>those who</u> are virtually unknown].

Those who are world-renowned and *those who are virtually unknown* are **pronoun phrases**. [Each of them contains a pronoun (*those*) modified by an relative clause (*who…*).]

8. We were dismayed to learn that our neighbors were [untidy (,) disagreeable (, and) <u>uninterested in making</u> new friends].

Untidy and *disagreeable* are **adjectives**. *Uninterested in making new friends* is a **participial phrase** formed from a past participle. This participial phrase acts as an adjective and is parallel to the two adjectives.

9. The students did poorly on the test [(more) because they had not studied (than) <u>because the material</u> was difficult.

Because they had not studied and *because the material was difficult* are **subordinate clauses**. [You can tell they are <u>clauses</u> because each of them contains a subject (*they*) and a verb (*had…studied, did…understand*). These clauses do the work of adverbs—in this case modifying the verb *did*.]

10. The blizzard deposited more than a foot of snow on the train tracks, [prompting the transit authority to shut down service temporarily (and) causing discontent among commuters who were left stranded for hours].

Prompting…temporarily and *causing…hours* are **participial phrases** formed from present participles. They both function as adverbs, modifying the verb in the main clause (*deposited*).

11. The experiences we have in childhood influence our behavior in adulthood.

In childhood and *in adulthood* are **prepositional phrases**. This sentence does not have any parallelism signals for us to circle. We know that *in childhood* should be parallel in structure to *in adulthood* because of logical considerations: the sentence is meant to highlight a connection between childhood and adulthood.

12. The band chosen for the annual spring concert appealed to [(both) the student body (and) the administration].

The student body and *the administration* are **noun phrases**. [It would normally be correct to write *The band…appealed to the student body as well as to the administration*. However, the word *both* was not underlined in the original question, so we are forced to choose *both X and Y* idiom as our parallelism signal.]

13. [Dr. King's "Letter from a Birmingham Jail" (is) [a condemnation of racial injustice (and) a call for nonviolent resistance to that injustice]].

The verb *is* equates the two parallel halves of this sentence, both of which are **action noun phrases**. In order to maximize parallelism between the latter half of the sentence and the first half, we prefer simple, common action nouns (*condemnation, call*) to gerunds (*condemning, calling*).

Note that the latter half of the sentence is one noun phrase that contains within itself two parallel noun phrases, *a condemnation of racial injustice* and *a call for resistance to that injustice*.

14. Tobacco companies, [which have been shaken by a string of legal setbacks in the United States (, but) which retain strong growth prospects in the developing world], face an uncertain future.

Which have…United States and *which retain…developing world* are both **subordinate clauses**. [You can tell they are clauses because each of them has a subject (*which*, a relative pronoun that refers to *companies*) and a verb (*have been shaken, retain*). These clauses both describe the noun *companies*.]

The original sentence was wrong because it attempted to put a **participial phrase** (*shaken by…United States*) in parallel with an **subordinate clause** (*which retain…developing world*).

15. Voters want to elect a president [who genuinely cares about [health care (,) the environment (, and) the travails of ordinary [men (and) women]] (, and) who has the [experience (,) wisdom (, and) strength of character] required for the job].

At the most fundamental level we have two **subordinate clauses** modifying *president*: (1) *who genuinely…women* and (2) *who has…job*. The two clauses are joined by the parallelism signal *and*. (Normally there is normally no comma before an *and* that joins only two parallel elements. However, we should use a comma in this case to separate the two clauses, since the first clause ends in a list, *men and women*, that we do not want to mingle with the beginning of the second clause.)

Within the first adjective clause we have three **noun phrases** in parallel: (a) *health care*, (b) *the environment*, and (c) *the travails...women*. These are not action nouns, so we would classify them as concrete nouns. Inside (c) we have two nouns in parallel: *men* and *women*.

Within the second adjective clause we have three **nouns or noun phrases** in parallel: (d) *experience*, (e) *wisdom*, and (f) *strength of character*. Although these nouns are all abstract, they are not action nouns; as a result, we would classify them as concrete nouns.

16. The consultant is looking for a café [that has comfortable chairs (and) that provides free internet access].

That has comfortable chairs and *that provides free internet access* are **subordinate clauses**. [You can tell they are clauses because each of them has a subject (*that*) and a verb (*has, provides*). These clauses both describe the noun *café*. Note that parallel clauses should normally start with the same word. In this case, the word is *that*.]

17. The network security team is responsible for [the detection of new viruses (and) the creation of software patches to block those viruses].

The detection of new viruses and *the creation of software patches to block those viruses* are **parallel noun phrases**. Both are centered on **action nouns** (*detection, creation*). The original sentence was incorrect because it attempted to put a **simple gerund phrase** (*detecting new viruses*) in parallel with an **action noun phrase**.

18. He received a medal for [the sinking of an enemy ship (and) the capture of its crew].

The sinking of an enemy ship is a **complex gerund phrase** and *the capture of its crew* is a **noun phrase** that centers on an **action noun** (*capture*). The original sentence was incorrect because it attempted to put a **simple gerund phrase** (*sinking an enemy ship*) in parallel with an **action noun phrase**.

[Why do we not use an **action noun phrase** instead of a **complex gerund phrase** in this answer? Simply because no appropriate **action noun** exists for the verb *to sink*. "Sinkage" is an English word, but it does mean the <u>act</u> of causing something to sink.]

19. Dr. Crock's claims [have (not) been [corroborated by other scientists (or) published in a prestigious journal] (but) have nonetheless garnered a great deal of attention from the public].

The parallelism signal *Not/But* links two **working verb phrases**: *have...been corroborated by...journal* and *have nonetheless garnered...from the public*.

In the first of these verb phrases, the word *not* must come <u>after</u> the <u>first helping verb</u> (*have*). Notice also that the first of our verb phrases contains two parallel phrases formed from **past participles** (*corroborated, published*).

Sentence Correction

Now that you have completed your study of PARALLELISM, it is time to test your skills on problems that have actually appeared on real GMAT exams over the past several years.

The problem set that follows is composed of past GMAT problems from two books published by GMAC (Graduate Management Admission Council):

The Official Guide for GMAT Review, 11ᵗʰ Edition (pages 39–43 & 638–660)
The Official Guide for GMAT Verbal Review (pages 234–253)

The problems in the set below are primarily focused on PARALLELISM issues. For each of these problems, identify parallel markers (that signal parallelism) and parallel elements (the parts that need to be parallelism). Do not fall victim to superficial parallelism! Also, identify the parallelism categories that the elements belong to.

<u>Note</u>: Problem numbers preceded by "D" refer to questions in the Diagnostic Test chapter of *The Official Guide for GMAT Review, 11ᵗʰ Edition* (pages 39–43).

Parallelism

11ᵗʰ Edition: 9, 11, 17, 18, 19, 22, 35, 39, 46, 47, 49, 54, 56, 60, 64, 65, 84, 86, 87, 88, 91, 106, 112, 113, 117, 119, 129, 130, 132, 134, 136, D36, D39, D46, D48, D50, D51

Verbal Review: 1, 4, 6, 11, 22, 25, 27, 46, 47, 51, 52, 56, 62, 64, 66, 70, 81, 82, 84, 93, 97, 99, 100, 108

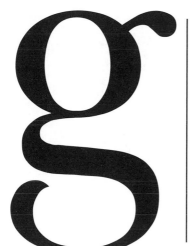

Chapter 5
of
SENTENCE CORRECTION

PRONOUNS

In This Chapter . . .

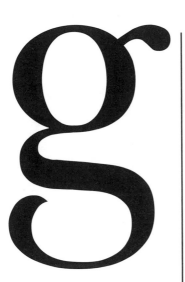

- The Antecedent Must Exist
- The Antecedent & Pronoun Must Make Sense Together
- The Antecedent Must Be Unambiguous
- The Antecedent & Pronoun Must Agree in Number
- Pronoun Case
- The Deadly Five: *It, Its, They, Them, Their*
- *This, That, These,* and *Those*
- Other Pronouns
- Placeholder *It*
- Avoiding Pronouns Altogether
- Nuances of Pronoun Reference (Advanced)

PRONOUNS

A pronoun is a word that takes the place of a noun, so that we do not have to repeat that noun elsewhere in the sentence.

> <u>Gasoline</u> has become so expensive that <u>IT</u> now consumes as much as 16% of personal income in some rural areas.

In the sentence above, the pronoun *it* takes the place of the noun *gasoline*. Alternatively, we can say that *it* refers to *gasoline*. The noun *gasoline* is known as the <u>antecedent</u> of *it*.

Pronoun errors are so frequent on the GMAT that every time you see a pronoun, such as *it, its, they, them,* or *their*, you should be sure to check whether it is being used correctly.

The first question you must ask yourself is this: **What is the antecedent of this pronoun?** Once you have found the antecedent, you must make sure that it makes sense, that it is the only possible antecedent, and that it agrees in number with the pronoun.

Notice that these questions are essentially the same as those you should ask with subjects and verbs: "what is the subject of this verb, does it make sense with the verb," etc.

The Antecedent Must Exist

The first task is to find the antecedent in the sentence.

> The park rangers discussed measures to prevent severe wildfires, which would be devastating to <u>IT</u>.

What noun does *it* refer to? We might guess the *park*. However, you should note that in this sentence, *park* is not truly a noun. Rather, *park* is acting as an <u>adjective</u> in the phrase *the park rangers*. As a result, *park* cannot be the antecedent of *it*. Moreover, there is no other possible antecedent in the sentence. Thus, as written, this sentence is incorrect.

One simple way to fix this sentence is to eliminate the pronoun, replacing it with the noun you want to refer to.

> Right: The rangers discussed measures to prevent severe wildfires, which would be devastating to THE PARK.

We eliminated the first mention of *park* to avoid repetition (after all, the noun *rangers* seems specific enough), but we could have left the subject as *the park rangers*.

Watch out for nouns used as adjectives! They cannot be antecedents of pronouns.

The antecedent to which you want to refer must actually exist in the sentence and be functioning as a noun.

Every pronoun must refer to an antecedent in the sentence.

The Antecedent & Pronoun Must Make Sense Together

The next task is to check whether the antecedent and the pronoun agree <u>logically</u>. That is, if you replace the pronoun with the noun, will you get a sensible sentence?

> Although the term "supercomputer" may sound fanciful or exaggerated, <u>IT</u> is simply an extremely fast mainframe that can execute trillions of calculations every second.

Looking for the antecedent, we find *the term "supercomputer."* Now we replace the pronoun:

> ... <u>the term "supercomputer"</u> is simply an extremely fast mainframe...

The error in meaning is subtle but unmistakable. The term <u>is not</u> a mainframe; rather, the term <u>refers to</u> a mainframe. Therefore, you must change the verb or make some other edit.

> Right: Although <u>the term "supercomputer"</u> may sound fanciful or exaggerated, <u>IT</u> simply REFERS TO an extremely fast mainframe that can execute trillions of calculations every second.

As you might recall, these issues are aspects of the <u>Meaning</u> principle. The GMAT tries to trick you into "assuming away" little wrinkles in meaning. After all, you knew what the author of the first sentence meant to say, right? But make no assumptions. **Whenever you find an antecedent, always check that it makes sense in place of the pronoun.**

The Antecedent Must Be Unambiguous

Every pronoun on the GMAT must clearly refer to only one antecedent. Sentences in which there are two or more possible antecedents for any pronoun should be rewritten.

> Researchers claim to have developed new "nano-papers" incorporating tiny cellulose fibers, which <u>THEY</u> allege give <u>THEM</u> the strength of cast iron.

What nouns do *they* and *them* refer to? We might <u>assume</u> that *they* refers to *researchers* (who *claim* something) and that *them* refers to *new "nano-papers."* However, in reality, both *they* and *them* have ambiguous antecedents. Either pronoun could refer to *researchers* <u>or</u> to *"nano-papers."*

Resolve the ambiguity by recasting the sentence. In this case, eliminate *they* and *them*.

> Right: Researchers claim to have developed <u>new "nano-papers"</u> incorporating tiny cellulose fibers, which allegedly give <u>THESE MATERIALS</u> the strength of cast iron.

Make sure that every pronoun has only one possible antecedent.

The Antecedent & Pronoun Must Agree in Number

After finding the antecedent, ask yourself if the pronoun agrees with the antecedent in number. If the antecedent is singular, the pronoun that refers to it must be singular. If the antecedent is plural, the pronoun that refers to it must be plural.

> Confronted by radical changes in production and distribution, modern Hollywood studios are attempting various experiments in an effort to retain <u>ITS</u> status as the primary arbiter of movie consumption.

The antecedent of *its* is *modern Hollywood studios*. However, *its* is singular, while *studios* is plural. We must change either the pronoun or the noun to make the number match.

> Right: Confronted by radical changes in production and distribution, <u>modern Hollywood studios</u> are attempting various experiments in an effort to retain <u>THEIR</u> status as the primary arbiters of movie consumption.

> Right: Confronted by radical changes in production and distribution, <u>the modern Hollywood studio</u> is attempting various experiments in an effort to retain <u>ITS</u> status as the primary arbiter of movie consumption.

Either sentence is correct. We can speak about *modern Hollywood studios* (plural) or the "generic" *modern Hollywood studio* (singular). Either way, we must match the number of the pronoun and its antecedent. Note that the GMAT tends to test number agreement when you can easily express the relevant concepts either in singular or in plural form. Also, we saw in Subject–Verb Agreement that the GMAT can disguise the subject and its number in various ways (e.g., additive phrases such as *along with*). The same disguises apply to pronoun antecedents. Be sure to identify the antecedent properly.

Pronoun Case

Occasionally, you need to think about the <u>case</u> of the pronoun or antecedent. "Case" means grammatical role or function. There are 3 cases in English: subject, object, and possessive.

1) <u>Subject</u> pronouns can be the subjects of sentences.
   I you he she it we they who   *They arrived late.*

2) <u>Object</u> pronouns can be the objects of verbs or prepositions.
   me you him her it us them whom   *No one saw them or talked to them.*

3) <u>Possessive</u> pronouns indicate ownership or a similar relation.
   my/mine your/yours his her/hers its
   our/ours their/theirs whose   *Their presence went unnoticed.*

Its is a possessive pronoun. *It's* is a contraction, meaning *it is*.

The GMAT does not force you to pick pronoun cases directly, since this task is too easy. For instance, *Them arrived late* and *No one saw they* sound terrible to the native ear and are simple to fix. However, we need to consider the topic of case for a couple of reasons.

a) Sometimes (though <u>not</u> always), pronouns show a tendency to refer to nouns in the same case, especially when they are embedded in parallel structures. In particular, **a pronoun in subject position in one clause may often be presumed to refer to the subject of a parallel clause**, even if that subject is relatively far away.

> Right: <u>Supernovas</u> destroy their immediate environments in vast explosions, BUT by synthesizing heavy chemical elements, <u>THEY</u> provide the universe with the possibility of biochemistry-based life as we know it.

Supernovas is the subject of the first clause. The *they* is also in subject position in the second clause, which is parallel to the first clause. Even though there are at least two closer possible antecedents (*environments* and *explosions*), we know that *they* clearly refers to *supernovas*.

b) **Nouns in the possessive case** (with *'s* or *s'*) **are often poor antecedents**.

> Wrong: The board is investigating several executives' compensation packages in order to determine how much may have been improperly awarded to <u>THEM</u>.

In this sentence, the pronoun *them* actually refers better to *packages* than to *executives'*. In fact, according to the <u>Possessive Poison</u> rule, *them* <u>cannot</u> refer to *executives'*. The Possessive Poison rule states that possessive nouns can serve as antecedents only to possessive pronouns, not to subject or object pronouns.

As a result of a controversy a few years ago with another major standardized test, the GMAT will almost certainly steer away from having this rule be the "make or break" for any question.

However, you should avoid the possibility of ambiguity by **taking the possessing noun out of the possessive case**.

> Better: The board is investigating the compensation packages of <u>several executives</u> in order to determine how much <u>THEY</u> may have been improperly awarded.

Since the reference of the pronoun *they* is still somewhat ambiguous (*executives* or *packages*?), an even better way to fix the issue is to replace *they* with a noun:

> Best: The board is investigating the compensation packages of <u>several executives</u> in order to determine how much <u>THESE EXECUTIVES</u> may have been improperly awarded.

The Deadly Five: *It, Its, They, Them, Their*

The most common pronoun mistakes involve <u>Third Person Personal Pronouns</u>—the singular *it* and *its*, together with the plural *they, them* and *their*. Whenever you see one of these five pronouns, you should find the antecedent and check its viability ("is the antecedent sensible, unambiguous, and in agreement with the pronoun?"). Be particularly careful with *their*, which is often used in everyday speech to refer to singular subjects.

Wrong: Whenever <u>a student</u> calls, take down <u>THEIR</u> information.
Right: Whenever <u>a student</u> calls, take down <u>HIS or HER</u> information.
Right: Whenever <u>students</u> call, take down <u>THEIR</u> information.

This, That, These, and *Those*

The <u>Demonstrative Pronouns</u> are *this, that, these,* and *those*. You may use any of these pronouns as <u>adjectives</u> in front of nouns, as we have already seen.

<u>New "nano-papers"</u> incorporate fibers that give <u>THESE MATERIALS</u> strength.

You may also use *that* or *those* to indicate a "New Copy" or copies of the antecedent.

<u>The money</u> spent by her parents is less than <u>THAT</u> spent by her children.

In this example, *that spent by her children* means *the money spent by her children*. Note that the two pots of money are NOT the same. One pot of money is spent by the parents; another pot of money, spent by the children, is the New Copy. In contrast, when you use *it, they,* or other personal pronouns, you mean the <u>same actual thing</u> as the antecedent.

<u>The money spent by her parents</u> is more than <u>IT</u> was expected to be.

That or *those* indicating a New Copy or copies must be <u>modified</u>. In other words, you have to add a description to indicate how the new copy is different from the previous version.

<u>The money</u> spent by her parents is less than <u>THAT SPENT</u> by her children.
<u>Her company</u> is outperforming <u>THAT OF her competitor</u>.

A little oddly, the GMAT insists that any "New Copy" *that* or *those* agree in number with the previous version. If you must change number, repeat the noun.

Wrong: <u>Her company</u> is outperforming <u>THOSE OF her competitors</u>.
Right: <u>Her company</u> is outperforming <u>THE COMPANIES OF her competitors</u>.

Finally, on the GMAT, do not use *this* or *these* in place of nouns. Also, do not use *that* or *those* in place of nouns (unless you modify *that* or *those*). Use *it, they,* or *them* instead.

Wrong: <u>Her products</u> are unusual; many consider <u>THESE</u> unique.
Right: <u>Her products</u> are unusual; many consider <u>THEM</u> unique.

Never skip past *It, Its, They, Them,* or *Their* in a sentence. Stop and check whether the pronoun is being used correctly.

Other Pronouns

There

Technically an adverb, *there* means "in that place." Thus, *there* acts a lot like a pronoun. The antecedent place is often referred to in a prepositional phrase and should be a noun, not an adjective.

> Wrong: At current prices, Antarctic oil may be worth drilling for, if wells can be dug <u>THERE</u> and environmental concerns addressed.
>
> Right: At current prices, oil <u>in Antarctica</u> may be worth drilling for, if wells can be dug <u>THERE</u> and environmental concerns addressed.

Note that we also use *there* as a "dummy" pronoun in expressions such as *There is a cat in a tree* or *There are roses on my doorstep.* In these cases, you do not need an antecedent.

Itself, Themselves, One Another, Each Other

The <u>Reflexive Pronouns</u> *itself* and *themselves* are used as objects to refer directly back to the subject: *The panda groomed <u>itself</u>.* Since you must use a reflexive pronoun to indicate when the subject acts upon itself, another pronoun may be less ambiguous than you think.

> Right: After <u>the agreement</u> surfaced, the commission dissolved <u>IT</u>.

It must refer to *the agreement*, because *it* cannot refer to *the commission.* If you wish to refer to the commission, you must use *itself*. Note the difference in meaning below.

> Right: After the agreement surfaced, <u>the commission</u> dissolved <u>ITSELF</u>.

Itself and *themselves* are also used to intensify a noun: *The commission <u>itself</u> was wrong.*

The <u>Reciprocal Pronouns</u> *one another* and *each other* are used to indicate <u>interaction</u> between parties. These pronouns are not interchangeable with *Themselves*.

> Wrong: The <u>guests</u> at the party interacted with <u>THEMSELVES</u>.
>
> Right: The <u>guests</u> at the party interacted with <u>ONE ANOTHER</u>.

Such and *Other/Another*

The words *such* and *other/another* often combine with a general noun to indicate an antecedent. *Such* means "like the antecedent."

> After <u>the land-use agreement</u> surfaced, the commission decided to subject any <u>SUCH contracts</u> to debate in the future.

In this example, *the land-use agreement* is a <u>type</u> of *contract.* Similarly, *other* and *another* mean "additional of the same type," though not necessarily "exactly alike."

> After <u>the land-use agreement</u> surfaced, the commission decided to subject any <u>OTHER contracts</u> to debate in the future.

One
One indicates an <u>indefinite</u> copy or a single, <u>indefinite</u> part of a collection.

> After walking by <u>the chocolates</u> so many times, Roger finally had to eat <u>ONE</u>.

The particular chocolate was not delineated ahead of time. In contrast, the personal pronouns *it* and *they/them* indicate <u>definite</u> selection of an <u>entire</u> object or collection.

> After walking by <u>the chocolates</u> so many times, Roger finally had to eat <u>THEM</u>.

In this case, Roger ate <u>all</u> the chocolates! Notice that after Roger has selected a chocolate, we now refer to that particular chocolate using the definite pronoun *it*.

> After walking by <u>the chocolates</u> so many times, Roger finally had to eat <u>ONE</u>.
> <u>IT</u> was delicious, but <u>HE</u> could eat only half of <u>IT</u>.

Do So versus *Do It*
Do so can refer to an entire action, including a verb, its objects, and its modifiers.

> Quinn <u>did not eat dinner quickly</u>, but her brother <u>DID SO</u>.

This sentence means that Quinn's brother *ate dinner quickly*. In referring to an earlier part of the sentence, the expression *do so* functions like a pronoun. (Technically, *do so* is called a "pro-verb," since it stands for a verb or even an entire predicate.)

Alternatively, you can simply repeat the helping verb without *so*.

> Quinn <u>DID NOT eat dinner quickly</u>, but her brother <u>DID</u>.

On the other hand, in the phrase *do it*, the pronoun *it* must refer to an actual noun antecedent.

> Quinn failed to do <u>the homework</u>, but her brother did <u>IT</u>.

It refers specifically to *the homework*. Of course, the verb does not have to be *do:*

> Quinn did not eat <u>the soup</u>, but her brother ATE <u>IT</u>.

Whenever you see *Do It* in a GMAT sentence, make sure that *It* has a good antecedent.

Placeholder *It*

Sometimes we need to move an awkward subject or object to the back of the sentence. In these cases, we put an *it* in the sentence where the subject or object used to be. We call this use of *it* "Placeholder *It*." Do <u>not</u> look for a noun antecedent for a Placeholder *It*.

Here are the three situations in which you should use Placeholder *It* on the GMAT.

<u>(1) Postpone Infinitive Subjects</u>

    Awkward: <u>TO RESIST temptation</u> is futile.

The subject of the sentence is the infinitive phrase *to resist temptation*. Although this sentence is grammatically correct, the GMAT rejects similar sentences on stylistic grounds.

    Right: <u>IT</u> is futile <u>TO RESIST temptation</u>.

It is now the grammatical subject. As a pronoun, it refers to the infinitive phrase. Under other circumstances, *it* cannot normally refer to an infinitive.

<u>(2) Postpone *That*-Clause Subjects</u>

    Awkward: <u>THAT we scored at all</u> gave us encouragement.

The subject of the sentence is a *That*-Clause, namely *That we scored at all*. Again, this sentence is grammatically correct, since some *That*-Clauses can function as nouns. However, the position is awkward. Postpone a *That*-Clause in subject position with an Placeholder *It*.

    Right: <u>IT</u> gave us encouragement <u>THAT we scored at all</u>.

It cannot normally refer to a clause under other circumstances.

<u>(3) Postpone Infinitive or *That*-Clause Objects</u>

    Right: She made <u>IT</u> possible <u>for us TO ATTEND the movie</u>.

You cannot say this sentence any other way, unless you change the infinitive phrase *to attend* into the action noun *attendance*. Then you should drop the Placeholder *It:*

    Right: She made possible <u>our attendance at the movie</u>.
    Right: She made <u>our attendance at the movie</u> possible.

Again, the point of this discussion is that these uses of Placeholder *It* are legal and even strongly encouraged. If you come across Placeholder *It*, do not be anxious because you cannot find a noun antecedent for the *it*. There is no such noun antecedent for this use of *it*.

Avoiding Pronouns Altogether

Sometimes, the best way to deal with a pronoun problem is to <u>eliminate</u> pronouns, as we have seen. For instance, at the end of a long sentence, a pronoun such as *it* or *them* might inevitably have ambiguous antecedents, no matter how you try to recast the sentence.

> Wrong: After roasting the deer, the hunter extinguished the fire and then searched for a tree to hang <u>IT</u> from.

From the sense of the words, we know that the hunter intends to hang *the deer*, not *the fire*. But *it* could in theory refer to *the fire*, so we have a classic case of antecedent ambiguity that we must fix.

Repeating the antecedent noun is always an option, if not necessarily the most elegant.

> Right: After roasting <u>the deer</u>, the hunter extinguished the fire and then searched for a tree to hang <u>THE DEER</u> from.

It is often smoother—and much more GMAT-like—to **use a generic synonym for the antecedent** than to repeat the noun exactly. Such a synonym stands in for the antecedent and functions just like a pronoun, but with none of the drawbacks. The synonym is often more general than the antecedent, which refers to an <u>example</u> of the generic synonym. We have already observed such synonyms more than once:

> Right: New <u>"nano-papers"</u> incorporate fibers that give <u>THESE MATERIALS</u> strength.

The generic synonym *materials* refers to *new "nano-papers,"* which are <u>types</u> of *materials*.

> Right: After <u>the land-use agreement</u> surfaced, the commission decided to subject any <u>SUCH CONTRACTS</u> to debate in the future.

Likewise, *contracts* refers to *the land-use agreement*, which is an <u>example</u> of a *contract*.

You do not always have to use *these* or *such*. Often, simply the article *the* will suffice.

> Right: After roasting <u>the deer</u>, the hunter extinguished the fire and then searched for a tree to hang <u>THE MEAT</u> from.

The generic synonym *meat* refers to *the deer*, which is or provides a <u>type</u> of meat.

Remember that a correct answer can eliminate the pronoun in this manner.

Do not be afraid to get rid of pronouns altogether by using generic synonyms to refer to nouns.

Nuances of Pronoun Reference (Advanced)

As you search for the antecedent of a particular pronoun, you should realize that several principles determine how suitable a noun may be as an antecedent. The most important principles are number and gender agreement, as you might expect. These two principles determine which nouns are <u>eligible</u> antecedents.

1. Number   The antecedent <u>must</u> agree in number (singular, plural) with the pronoun.

2. Gender   The antecedent <u>must</u> agree in gender (masculine, feminine, neuter) with the pronoun. *He* and *his* are masculine; *she, her,* and *hers* are feminine. *It* and *its* are neutral. *They, them,* and *their* can be any gender.

The remaining three principles are not absolute. They occur in this order of importance:

3. Repeats   Repeated pronouns are presumed to refer to the <u>same</u> antecedent. That is, every *it* and *its* in the sentence should generally mean the same thing.

4. Proximity   The pronoun should normally refer to the <u>closest</u> eligible antecedent. Note that there is such an idea as "too close." In the sentence *In the station house* <u>*IT*</u> *is considered taboo,* the <u>*IT*</u> cannot refer to *station house*. Also, the antecedent normally occurs earlier in the sentence. Rarely, the antecedent may come shortly after the pronoun (e.g., *After he dried his tears, Jack made a vow*). However, you should usually place the antecedent first.

5. Case   The pronoun and the antecedent should agree in case if they are in parallel structures. In particular, a subject pronoun in one clause often refers to a noun in subject position in another parallel clause.

These three principles do not have to agree for there to be unambiguous pronoun reference.

> Although the company has had increasing revenues for years because of <u>ITS</u> well-designed products and <u>ITS</u> excellent management team, in the current economic climate <u>IT</u> may finally experience sales declines.

What is the antecedent of the *IT*? And is there ambiguity?

First, apply the filters of <u>Number</u> (singular) and <u>Gender</u> (neutral). The three eligible antecedents are therefore *company, team,* and *climate.* Now apply the other principles.

<u>Repeats</u>: The earlier two *Its* (*It* and *Its* count as repeats) refer to *company.* Points to *company.*

<u>Proximity</u>: *Climate* is "too close." *Team* is closer than *company.* Points to *team.*

<u>Case</u>: *Company* and *IT* are both the subjects of their clauses. Points to *company.*

Company clearly wins on "repeats" alone. The pronoun reference of *IT* is not ambiguous.

Manhattan **GMAT** Prep
the new standard

Problem Set

(Circle) all the pronouns in the following sentences. Underline the antecedent, if there is one, of each pronoun. If you notice any pronoun errors in a sentence, correct the sentence by altering the pronoun(s). Explain what rules are violated by the incorrect sentences. If a sentence is correct, mark it with the word CORRECT.

1. When the guests finished their soup they were brought plates of salad.

    correct

2. Everyone here needs their own copy of the textbook in order to take this class.

    his/her (number agreement)

3. Jim may not be elected CEO by the board because he does not meet their standards.

    its (number agreement)

4. Meg left all her class notes at school because she decided that she could do her homework without it.

    them (number agreement)

5. Some people believe that the benefits of a healthy diet outweigh that of regular exercise.

    those (demonstrative pronouns - number agreement)

6. Caroline receives e-mail from friends who she knows well, from acquaintances who's names are only vaguely familiar, and from strangers about who she knows nothing at all.

    whom   whom   whose

    ...from acquaintances who she only knows vaguely, and from strangers who she does not know at all

7. The police have significantly reduced violent crime and are pleased with them for doing it.

    themselves (need proper reflexive pronoun)

8. The players' helmets need to be repainted before they are used in Sunday's game.

    correct

9. We finally chose the coffee table towards the back of the store, which we thought would complement our living room furniture.

    refers to store
    because we thought it...
    correct

10. Oil traders have profited handsomely from the recent rise in its price.

    missing antecedent ⇒   in the price of oil.

11. A few Shakespearean scholars maintain that he borrowed some of his most memorable lines from Christopher Marlowe.

    shakespear

12. The Smiths avoid the Browns because they dislike their children.

    the Browns or the Smiths

13. A careful analysis of the students' test scores reveals that some of them must have cheated.

    the students

14.   Our cat is cuter than those in the shelter.

(handwritten: the cats   (demonstrative pronoun - new copy, number agreement))

15.   The rapid <u>development</u> of India in the twenty-first century is like England in the eighteenth century.

(handwritten: that of   (demonstrative pronoun - new copy))

16.   When Norma and her husband read an article about Florida's adorable manatees, they promised each other that they would one day go there and see one.

(handwritten: to Florida   the animals)

17.   Most European countries—including those of Bulgaria and Romania—have joined the European Union; Norway and Switzerland, however, have steadfastly refused to do it.

(handwritten: (do it must refer to a noun)   so)

18.   It would hardly be fair for the <u>meatpacking industry</u> to <u>blame regulators for the harm that it has inflicted upon itself in the sub-prime meat sector.</u>

(handwritten: correct)

19.   She took her laptop and her books with her on the airplane because she thought she could use these to get some work done.

(handwritten: them   herself)

1.   When the <u>guests</u> finished (their) soup (they) were brought plates of salad.

    CORRECT.
    Guests is the antecedent of *their* and *they*.

2.   (Everyone) here needs (his or her) own copy of the textbook in order to take this class.

    Everyone is an indefinite pronoun. It is the antecedent of *his or her*. (*Their* is <u>incorrect</u>, because *everyone* is singular.)

3.   Jim may not be elected CEO by the <u>board</u> because he does not meet (its) standards.

    Board is the antecedent of *its*. (*Their* is <u>incorrect</u>, because *board* is a singular collective noun.)

4.   <u>Meg</u> left all (her) class <u>notes</u> at school because (she) decided that (she) could do (her) homework without (them.)

    Meg is the antecedent of *her* and *she*.
    Notes is the antecedent of *them*. (*It* is incorrect because *notes* is plural.)

5.   Some people believe that the <u>benefits</u> of a healthy diet outweigh (those) of regular exercise.

    Benefits is the antecedent of *those*. (*That* is <u>incorrect</u>, because *benefits* is plural.)

6.   <u>Caroline</u> receives e-mail from <u>friends</u> (whom) (she) knows well, from <u>acquaintances</u> (whose) names are only vaguely familiar, and from <u>strangers</u> about (whom) (she) knows nothing at all.

    Caroline is the antecedent of both *she's*.

    Friends is the antecedent of the first *whom*. (*Who* is <u>incorrect</u> because the objective case is required here. *Whom* is the <u>direct object</u> of the verb *knows*; we would say that *she knows <u>them</u>*.)

    Acquaintances is the antecedent of *whose*. (*Who's* is <u>incorrect</u>, because *who's* means "*who is*". We need the possessive pronoun *whose* to indicate that the *names* belong to the acquaintances.)

    Strangers is the antecedent of *whom*. (*Who* is <u>incorrect</u> because we need the objective case here. *Whom* is the object of the preposition *about*.)

7.   The <u>police</u> have significantly reduced violent crime and are pleased with (themselves) for doing so.

    Police is the antecedent of *themselves*. (*Them* is <u>incorrect</u> here because we need a <u>reflexive</u> pronoun here.)

    It in the original sentence is <u>incorrect</u>. Its only possible antecedent, *violent crime*, does not make logical sense. The author's intention is to refer to the verb phrase *have significantly reduced violent crime*, but a pronoun cannot have such an antecedent. To solve this problem, we can write *doing so* instead of *doing it*. Alternatively, we can replace *doing it* with an appropriate noun, such as *this achievement*.

8.   The players' <u>helmets</u> need to be repainted before (they) are used in Sunday's game.

CORRECT.

Helmets is the antecedent of *they*. You need not worry that *they* could refer to *players'*, because (1) *helmets* is closer to *they*, and (2) *players'* is a possessive noun, and is therefore not a good antecedent for a pronoun in the subjective case.

9.   (We) finally chose the coffee <u>table</u> towards the back of the store, because (we) thought it would complement our living room furniture.

We is a pronoun that never has an antecedent in the sentence, because *we* is first person (*we* refers to the people speaking).

Table is the antecedent of *it*. (Why is *store* not the antecedent? *Table* is a more "attractive" antecedent for *it* because: (1) *table* and *it* are in the same case (objective), and have similar roles in the sentence: both are the objects of verbs (*chose, thought*) of which *we* is the subject, and (2) *store* is in a particularly unattractive place for an antecedent—it is buried inside a prepositional phrase (*towards the back of the store*).

The original sentence is <u>incorrect</u> because the pronoun *which* refers to *store*. *Store* is an illogical antecedent for *which*, because the *table*, not the *store*, is what would complement someone's living room furniture.

10.   Oil traders have profited handsomely from the recent rise in the price of oil.

This new, correct version of the sentence contains no pronouns.

The original sentence is <u>incorrect</u> because *its* has no antecedent. *Oil* is an adjective in the expression *oil traders*, and therefore cannot be the antecedent of *its*.

11.   A few Shakespearean scholars maintain that Shakespeare borrowed some of (his) most memorable lines from Christopher Marlowe.

Shakespeare is the antecedent of *his*.

The original sentence is incorrect because *he* has no antecedent. *Shakespearean* is an adjective, and therefore cannot be the antecedent. We are thus forced to replace *he* with *Shakespeare* in the correct sentence.

12.   The original sentence is ambiguous. The antecedent of *they* could be *the Smiths* or *the Browns*. Likewise, the antecedent of *their* could be *the Smiths* or *the Browns*. To correct this sentence, we would need to get rid of the pronouns. One possible version: *The Smiths avoid the Browns because the Browns dislike the Smiths' children*. We cannot be sure, however, that this version accurately represents what the author intended, because he or she might have meant that *The Smiths avoid the Browns because the Smiths dislike the Browns' children*.

13.   A careful analysis of the students' test scores reveals that some students must have cheated.

      This new, correct version of the sentence contains no pronouns.

      The original sentence is <u>incorrect</u> because *them* refers to *test scores*. *Them* fails to refer to *students'*, because (1) *test scores* is closer to *them*, and (2) *students'* is a possessive noun, and is therefore relatively unattractive as an antecedent for a non-possessive pronoun such as *them*.

14.   Our cat is cuter than the cats in the shelter.

      This new, correct version of the sentence contains no third-person pronouns. (*Our* is a pronoun, but first-person pronouns such as *our* never have antecedents in the sentence.)

      The original sentence is <u>incorrect</u> because *those* has no antecedent. *Those* is plural, and therefore cannot refer to *cat*.

15.   The rapid <u>development</u> of India in the twenty-first century is like (that) of England in the eighteenth century.

      Development is the antecedent of *that*.

      The original sentence is <u>incorrect</u> because it makes an illogical comparison. India's *development* is not like *England*. It is like England's <u>development</u>, or *that of England*.

16.   When <u>Norma and (her) husband</u> read an article about Florida's adorable manatees, (they) promised (each other) that (they) would one day go to Florida and see (one.)

      Norma is the antecedent of *her*.

      Norma and her husband is the antecedent of they and of *each other*.

      Manatees is the antecedent of *one*. Recall that *one*, although singular, can take either a singular or a plural antecedent.

      There in the original sentence is <u>incorrect</u>. *There* is an adverb that behaves much like a pronoun. The problem with *there* in the original sentence is that it cannot refer to Florida, because *Florida's* is in the possessive case.

17.   Most European countries—including Bulgaria and Romania—have joined the European Union; Norway and Switzerland, however, have steadfastly refused to do so.

      This new, correct version of the sentence contains no pronouns.

      The original sentence is <u>incorrect</u> for three reasons: (1) *those* has no antecedent, (2) *those of* is redundant, since Bulgaria and Romania <u>are</u> European countries, and (3) the sentence attempts to use a pronoun, *it*, to refer to the verb phrase *joined the European Union*.

18.   (It) would hardly be fair for the meatpacking <u>industry</u> <u>to blame regulators for the harm that</u> (it) <u>has</u> <u>inflicted upon</u> (itself) <u>in the sub-prime meat sector.</u>

CORRECT.

The antecedent of the first *it* (which is a Placeholder *It*) is the long infinitive phrase *to blame…mortgage sector*.

The antecedent of the second *it* and of *itself* is *industry*.

19.   (She) took (her) laptop and (her) books with (her) on the airplane because (she) thought (she) could use (them) to get some work done.

The first *she* is the antecedent of all three *her's*.

The three uses of *she* lack an antecedent, but are correct. The subject of the sentence is simply an unnamed *she*. Note that the GMAT will generally name any personal antecedent, rather than leave this person nameless as in the example above.

Her laptop and her books is the antecedent of *them*. (The original *these* is incorrect because *these* is never used as a stand-alone pronoun without a noun following.)

Sentence Correction

Now that you have completed your study of PRONOUNS, it is time to test your skills on problems that have actually appeared on real GMAT exams over the past several years.

The problem set that follows is composed of past GMAT problems from two books published by GMAC (Graduate Management Admission Council):

The Official Guide for GMAT Review, 11th Edition (pages 39–43 & 638–660)
The Official Guide for GMAT Verbal Review (pages 234–253)

The problems in the set below are primarily focused on PRONOUN issues. For each of these problems, identify each pronoun and its antecedent. Eliminate any answer choices that contain errors in pronoun use, including missing or unclear antecedents and agreement errors.

Note: Problem numbers preceded by "D" refer to questions in the Diagnostic Test chapter of *The Official Guide for GMAT Review, 11th Edition* (pages 39–43).

Pronouns

   11th Edition: 5, 43, 127, 133, D42
   Verbal Review: 12, 15, 19, 29, 41, 44, 49, 53, 60, 65, 67, 71, 72, 74, 102, 107

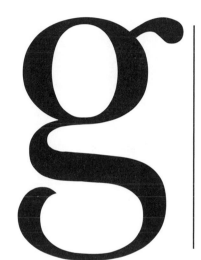

Chapter 6
of
SENTENCE CORRECTION

MODIFIERS

In This Chapter . . .

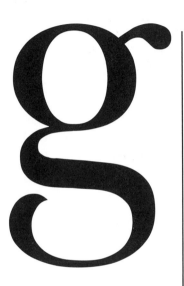

MODIFIERS

A modifier describes or "modifies" someone or something in the sentence. Although modifiers can be as simple as a single word (an adjective or an adverb), GMAT sentences often contain several complex modifiers.

> <u>Tired out from playing basketball</u>, <u>Charles</u> decided to take a nap.

The modifier *Tired out from playing basketball* describes the noun *Charles*. Be on the lookout for opening modifiers, which appear at the beginning of a sentence. In the example above, *tired out from playing basketball* is an opening modifier separated from the rest of the sentence by a comma. Many modifying phrases in GMAT sentences are separated by commas from the noun being modified.

Adjectives and Adverbs

Adjectives and adverbs are one-word modifiers. An <u>Adjective</u> modifies <u>only</u> a noun or a pronoun, whereas an <u>Adverb</u> modifies almost anything <u>but</u> a noun or a pronoun. An adverb often modifies a verb, but it can also describe an adjective, another adverb, a preposition, a phrase, or even a whole clause.

> The SMART student works QUICKLY.

Here the adjective *smart* modifies the noun *student*, while the adverb *quickly* modifies the verb *works*. Many adverbs are formed by adding *-ly* to the adjective.

Be sure not to use an adjective where an adverb is grammatically required, and vice versa. Note that adjectives, not adverbs, follow linking verbs such as *feel*. These adjectives do not modify the verb but rather identify a quality with the noun subject. All of the following examples are correct, although they differ in meaning:

> Amy is a <u>GOOD</u> person. (*Good* is an adjective that modifies the noun *person*.)
> <u>Amy</u> is feeling <u>GOOD</u>. (*Good* is an adjective that modifies the noun *Amy*.)
> <u>Amy</u> is feeling <u>WELL</u>. (*Well* is an adjective that modifies the noun *Amy*.)
> Amy <u>writes</u> <u>WELL</u>. (*Well* is an <u>adverb</u> that modifies the verb *writes*.)

Often, the GMAT provides two grammatically correct phrasings. For instance, one phrasing might be [Adjective + Adjective + Noun], in which the two adjectives both modify the noun. The other phrasing would be [Adverb + Adjective + Noun], in which the adverb modifies the adjective, which in turn modifies the noun. These two phrasings do <u>not</u> mean the same thing. Pick the phrasing that reflects the author's intent.

> Wrong: James Joyce is Max's SUPPOSEDLY Irish ancestor.
> Right: James Joyce is Max's <u>SUPPOSED</u> Irish <u>ancestor</u>.

James Joyce may or may not be Max's ancestor, but James Joyce was certainly Irish. Thus, we want the adjective *supposed,* so that we can modify the noun *ancestor*.

Modifiers are often set off by commas from the rest of the sentence.

Wrong: Max's grandmother is his SUPPOSED Irish ancestor.
Right: Max's grandmother is his SUPPOSEDLY Irish ancestor.

What is in question here is whether Max's grandmother was Irish, not whether she is Max's ancestor. Thus, we want the adverb *supposedly,* so that we can modify the adjective *Irish.*

Adjectives that have been observed alternating with their corresponding adverbs (in *-ly*) in released GMAT problems include *corresponding, frequent, independent, rare, recent, seeming, separate, significant, supposed,* and *usual.* It is easy to miss an *-ly* added in some of the answer choices; be sure not to miss this difference among the choices.

Noun modifiers describe nouns. They tell you more about the noun, or which noun is under discussion.

Noun Modifiers

Phrases or clauses that modify nouns or pronouns are called Noun Modifiers. Noun modifiers act like long adjectives. The first word or two of a noun modifier determines its type, as seen in the chart below. The modifier and the modified noun are both underlined.

Type / First Words	Position	Example
Adjective	Before noun	The LAZY cat took a nap.
	After noun	The cat, LAZY from overeating, took a nap.
Preposition	Before noun	ON the couch, the cat took a nap.
	After noun	The cat ON the couch took a nap.
Past Participle	Before noun	The TIRED cat took a nap.
		TIRED from chasing mice, the cat took a nap.
	After noun	The cat, TIRED from chasing mice, took a nap.
Present Participle without commas	Before noun	The SLEEPING cat took a nap.
	After noun	The cat SLEEPING on the rug is named "Sue."
Relative Pronoun	After noun	The grey cat, WHICH loves tuna, took a nap.
		The cat THAT lives next door is noisy.
		The person WHO lives next door is noisy.
		The city WHERE I live is noisy.
Another Noun (→ Appositive)	Before noun	A LOVER of mice, my cat hunts night and day.
	After noun	The cat, a TABBY raised on a farm, took a nap.

A noun used to modify another noun is called an Appositive. In the last example, the appositive noun *tabby* was itself modified by a past participle modifier (*raised on a farm*). Even modifiers of moderate length (*a tabby raised on a farm*) can contain other modifiers.

In the chart above, notice that many modifiers are separated from the noun by commas. Again, pay particular attention to opening modifiers, which appear at the beginning of a sentence. It may seem unnatural to say an unprepared sentence with a long opening modifier, but it is perfectly fine to write such a sentence.

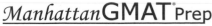

Right: <u>TIRED from chasing mice</u>, the <u>cat</u> took a nap.

Because your ear is not accustomed to sentences with opening modifiers, the GMAT loves to play tricks with these kinds of modifiers.

Position of Noun Modifiers

When you see a noun modifier, ask yourself what noun should be modified. Then check to make sure that the modifier is next to that noun. Follow the <u>Touch Rule</u>:

A NOUN and its MODIFIER should TOUCH each other.

If the modifier is next to a different noun, we have a <u>Misplaced Modifier</u>.

Wrong: Jim biked along an old dirt <u>road</u> to get to his house, <u>which cut through the woods</u>.

In the preceding example, the modifying phrase *which cut through the woods* is meant to describe the *road*, not the *house*. Thus, you should move the modifier next to *road*.

Right: To get to his house, Jim biked along an old dirt <u>road</u>, <u>which cut through the woods</u>.

If the noun we want to modify is not even in the sentence, we have a <u>Dangling Modifier</u>.

Wrong: <u>Resigned to the bad news</u>, there was no commotion in the office.
Wrong: There was no commotion in the office, <u>resigned to the bad news</u>.

The modifier *Resigned to the bad news* should modify someone or some group of people who were actually resigned to the news. However, no noun referring to a person appears in the sentence (*office* means the physical place in this context). Instead, the phrase *resigned to the bad news* seems to modify *there* or *the office*. To correct this issue, we insert a reasonable noun as the noun modified by *resigned*:

Right: <u>Resigned to the bad news</u>, the <u>people</u> made no commotion.

A present participle (-*Ing* form) at the beginning of a sentence is often made to be dangling. Although these forms are technically verb modifiers, they need a subject that makes sense.

Wrong: <u>Using the latest technology</u>, the <u>problem</u> was identified.
Wrong: The <u>problem</u> was identified, <u>using the latest technology</u>.

Errors such as these are common in speech. The modifier *using the latest technology* needs to modify someone who actually used the technology. To correct this issue, we insert a reasonable noun as the subject of *using*:

Right: <u>Using the latest technology</u>, the <u>engineer</u> identified the problem.

Noun modifiers should touch the noun they modify.

Notice that you can move the *using* phrase to the end of the sentence.

Right: The <u>engineer</u> identified the problem, <u>using the latest technology</u>.

Unlike a noun modifier, a verb modifier does not have to touch the subject. However, the subject must make sense with the verb modifier used in this way.

Avoid long sequences of modifiers that modify the same noun. Putting two long modifiers in a row before or after a noun can lead to awkward or incorrect phrasings.

Wrong: <u>George Carlin</u>, <u>both shocking and entertaining audiences across the nation</u>, <u>who also struggled publicly with drug abuse</u>, influenced and inspired a generation of comedians.

The misplaced modifier *who also struggled publicly with drug abuse* should be next to *George Carlin*, not *nation*. But the simple fix (putting the modifiers on either side of *George Carlin*) may still be awkward, if the main verb is delayed or if the ideas are not connected clearly.

Better: <u>Both shocking and entertaining audiences across the nation</u>, <u>George Carlin</u>, <u>who also struggled publicly with drug abuse</u>, influenced and inspired a generation of comedians.

An even better alternative may be to rephrase the sentence so that one of the modifiers is no longer a modifier.

Best: <u>Both shocking and entertaining audiences across the nation</u>, <u>George Carlin</u> influenced and inspired a generation of comedians, even as he struggled publicly with drug abuse.

In this version, the modifier *Both shocking and entertaining...* clearly links to the subject *George Carlin* and explains how he *influenced and inspired*. The contrasting thought (*struggled publicly...*) is put at the end of the sentence in a subordinate clause headed by *even as*.

Watch Out For Possessives

Just as possessive nouns are often dangerous with regard to pronoun reference, they are also dangerous in sentences with modifiers. Misplaced modifiers sometimes appear in sentences that have possessive nouns (nouns that end in *'s* or *s'*).

Wrong: <u>Unskilled in complex math</u>, Bill's <u>score</u> on the exam was poor.

Here, the modifier *unskilled in complex math* should describe *Bill*. However, this modifier cannot "reach inside" the possessive form *Bill's* and modify *Bill*. As it stands, the sentence is saying that *Bill's score* itself is *unskilled in complex math*. This meaning is not what the author intended. To solve the problem, we should replace the possessive *Bill's score* with *Bill*.

Right: <u>Unskilled in complex math</u>, <u>Bill</u> did not score well on the exam.

Avoid dangling modifiers by making sure the noun you want to modify is in the sentence. To avoid misplaced modifiers, place them next to the nouns they are meant to modify.

Do not ignore the noun *development* or other abstract nouns. They follow the same rules as all other nouns: modifiers that touch them should be intended to modify them.

> Wrong: Only in the past century has origami's <u>development</u>, <u>a ceremonial activity invented millennia ago</u>, into a true art form taken place.

We do not mean that the *development* of origami was *a ceremonial activity*. Thus, we need to rephrase the sentence to modify the noun *origami* itself.

> Right: <u>Origami—a ceremonial activity invented millennia ago</u>—has developed into a true art form only in the past century.

While we are on the subject of possessives (which are in fact noun modifiers), you should note that you should not choose *OF X's* on the GMAT. Choose <u>either</u> the form *OF X* <u>or</u> the form *X's*. Other grammar authorities allow *OF X's*, but this construction is considered redundant by the GMAT.

> Wrong: The orca, a relative <u>of the blue whale's</u>, is found throughout the globe.
> Right: The orca, a relative <u>of the blue whale</u>, is found throughout the globe.

Finally, as a guessing rule of thumb, try to steer clear of the plural possessive form (*-s'*) in answer choices. In roughly 80–90% of publicly released problems that contain the plural possessive in the underlined portion, the GMAT avoids the plural possessive answer choice or choices for a variety of reasons:

(1) You cannot easily modify the noun that is in the possessive.
(2) With a possessive, you cannot express a relationship other than *of*.
(3) The plural possessive can be easily misread, especially within a prepositional phrase. For one thing, it sounds the same as the singular possessive, and you can easily miss the added-on apostrophe after the final *-s*.

> Wrong: Certain <u>humans'</u> parasites have been shown to provide bacterial resistance and protection against auto-immune disorders.
> Right: Certain parasites <u>in humans</u> have been shown to provide bacterial resistance and protection against auto-immune disorders.

The correct version clears up the ambiguity about what the adjective *certain* modifies (do we mean *certain humans* or *certain parasites*?). The correct version also properly identifies the relationship between *parasites* and *humans* (it is more precise to say *parasites IN humans* than *parasites OF humans*).

Obviously, do not select an answer only to rule out plural possessives. But if you are stuck between choices and time is short, guess anything but the plural possessive option.

Modifiers cannot normally modify a noun in the possessive case.

Exceptions to the Touch Rule

In general, noun modifiers must touch their nouns. However, there are a few exceptions to the Touch Rule.

1) A "mission-critical" modifier falls between. This modifier is often an *Of*-phrase that defines the noun. The less important modifier refers to the noun plus the first modifier.

> Right: He had <u>a way OF DODGING OPPONENTS</u> <u>that impressed the scouts</u>.

Here, the "mission-critical" modifier *of dodging opponents* defines the noun *way*. Without this modifier, the noun *way* is almost meaningless. In turn, the modifier *that impressed the scouts* modifies the entire noun phrase *a way of dodging opponents*. It helps that the relative pronoun *that* cannot refer to human *opponents*, according to the GMAT. Moreover, the reversed order is nonsensical:

> Wrong: He had <u>a way that impressed the scouts</u> <u>OF DODGING OPPONENTS</u>.

Of course, try to sidestep the issue altogether by rephrasing the sentence.

> Best: His <u>way</u> <u>OF DODGING OPPONENTS</u> impressed the scouts.

Other examples include parts of a whole.

> Right: An ice sheet covers <u>80 percent OF THE SURFACE OF GREENLAND</u>, <u>an area roughly the size of Alaska</u>.

The modifier *an area roughly the size of Alaska* modifies not the noun *Greenland*, but rather the whole phrase *80 percent of the surface of Greenland*. The "mission-critical" modifier *of the surface of Greenland* is required next to *80 percent* in order to define that percentage.

2) A very short predicate falls between, shifting a very long modifier back.

> Right: A new <u>CEO</u> has been hired <u>who will transform the company by decentralizing authority to various division heads while increasing their accountability through the use of public scorecards</u>.

The alternative construction is confusing, because the modifier is extremely lengthy:

> Awkward: A new <u>CEO</u> <u>who will transform the company by decentralizing authority to various division heads while increasing their accountability through the use of public scorecards</u> has been hired.

3) A short <u>non-essential</u> phrase intervenes and is set off by commas.

> Right: Our system of Presidential elections favors <u>states</u>, <u>such as Delaware</u>, <u>that by population are over-represented in the Electoral College</u>.

The short phrase *such as Delaware* sneaks between the noun *states* and its modifier *that by population are over-represented in the Electoral College.* There is nowhere else logical to put the phrase *such as Delaware.* Because this phrase is short, its insertion is acceptable.

4) The modifier is part of a series of parallel modifiers, one of which touches the noun.

Right: In heraldry, the term "tincture" refers to a <u>color</u> <u>emblazoned on a coat of arms</u> and <u>labeled with a special French word</u>.

The second modifier, *labeled with a special French word*, is not positioned right next to the noun it modifies, namely *color*. However, this modifier is in a parallel construction with another modifier, *emblazoned on a coat of arms*, that <u>is</u> positioned right next to the noun *color*. Thus, the second modifier is considered well-placed.

To summarize, noun modifiers must touch the modified noun, with a few minor exceptions. These exceptions all "read" well; simply use your judgment as you apply the Touch Rule.

Noun Modifiers with Relative Pronouns

Noun modifiers are often introduced by <u>Relative Pronouns</u> such as the following:

Which That Who Whose Whom Where When

Such modifiers are called relative clauses. Relative pronouns are subject to several restrictions. The pronouns *who* and *whom* must modify people. On the other hand, the pronoun *which* must modify things.

According to the GMAT, clauses led by the pronoun *that* cannot modify people. Other grammatical authorities disagree, but what matters on test day is the GMAT's point of view.

Wrong: The scientists <u>THAT made the discovery</u> were rewarded.
Right: The scientists <u>WHO made the discovery</u> were rewarded.

It is very easy to make a mistake on this issue. In fact, the 10th Edition of the Official Guide includes such an error in the commentary on one Sentence Correction problem.

Surprisingly, the pronoun *whose* <u>can</u> modify either people or things, according to the GMAT: *the town <u>whose water supply was contaminated</u>.*

Which or *whom* sometimes follow prepositions: *the canal <u>through which water flows</u>; the senator <u>for whom we worked</u>.*

Who is used as the subject of the verb in a relative clause, whereas *whom* is used as the object of the verb or of a preposition.

Wrong: The security guard <u>WHO we met</u> was nice.
Right: The security guard <u>WHOM we met</u> was nice.

> Use *Who, Whose* or *Whom* to modify people.
> Do not use *That* or *Which* to modify people.

That or *whom* can be dropped when the modified noun is the object of the modifying clause.

 Right: The movie <u>THAT we watched last Friday</u> was scary.
 Right: The movie <u>we watched last Friday</u> was scary.

The pronoun *where* can be used to modify a noun place, such as *area, site, country* or *Nevada. Where* cannot modify a "metaphorical" place, such as *condition, situation, case, circumstances,* or *arrangement.* In these cases, use *in which* rather than *where.*

 Wrong: We had an arrangement <u>WHERE he cooked and I cleaned.</u>
 Right: We had an arrangement <u>IN WHICH he cooked and I cleaned.</u>

The pronoun *when* can be used to modify a noun event or time, such as *period, age, 1987,* or *decade.* In these circumstances, you can also use *in which* instead of *when.*

Study the three right ways and the three wrong ways to describe a subgroup.

Subgroup Modifiers

When you want to describe a part of a larger group with a modifier, use one of the following three <u>Subgroup Modifier</u> constructions.

 Right: This model explains all known subatomic particles, <u>SOME OF WHICH WERE only recently discovered</u>.

 Right: This model explains all known subatomic particles, <u>SOME OF THEM only recently discovered</u>.

 Right: This model explains all known subatomic particles, <u>SOME only recently discovered</u>.

Notice that only the *which* construction has a working verb (*were*) in it. In contrast, wrong answer choices often include the following three <u>incorrect</u> constructions, which scramble the correct forms.

 Wrong: This model explains all known subatomic particles, <u>OF WHICH SOME WERE only recently discovered</u>.

 Wrong: This model explains all known subatomic particles, <u>SOME OF THEM WHICH WERE only recently discovered</u>.

 Wrong: This model explains all known subatomic particles, <u>SOME OF WHICH only recently discovered</u>.

In place of *some,* you can substitute the other SANAM pronouns (*any, none, all, more/most*), as well as *many, each, either, neither, half, one,* and any other number or pronoun that picks out a subgroup.

Essential vs. Non-essential Noun Modifiers

Noun modifiers are either **essential** or **non-essential**.

As their name suggests, <u>Essential Modifiers</u> provide necessary information. Use an essential modifier to identify the noun (out of many possibilities) or to "attach" the modifier to the noun from that point onward.

> Essential: The <u>mansion</u> <u>PAINTED RED</u> is owned by the Lees.

The modifier *painted red* is necessary to identify the mansion, perhaps from among a row of differently painted mansions along a street. In other words, you cannot remove *painted red* without creating confusion and distorting the meaning of the sentence. To answer the question *What is owned by the Lees?*, you would say *The mansion painted red.*

In contrast, <u>Non-essential Modifiers</u> provide extra information. You do not need this information to identify the noun, since it is already identified in some other way. Moreover, you can forget about a non-essential modifier afterward, in a sense; any later reference to the noun does not include that extra information.

> Non-essential: This <u>mansion</u>, <u>RECENTLY PAINTED RED</u>, is owned by the Lees.

The modifier *recently painted red* is not necessary; we already know which mansion is under discussion because of the word *this*. So you can remove *recently painted red* and preserve the sentence's core meaning. To answer the question *What is owned by the Lees?*, you would simply say *This mansion*, leaving out the information about the color of its paint.

Punctuation distinguishes between essential and non-essential modifiers:

> ⚓ **Put COMMAS between NON-ESSENTIAL modifiers and their nouns.** ✶
> ⚓ **Put NO COMMAS between ESSENTIAL modifiers and their nouns.** ✈

Furthermore, if you have a choice between *which* and *that*, then follow this rule:

> ✶ Use *WHICH* (and **commas**) if the modifier is <u>non-essential</u>. ✶
> ✶ Use *THAT* (and **no commas**) if the modifier is <u>essential</u>. ✶

> Non-essential: This <u>mansion</u>, <u>WHICH HAS BEEN RECENTLY PAINTED RED</u>, is
>   owned by the Lees.
> Essential: The <u>mansion</u> <u>THAT HAS BEEN PAINTED RED</u> is owned by the Lees.

In some circumstances, you do not have a simple choice between *Which* and *That* (e.g., when *Which* is used with a preposition). However, you should still obey the comma rule: use commas with non-essential uses of *Which*, but not with essential uses of *Which.*

> Non-essential: This <u>mansion</u>, <u>FOR WHICH I YEARN</u>, is owned by the Lees.
> Essential: The <u>mansion</u> <u>FOR WHICH I YEARN</u> is owned by the Lees.

Essential modifiers are not separated from their nouns by commas. Non-essential modifiers <u>are</u> separated by commas.

*Manhattan*GMAT*Prep
the new standard

107

Other relative pronouns, such as *who*, can be used in essential or in non-essential modifiers. With these other pronouns, continue to observe the comma rule: use commas only with non-essential modifiers.

Verb Modifiers

As their name indicates, <u>Verb Modifiers</u> modify verbs. These modifiers answer questions about the verb, such as "how," "when," "where," "why," etc. The most basic verb modifier is an adverb. Other verb modifiers act in much the same way as adverbs.

Type / First Words	Position	Example
Adverb	Before verb	<u>FREQUENTLY</u>, I <u>walk</u> to the store.
		I <u>FREQUENTLY</u> <u>walk</u> to the store.
	After verb	I <u>walk</u> to the store <u>FREQUENTLY</u>.
Preposition	Before verb	<u>ON Mondays</u>, I <u>walk</u> to the store.
	After verb	I <u>walk</u> to the store <u>ON Mondays</u>.
Subordinator	Before verb	<u>WHEN my car is broken</u>, I <u>walk</u> to the store.
	After verb	I <u>walk</u> to the store <u>WHEN my car is broken</u>.

Subordinators include words such as *because, although, if, unless, while, so that, while*, and so on. These words begin subordinate clauses, which cannot stand alone as sentences, but rather are attached to main clauses.

Some verb modifiers may apply to both the verb and the verb's subject. In these cases, you must make sure that the subject makes sense with the modifier.

Type / First Words	Position	Example
Present Participle with commas	Before verb	<u>WHISTLING "Beat It,"</u> I <u>lifted</u> the weight.
	After verb	I <u>lifted</u> the weight, <u>WHISTLING "Beat It."</u>
Preposition + Simple Gerund	Before verb	<u>BY CONCENTRATING</u>, I <u>lifted</u> the weight.
	After verb	I <u>lifted</u> the weight <u>BY CONCENTRATING</u>.
Infinitive of Purpose	Before verb	<u>TO FREE my leg</u>, I <u>lifted</u> the weight.
	After verb	I <u>lifted</u> the weight <u>TO FREE my leg</u>.

In each case, the subject *I* makes sense: *I* was *whistling "Beat It," I* was *concentrating, I* wanted *to free my leg*. Make sure that these modifiers have a sensible subject in the sentence.

Wrong: The weight was lifted <u>by concentrating</u>.
Wrong: The weight was lifted <u>to free my leg</u>.

Whoever lifted the weight should be in each of these sentences.

> Verb modifiers can generally be placed further away from what they modify than noun modifiers can be placed.

Manhattan **GMAT** Prep
the new standard

There is an important difference between verb modifiers and noun modifiers. **Verb modifiers can be placed more freely than noun modifiers**, which must generally touch the modified noun. However, you should always place a verb modifier so that it modifies the right verb, without ambiguity.

> Wrong: The nameless symphony was at last performed, decades after it was composed, <u>yesterday</u>.
>
> Right: The nameless symphony <u>was</u> at last <u>performed</u> <u>yesterday</u>, decades after it was composed.

In the first example, the adverb *yesterday* is at best awkwardly placed. The concerto seems to have been composed yesterday, a meaning that does not make sense with the rest of the sentence. In the second example, *yesterday* has been moved closer to the verb that ought to be modified—namely, *was performed*.

Which vs. the Present Participle *-Ing*

Sentences such as the following are common in speech, but they are wrong in writing.

> Wrong: Crime has recently decreased in <u>our neighborhood</u>, <u>WHICH has led to a rise in property values</u>.

What you want to say is that the recent decrease in crime has led to a rise in property values. However, whenever you use *which*, you must be referring to a noun—the noun that comes just before the *which*. Here, the *neighborhood* itself has not led to anything!

Use *WHICH* <u>only</u> to refer to the noun immediately preceding it—never to refer to an entire clause.

One way to correct the sentence is to turn the first thought into a noun phrase and make this phrase the subject of the verb in the *which* clause, eliminating *which* altogether:

> Right: The recent <u>decrease</u> in crime in our neighborhood <u>has led</u> to a rise in property values.

Another way to correct the sentence is to use a present participle, the *-Ing* verb form:

> Right: <u>Crime has recently decreased in our neighborhood</u>, <u>leading</u> to a rise in property values.

The *-Ing* form is very flexible. It can modify nouns directly (e.g., *the <u>changing</u> seasons*). It can modify verbs and their subjects (e.g., *I <u>lifted</u> the weight, <u>whistling</u>*). It can even modify an entire clause as above, as long as the entire clause <u>converted into a noun phrase</u> could function as the subject of the verb that is now in *-Ing* form. The two previous examples illustrate this process. Since we can say that *the recent <u>decrease in crime</u>…<u>has led</u> to a rise*, we can also say *<u>crime</u> <u>has</u> recently <u>decreased</u>… <u>leading</u> to a rise*. This use of the *-Ing* form works best when you want to express the <u>result</u> of the main clause.

Be careful with *Which* at the end of a sentence. Make sure that it refers <u>only</u> to the preceding noun, not the entire preceding clause.

Again, in speech we often break these rules—we use *which* to refer to a previous thought that is <u>not</u> a noun. Do not use your ear. Always test *which* clauses to make sure that the *which* refers to the noun immediately preceding the *which*.

More on Relative Clauses vs. Participles (Advanced)

In many cases, a relative clause (a clause headed by a relative pronoun) and a present participle modifier are practically interchangeable.

> Right: The man <u>WHO IS CLEANING the steps</u> is my uncle.
> Right: The man <u>CLEANING the steps</u> is my uncle.

However, consider these examples:

> (A)   The rate of language extinction is accelerating, a tendency ultimately culminating in the survival of just a few languages, according to some.
> (B)   The rate of language extinction is accelerating, a tendency that will ultimately culminate in the survival of just a few languages, according to some.

Which sentence is correct? Choice (**B**): *a tendency THAT WILL ultimately CULMINATE...* The reason is that the adverb *ultimately* tells us that the action of *culminate* or *culminating* is meant to happen <u>in the future</u>. However, *culminating* by itself, in the context of choice (**A**), indicates the <u>present</u> time. Why? The reason is that the main verb of the sentence, *is accelerating*, is in the present tense. In contrast, through the use of the word *will*, choice (**B**) correctly establishes when the action is meant to occur (that is, in the future).

Present participles get their tense from the main verb in the sentence.

> Past: I SAW a man <u>CLEANING</u> the steps.   (*cleaning* takes place in the past)
> Present: I SEE a man <u>CLEANING</u> the steps.   (*cleaning* takes place in the present)
> Future: I WILL SEE a man <u>CLEANING</u> the steps.   (*cleaning* takes place in the future)

Thus, if you want the *cleaning* to take place <u>at a different time</u> from the *seeing*, then use the relative clause, not the present participle.

> Wrong: I SEE the man <u>CLEANING</u> the steps yesterday.
> Right: I SEE the man <u>WHO CLEANED</u> the steps yesterday.

*Present participles do not necessarily indicate present tense. They indicate the **same** tense as the main verb.*

Absolute Phrases (Advanced)

A few GMAT sentences use a sophisticated modifier called an <u>Absolute Phrase</u>. Absolute phrases are composed of a noun plus a noun modifier. These phrases do not have to modify what they touch; rather, they modify the main clause in some way.

> Right: <u>His head held high</u>, Owen walked out of the store.

The absolute phrase *His head held high* is composed of a noun (*His head*) and a noun modifier (*held high*) that describes the noun. The phrase *His head held high* describes <u>how</u> Owen walked out of the store. Thus, this absolute phrase acts as a verb modifier.

You might argue that the noun *Owen* is directly described by *His head held high*, especially since the pronoun *His* refers to *Owen*. However, you should note that *His head held high* is not an appositive noun modifier. We are not placing *His head held high* next to *Owen* to equate them. Moreover, we can easily move the modifier to the end of the sentence; we cannot do so with normal noun modifiers. We can also vary the phrase slightly by adding *with*.

> Right: Owen walked out of the store, <u>his head held high</u>.
> Right: Owen walked out of the store <u>with his head held high</u>.

Consider another example:

> Right: Scientists have found high levels of iridium in certain geological formations around the world, <u>results that suggest the cataclysmic impact of a meteor millions of years ago</u>.

The absolute phrase in this sentence, *results that suggest the cataclysmic impact of a meteor millions of years ago,* is composed of the noun *results* and the noun modifier *that suggest... years ago*. Notice that the noun *results* does not modify *world*, the closest noun in the main clause. The noun *results* refers to either *high levels of iridium* or the act of finding these levels. The absolute phrase construction gives us a way to link a second sentence to the first.

> Right: Scientists have found high levels of iridium in certain geological formations around the world. <u>These results suggest the cataclysmic impact of a meteor millions of years ago</u>.

You will never see two separate sentences in a Sentence Correction problem. However, the example illustrates how an absolute phrase at the end of a sentence gives you a legitimate way to tack on a second thought. Remember, never use *Which* to do so!

> Wrong: Scientists have found high levels of iridium in certain geological formations around the world, <u>which suggests the cataclysmic impact of a meteor millions of years ago</u>.

Again, the relative pronoun *Which* must refer to the noun just before the *Which*. In speech, you might say something like the next example, although it would be wrong on the GMAT.

Absolute phrases are uncommon in speech. As a result, the GMAT likes to use them on advanced problems.

Wrong: Scientists have found high levels of iridium in certain geological forma-
             tions around the world, <u>AND THIS suggests the cataclysmic impact of a</u>
             <u>meteor millions of years ago</u>.

The problem with this sentence is that the GMAT does not like *this* or *that* by themselves, since these pronouns have vague antecedents unless they are attached to a noun (e.g., *these results*). If you find yourself wanting to say *and this...* or *and that...* to add a second thought, then you need to write an absolute phrase or find another legitimate way to refer to the previous thought.

In fact, we do have one more legal way to refer to the whole previous clause and indicate the result of that clause: an *-Ing* form placed after a comma.

Right: Scientists have found high levels of iridium in certain geological forma-
             tions around the world, <u>SUGGESTING the cataclysmic impact of a meteor</u>
             <u>millions of years ago</u>.

In some cases, you can use an *-Ing* form (with a comma) in place of an absolute phrase. At the end of a sentence, either an *-Ing* form or an absolute phrase can indicate a result of the preceding clause.

At the end of a sentence, a result of the main clause can be written with either an absolute phrase or an *-Ing* form.

Problem Set

Each of the following sentences contains one or more underlined modifiers. For each of these modifiers, (1) identify the word or words, if any, that it modifies, and (2) indicate whether the modifier is correct. If the modifier is incorrect, suggest a way to correct the error. For an additional challenge, (3) identify the type of the modifier by choosing a letter from the table below.

Noun Modifiers	Verb Modifiers
(A) Adjective or adjective phrase	(G) Adverb
(B) Prepositional phrase	(H) Prepositional phrase
(C) Participle or participial phrase	(I) Participle or participial phrase
(D) Relative clause	(J) Adverbial clause (starts with a
(E) Appositive	subordinator)
(F) Subgroup modifier	(K) Absolute phrase

1. Upon setting foot in the Gothic cathedral, the spectacularly stained-glass windows amazed the camera-wielding tourists.

2. Although the ballerina seems healthily, she feels very unwell and is unlikely to dance well at tonight's performance.

3. A recent formed militia, consisting of lightly armed peasants and a few retired army officers, is fighting a bitterly civil war against government forces.

4. Angola, which was ravaged by civil war for many years after it gained independence from Portugal, which is now one of Africa's success stories, has an economy that grew by 21% last year, where parliamentary elections are to be held later this week.

5. Some critics of the Olympian Party candidate Zeus Pater's are pleased that he has chosen Artemis Rhodes, the prefect of Alexandria, to be his running mate; as many commentators have pointed out, her views on social issues are more in line with the Olympian Party platform than are Pater's.

6. The principal tried to calm the worried students' parents, as a result of those students disappearing in the storm.

7. Kelp is a natural fertilizer that has become popular among growers of heirloom tomatoes, who generally are willing to pay a premium for organic products.

8. After many years of difficult negotiations, a deal has been reached that will lower tariffs and end many subsidies, potentially changing the lives of millions of people in both the developed and the developing world.

9. Mary buys cookies made with SugarFree, an artificial sweetener, which tastes as sweet as the corn syrup that her brother loves but where there are fewer calories than in an equivalent amount of corn syrup.

10. People that are well-informed know that Bordeaux is a French region whose most famous export is the wine which bears its name.

11. The acquaintances who we like most are those that flatter us best.

12. The houses on Canal Street, of which many had been damaged in the storm, looked abandoned.

13. People, who talk loudly on their cell phones in crowded trains, show little respect for other passengers.

14. Of all the earthquakes in European history, the earthquake, which destroyed Lisbon in 1755, is perhaps the most famous.

15. The tallest mountain on Earth is Mount Everest that is on the border between Nepal and Tibet.

16. Based on the recent decline in enrollment, the admissions office decided to reevaluate its recruitment strategies.

17. Unaccustomed to the rigors of college life, James's grades dropped.

18. Regina returned the dress to the store, which was torn at one of the seams.

19. Last night our air conditioner broke, which caused great consternation.

20. The patient's rare disease was treated using novel techniques developed at the medical school.

1. <u>Upon setting foot in the Gothic cathedral</u>, the <u>spectacularly</u> stained glass windows amazed the <u>camera-wielding</u> tourists.

Upon setting foot in the Gothic cathedral: **(H)** Prepositional phrase. INCORRECT. *Upon* is a preposition. The phrase *upon setting foot in the Gothic cathedral* contains the gerund *setting*. Who or what set foot in the cathedral? Logically, it must be the *tourists*, not the *windows*. However, the noun *windows* is the subject of the sentence, and so *windows* seems to be the subject of *setting*.

spectacularly: **(G) Adverb.** INCORRECT. An adverb can modify many parts of speech, but not a noun. The phrase *spectacularly stained-glass windows* seems to imply that the windows were *spectacularly stained*—that is, *spectacularly* seems to modify *stained*. However, *stained-glass* is a material. The author intended to say that either the *stained glass* itself or the *windows* were *spectacular*. The adverb should be replaced with the adjective *spectacular*.

camera-wielding: **(C) Participle or participial phrase.** CORRECT. This participle modifies *tourists*.

Correction: **<u>Upon entering the Gothic cathedral</u>, the <u>camera-wielding</u> tourists were amazed by the spectacular stained-glass windows.**

2. Although the ballerina seems <u>healthily</u>, she feels <u>very</u> <u>unwell</u> and is <u>unlikely</u> to dance <u>well</u> at tonight's performance.

Healthily: **(G) Adverb.** INCORRECT. *Healthily* should be replaced by an adjective, because *seems* is a linking verb. The appropriate adjective, *healthy*, would modify *ballerina*.

Very: **(G) Adverb.** CORRECT. The adverb *very* modifies the adjective *unwell*.

Unwell: **(A) Adjective.** CORRECT. *Unwell* is an adjective meaning "sick" or "ill." It modifies *she*, because *feel* is a linking verb.

Unlikely: **(A) Adjective.** CORRECT. Here, *unlikely* is an adjective. *Unlikely* modifies *she*, because *is* is a linking verb.

Well: **(G) Adverb.** CORRECT. Here, *well* is an adverb meaning "in a good manner." An adverb is required to modify *dance*, which is not a linking verb.

Correction: **Although the ballerina seems <u>healthy</u>, she feels <u>very</u> <u>unwell</u> and is <u>unlikely</u> to dance <u>well</u> at tonight's performance.**

3. A <u>recent</u> formed militia, consisting of <u>lightly</u> armed peasants and a few <u>retired</u> army officers, is fighting a <u>bitterly</u> civil war against government forces.

Recent: **(A) Adjective.** INCORRECT. The adjective *recent* modifies *militia*, whereas logic calls for an adverb, *recently*, to modify *formed*.

Lightly: **(G) Adverb.** CORRECT. The adverb *lightly* modifies the past participle *armed*, which is being used as an adjective (*armed* modifies the noun *peasants*).

Retired: **(A) Adjective.** CORRECT. *Retired* is an adjective that modifies *army officers.* (You can also argue that *retired* is a past participle being used as an adjective.)

Bitterly: **(G) Adverb.** INCORRECT. The adverb *bitterly* modifies *civil,* but the writer surely meant to use an adjective (*bitter*) to modify the noun phrase *civil war.*

Correction: **A <u>recently</u> formed militia, consisting of <u>lightly</u> armed peasants and a few <u>retired</u> army officers, is fighting a <u>bitter</u> civil war against government forces.**

4. Angola, <u>which was ravaged by civil war for many years after it gained independence from Portugal,</u> <u>which is now one of Africa's success stories,</u> has an economy that grew by 21% last year, <u>where parliamentary elections are to be held later this week.</u>

Which was ravaged... from Portugal: **(D) Relative clause.** CORRECT. This relative clause modifies the noun *Angola.*

Which is now one of Africa's success stories: **(D) Relative clause.** INCORRECT. This relative clause illogically modifies *Portugal.*

Where parliamentary... this week: **(D) Relative clause.** INCORRECT. A relative clause that begins with *where* must modify a noun that names a physical place, so this clause does not really modify *year.* The clause is too far away from *Angola,* however, to perform its intended role of modifying *Angola.*

Repairing this deeply flawed sentence involves rearranging its components and incorporating some of the modifiers into main clauses.

Correction: **<u>Ravaged by civil war for many years after it gained independence from Portugal,</u> Angola is now one of Africa's success stories: its economy grew by 21% last year, and parliamentary elections are to be held later this week.**

5. Some critics <u>of the Olympian Party candidate Zeus Pater's</u> are pleased that he has chosen Artemis Rhodes, <u>the prefect of Alexandria,</u> to be his running mate; as many commentators have pointed out, her views on social issues are more in line with the Olympian Party platform than are <u>Pater's.</u>

Of the Olympian Party candidate Zeus Pater's: **(B) Prepositional phrase.** INCORRECT. This prepositional phrase modifies the noun *critics.* The phrase is incorrect, according to the GMAT, because it uses two possessives (*of* and *'s*) when only one is necessary. The GMAT claims that you must say either *critics of Zeus Pater* or *Zeus Pater's critics.*

The prefect of Alexandria: **(E) Appositive.** CORRECT. This noun phrase modifies another noun, *Artemis Rhodes.*

Pater's: **(A) Adjective.** CORRECT. *Pater's* is the possessive form of the noun *Pater*; therefore, it can be thought of as an adjective. What does it modify? The last clause can be seen as an abbreviation of *her views on social issues are more in line with the Olympian Party platform than are Pater's <u>views on social issues</u>.* Thus, *Pater's* modifies the implied second occurrence of the noun phrase *views on social issues.*

Correction: **Some critics <u>of the Olympian Party candidate Zeus Pater</u> are pleased that he has chosen Artemis Rhodes, <u>the prefect of Alexandria</u>, to be his running mate; as many commentators have pointed out, her views on social issues are more in line with the Olympian Party platform than are <u>Pater's</u>.**

6. The principal tried to calm the <u>worried</u> students' parents, as a result of those <u>students</u> disappearing in the storm.

Worried: **(C) Participle.** INCORRECT. *Worried* is a past participle derived from the verb *to worry.* It is used here as an adjective, but its meaning is ambiguous. Its placement suggests that it modifies *students'*, but logic suggests that it should modify *parents.*

Students: **(A) Adjective.** INCORRECT. *Students*, in the phrase *those students disappearing*, is a noun that seems intended to modify the gerund *disappearing.* The reason is that what is worrying the adults is not the students themselves but their disappearance. A noun that modifies a gerund has to be in the possessive form, however, so *those students' disappearing* would be better. *Those students' disappearance* would be even better, because possessive nouns before gerunds tend to sound awkward.

The best way to salvage this sentence would be to rewrite it completely.

Correction: **The principal tried to calm the <u>worried</u> parents of the students who had disappeared in the storm.**

7. Kelp is a natural fertilizer <u>that has become popular among growers of heirloom tomatoes,</u> <u>who generally are willing to pay a premium for organic products.</u>

That has... heirloom tomatoes: **(D) Relative clause.** CORRECT. This clause modifies *fertilizer.*

Who generally... organic products: **(D) Relative clause.** CORRECT. Perhaps surprisingly, this clause correctly modifies *growers,* or more precisely the noun phrase *growers of heirloom tomatoes.* The prepositional phrase *of heirloom tomatoes* is a "mission-critical" modifier: it cannot be moved away from *growers,* the noun that is <u>defined</u> by the prepositional phrase. Moreover, *of heirloom tomatoes* is short, and the relative pronoun *who* cannot refer to objects such as *tomatoes.* For all these reasons, we are allowed to position the relative clause a few words away from *growers.*

No correction necessary.

8. After many years of difficult negotiations, a deal has been reached <u>that will lower tariffs and end many subsidies</u>, potentially changing the lives of millions of people in both the developed and the developing world.

That will lower tariffs and end many subsidies: **(D) Relative clause.** CORRECT. This clause modifies *a deal*. Normally a relative clause should touch its antecedent, but we are sometimes allowed to put a short verb phrase between a relative clause and its antecedent. In this sentence, the long participial phrase *potentially changing...world* needs to be close to the verbs that it modifies (*will lower...and end...*). The only alternative to the current configuration of the sentence would put *has been reached* at the end of the sentence, so far away from *a deal* that the sentence would be difficult to understand: *After many years of difficult negotiations, a deal that will lower tariffs and end many subsidies, potentially changing the lives of millions of people in both the developed and the developing world, has been reached.*

No correction necessary.

9. Mary buys cookies made with SugarFree, <u>an artificial sweetener,</u> <u>which tastes as sweet as the corn syrup</u> <u>that her brother loves</u> but <u>where there are fewer calories than in an equivalent amount of corn syrup.</u>

An artificial sweetener: **(E) Appositive.** CORRECT. This appositive noun phrase modifies *SugarFree*.

Which tastes...brother loves **(D) Relative clause.** CORRECT. This clause modifies *SugarFree*. Normally a relative clause should touch the noun that it modifies, but we are generally allowed to place an appositive between a relative clause and the modified noun.

Where there are...corn syrup **(D) Relative clause.** INCORRECT. This relative clause is wrong for two reasons. (1) The relative pronoun *where* must modify places. *SugarFree*, the intended antecedent, is not a geographic place. (2) The relative clause *where there...corn syrup* is meant to be parallel to the relative clause *which tastes...brother loves*. When relative clauses are parallel, they should start with the same relative pronoun.

Correction: **Mary buys cookies made with SugarFree, <u>an artificial sweetener, which tastes as sweet</u>** **<u>as the corn syrup that her brother loves</u> but <u>which contains fewer calories than does an</u>** **<u>equivalent amount of corn syrup.</u>**

10. People <u>that are well-informed</u> know that Bordeaux is a French region <u>whose most famous export is the</u> <u>wine which bears its name.</u>

That are well-informed: **(D) Relative clause.** INCORRECT. This clause uses the relative pronoun *that* to refer to people. *Who* must refer to human beings. Another problem with *that are well-informed* is that it is wordy. Avoid relative clauses whose only verb is a form of *to be*, because they can generally be expressed more succinctly.

Whose most famous...bears its name: **(D) Relative clause.** CORRECT. This clause modifies *region*. Notice that *whose*, unlike *who* and *whom*, can correctly modify non-human entities.

Which bears its name: **(D) Relative clause.** INCORRECT. The context of this sentence calls for an essential clause to modify the wine, since the point of the clause is to identify the wine. If the sentence ended with *the wine*, it would be incomplete. The clause should therefore begin with *that* rather than *which*.

*Manhattan*GMAT*Prep
the new standard

Correction: **<u>Well-informed</u> people know that Bordeaux is a French region <u>whose most famous export is the wine that bears its name.</u>**

11. The acquaintances <u>who we like most</u> are those <u>that flatter us best</u>.

Who we like most: **(D) Relative clause.** INCORRECT. The relative pronoun *who* should be *whom*, because *whom* is the object of the verb *like*. The word *whom* is in fact optional in this circumstance. We can say either *The acquaintances whom we like most* or *The acquaintances we like most*.

That flatter us best: **(D) Relative clause.** INCORRECT. *Who*, not *that*, should be used to refer to people (*acquaintances*).

Correction: **The acquaintances <u>whom we like most</u> are those <u>who flatter us best</u>.**

12. The houses <u>on Canal Street</u>, <u>of which many had been damaged in the storm</u>, looked <u>abandoned</u>.

On Canal Street: **(B) Prepositional phrase.** CORRECT. This phrase modifies *houses*.

Of which many…storm: **(F) Subgroup modifier.** INCORRECT. This is a subgroup modifier because it makes a statement about a subgroup of the houses on Canal Street. The wording is wrong, however. One corrected version is *many of which had been damaged in the storm*.

Abandoned: **(C) Participle.** CORRECT. This past participle modifies *houses*, because *looked* is a linking verb.

Correction: **The houses <u>on Canal Street</u>, <u>many of which had been damaged in the storm</u>, looked <u>abandoned</u>.**

13. People<u>, who talk loudly on their cell phones in crowded trains,</u> show little respect for other passengers.

Who talk… crowded trains: **(D) Relative clause.** INCORRECT. This clause is wrong because the commas that enclose it make it a non-essential clause. The logic of the sentence calls for an essential clause, because the rest of the sentence would change its meaning without the information in the relative clause. (The sentence *People show no respect for other passengers*, which we would get by removing the relative clause, makes a sweeping claim about every human being.) To correct this error, we need only to remove the commas.

Correction: **People <u>who talk loudly on their cell phones in crowded trains</u> show little respect for other passengers.**

14. Of all the earthquakes in European history, the earthquake<u>, which destroyed Lisbon in 1755,</u> is perhaps the most famous.

Which destroyed Lisbon in 1755: **(D) Relative clause.** INCORRECT. This clause is wrong because the commas that enclose it make it a non-essential clause. The logic of the sentence calls for an essential clause to make clear which earthquake is the most famous. (If you remove the relative clause, you get the very mysterious sentence *Of all the earthquakes in European history, the earthquake is perhaps the most famous.*) To correct the sentence, we must remove the commas and replace *which* with *that*.

Correction: **Of all the earthquakes in European history, the earthquake <u>that destroyed Lisbon in 1755</u> is perhaps the most famous.**

15. The tallest mountain on Earth is Mount Everest <u>that is on the border between Nepal and Tibet</u>.

That is on…Tibet: **(D) Relative clause.** INCORRECT. This clause is wrong because it is essential. The logic of the sentence calls for a non-essential clause for two reasons. (1) The information about Mount Everest being *on the border between Nepal and Tibet* is hardly necessary to identify which mountain we are talking about, since we are given both the mountain's name (*Mount Everest*) and a unique description of the mountain (*the tallest mountain on Earth*). (2) The meaning of the rest of the sentence would not change in any significant way if the information in the relative clause were removed. To correct this sentence, we need to put a comma after *Everest* and change *that* to *which*.

Correction: **The tallest mountain on Earth is Mount Everest, <u>which is on the border between Nepal and Tibet</u>.**

16. <u>Based on the recent decline in enrollment</u>, the admissions office decided to reevaluate its recruitment strategies.

Based on… enrollment: **(C) Participial phrase.** INCORRECT. As a noun modifier, the past participle *based* modifies *admissions office*. However, the intention of the sentence is not that the *admissions office* itself is *based on the recent decline in enrollment*. The phrase *based on X* is often incorrectly used in place of the prepositional phrase *because of*, which can correctly modify the verb phrase *decided to reevaluate*.

Correction: **<u>Because of the recent decline in enrollment</u>, the admissions office decided to reevaluate its recruitment strategies.**

17. <u>Unaccustomed to the rigors of college life</u>, James's grades dropped.

Unaccustomed to… college life: **(C) Participial phrase.** INCORRECT. As a noun modifier, the past participle *unaccustomed* modifies the noun phrase *James's grades*. However, the author of the sentence obviously intends for *unaccustomed* to modify *James* himself. If we wish to begin the sentence with the noun modifier, we must rephrase the sentence to make *James* the subject.

Correction: **<u>Unaccustomed to the rigors of college life</u>, James allowed his grades to drop.**

18. Regina returned the dress to the store, <u>which was torn at one of the seams</u>.

Which was... the seams: **(D) Relative clause.** INCORRECT. This modifier is misplaced. It seems to describe *store,* the adjacent noun; however, the modifier should modify *dress.* Thus, we must move the modifier next to *dress.* Since the modifier is relatively short, we can get away with simply inserting it and setting it off with commas.

Correction: **Regina returned the dress, <u>which was torn at one of the seams,</u> to the store.**

19. Last night our air conditioner broke, <u>which caused great consternation</u>.

Which caused great consternation: **(D) Relative clause.** INCORRECT. This modifier is dangling, since the sentence contains no noun correctly modified by the clause *which caused great consternation.* The author's intent is to comment on the event (the breakdown of the air conditioner). But the main clause does not name the event with a noun. Therefore, we need to change the modifier to a verb modifier, either a participle (*causing...*) or an absolute phrase (*an event that caused...*).

Correction: **Last night our air conditioner broke, <u>causing great consternation</u>.**

20. The patient's rare disease was treated <u>using novel techniques</u> <u>developed at the medical school</u>.

Using novel techniques: **(C) Participial phrase.** INCORRECT. This modifier is dangling, since the sentence contains no noun that is properly modified by *using novel techniques.* To fix the sentence, we can introduce an agent who actually used the novel techniques (e.g., a *doctor*), or we can switch to a prepositional phrase, such as *through the use of novel techniques*, that does not contain an *-Ing* verb form.

Developed at the medical school: **(C) Participial phrase.** CORRECT. This past participle modifies *techniques.*

Correction: **The patient's rare disease was treated <u>through the use of novel techniques</u> <u>developed at the medical school</u>.**

OR   **The doctor treated the patient's rare disease <u>by using novel techniques</u> <u>developed at the medical school</u>.**

Sentence Correction

Now that you have completed your study of MODIFIERS, it is time to test your skills on problems that have actually appeared on real GMAT exams over the past several years.

The problem set that follows is composed of past GMAT problems from two books published by GMAC (Graduate Management Admission Council):

The Official Guide for GMAT Review, 11th Edition (pages 39–43 & 638–660)
The Official Guide for GMAT Verbal Review (pages 234–253)

The problems in the set below are primarily focused on MODIFIER issues. For each of these problems, identify any modifiers and the words that they modify. Determine the type of modifier issues at work, including positioning, use of relative pronouns, and essential vs. non-essential modifiers.

Note: Problem numbers preceded by "D" refer to questions in the Diagnostic Test chapter of *The Official Guide for GMAT Review, 11th Edition* (pages 39–43).

Modifiers

> *11th Edition*: 7, 20, 24, 38, 67, 71, 72, 78, 89, 93, 98, 102, 105, 109, 110, 111, 114,
> D40, D44, D49
> *Verbal Review*: 7, 18, 32, 38, 63, 73, 78, 79, 91, 96, 110, 111, 112

Chapter 7
of
SENTENCE CORRECTION

VERB TENSE, MOOD, & VOICE

In This Chapter . . .

VERB TENSE, MOOD, & VOICE

In addition to subject–verb agreement, we must consider three other features of verbs that are tested on the GMAT: tense, mood, and voice.

Verb Tense indicates when the action of the verb takes place. In sentences with one action, verb tense is relatively easy. Knowing this, the GMAT tries to complicate sentences by incorporating more than one action.

Verb Mood indicates what the writer believes about, or wants to do with, the action. Two verb moods are tested on the GMAT: indicative and subjunctive. Most verbs are in the indicative mood, which we use to describe knowledge or beliefs. Occasionally, we use verbs in the subjunctive mood to express suggestions, desires, or hypothetical events.

Finally, Verb Voice indicates who or what is doing the action. Two verb voices are tested on the GMAT: active voice and passive voice. In the active voice, the subject of the sentence performs the action. In the passive voice, the subject of the sentence has an action performed on it by someone or something else.

> Use the simple tenses unless the sentence requires a more complex tense.

Simple Tenses

The three simple tenses express three basic times:

SIMPLE PRESENT   Sandy PLAYS well with her friends.
SIMPLE PAST   Sandy PLAYED well with her friends yesterday.
SIMPLE FUTURE   Sandy WILL PLAY well with her friends tomorrow.

The Simple Present tense is often used to express "eternal" states or frequent events. In the first example above, the sentence does not mean that Sandy is playing right now, but rather that as a general rule, Sandy plays well with her friends.

In general, the GMAT prefers the simple tenses, unless the sentence clearly requires one of the more complex tenses discussed below.

Progressive Tenses

To emphasize the ongoing nature of an action, we can use the Progressive tenses, which use the verb *to be* and the present participle (*-Ing* form):

PRESENT PROGRESSIVE   Sandy IS PLAYING soccer.
PAST PROGRESSIVE   Sandy WAS PLAYING soccer yesterday.
FUTURE PROGRESSIVE   Sandy WILL BE PLAYING soccer tomorrow.

The Present Progressive indicates action happening right now, whether the sentence contains words such as *right now* or not. The first example above means that at the present moment, if you look for Sandy, you will find her actually playing soccer. In contrast, the Simple Present version, *Sandy plays soccer*, means that she frequently plays, or that she knows how to play.

Do not use the Present Progressive for general definitions. Instead, use the Simple Present.

Wrong: Cherenkov radiation is light that particles ARE EMITTING when they ARE TRAVELING faster than the effective speed of light in any medium.

Right: Cherenkov radiation is light that particles EMIT when they TRAVEL faster than the effective speed of light in any medium.

In GMAT sentences, do not use the Present Progressive to indicate future actions. This usage is considered too colloquial. Instead, use the Simple Future.

Wrong: Quentin IS MEETING Harvey for lunch tomorrow.
Right: Quentin WILL MEET Harvey for lunch tomorrow.

Verbs that express general states do not normally take progressive forms. Such <u>State Verbs</u> include *know* or *signify*.

Wrong: This inscription IS SIGNIFYING the emperor's birth.
Right: This inscription SIGNIFIES the emperor's birth.

> When you encounter the Present Progressive, check to see whether another tense would be preferable.

Keep Verb Tenses Consistent

Sentences with more than one action do not necessarily require more than one verb tense. In fact, in any given sentence you should try to keep all verb tenses consistent, unless the meaning clearly dictates otherwise. For example:

She WALKED to school in the morning and RAN home in the afternoon.
She WALKS to school in the morning and RUNS home in the afternoon.
She WILL WALK to school in the morning and RUN home in the afternoon.

In the first sentence, both verbs are in the Simple Past tense. In the second sentence, both verbs are in the Simple Present tense. In the third sentence, both verbs are in the Simple Future tense. (Note that *run* is understood as *will run*; parallelism allows the *will* to apply to both verbs.) There is no reason to change tenses within any of these sentences, so the verb tenses are kept the same.

However, some sentences with more than one action do require you to switch verb tenses.

Right: He IS thinner now because he SPENT the last six months on a strict diet.

Here, the first verb (*is*) is in the Simple Present, while the second verb (*spent*) is in the Simple Past. This is a straightforward and logical switch, given the content of the sentence.

In a more subtle example, you can use the Past Progressive to describe a background event, while you use Simple Past to describe a more important event in the foreground.

Right: She WAS PLAYING with her friends when the babysitter ARRIVED.

In the previous example, the action *was playing* (in the Past Progressive) takes place in the background. *Arrived* (in the Simple Past) is the interrupting foreground event. Note that the following sentence is also correct, but it has a different meaning.

> Right: She PLAYED with her friends when the babysitter ARRIVED.

In this case, the action *played* took place <u>after</u> the babysitter *arrived*. Both actions are in the Simple Past and express equal levels of importance.

The Perfect Tenses: An Introduction

Sometimes, however, actions in a sentence involve more complex time sequences than can be expressed with the simple tenses or the simple progressive tenses.

These actions can be expressed using the PERFECT tenses: Present Perfect & Past Perfect. You must understand these tenses as they are tested on the GMAT.

Present Perfect: Still In Effect. . .

We use the <u>Present Perfect</u> tense for actions that started in the past but continue into the present, or remain true in the present. The Present Perfect tense has one foot in the past and one foot in the present.

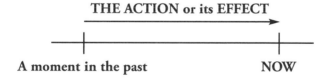

THE ACTION or its EFFECT

A moment in the past   NOW

> Right: We HAVE LIVED in a hut for three days.

This sentence means that we started living in the hut three days ago and that we are still living in that hut. In comparison, a sentence in the Simple Past has a different meaning.

> Right: We LIVED in a hut for three days.

This example means that we are no longer living in the hut. The three days are over. The Present Perfect tense is formed as follows:

> **Present Perfect = HAVE/HAS + Past Participle**

The past participle of a regular verb, such as *walk* or *live*, is simply the verb with an *-ed* ending: *walked, lived.* Irregular verbs, such as *go* or *see*, have unique past participles (*gone, seen*). If you are a native English speaker, you already know all the irregular forms. Otherwise, study the list of irregular past participles in the Glossary under "Past Participles."

Use the Present Perfect tense for an action that began in the past and continues (or whose result continues) into the present.

Here are some examples of actions in the Present Perfect tense:

> Right: This country HAS ENFORCED strict immigration laws <u>for thirty years</u>.
> Right: They HAVE KNOWN each other <u>since 1987</u>.

Each example involves an action that began in the past and continues into the present. This country enforced strict immigration laws in the past and still enforces them today. They knew each other in the past and still know each other today. In each case, the idea of "continuing action" is reinforced by a time phrase, such as *for thirty years* or *since 1987,* that states how long the action has been occurring.

Sometimes, the Present Perfect tense means that the action is definitely over, but its effect is still relevant or pertinent to the present moment.

> Right: The child HAS DRAWN a square in the sand.

In this example, the child is <u>no longer</u> drawing a square. The act of drawing is finished. However, the square must still be here somehow; the **effect** of the act is still operative. If the square has disappeared, you should use Simple Past.

> Right: The child DREW a square in the sand, but the ocean ERASED it.
> Right: The child DREW a square in the sand, but the ocean HAS ERASED it.
> Awkward: The child HAS DRAWN a square in the sand, but the ocean HAS ERASED it.

Note that the act of erasing could be in either Simple Past or Present Perfect. In the first example above (with *erased*), the current state of the sand is not known; in the second example (with *has erased*), the current state of the sand is square-free, since the Present Perfect *has erased* indicates that this action's effect is still true.

To summarize, we use Present Perfect to indicate either <u>continued action</u> or <u>continued effect</u> (of a completed action).

If you use *since,* you must use the Present Perfect to indicate continued action:

> Wrong: <u>Since 1986</u> no one BROKE that world record.
> Right: <u>Since 1986</u> no one HAS BROKEN that world record.

Likewise, Present Perfect should be used with *within* phrases, such as *within the past five minutes* or *within the last ten days,* to indicate continued action or continued effect.

If you want to talk about a specific, completed time period, use the Simple Past, not the Present Perfect:

> Wrong: Veronica HAS TRAVELED all over the world <u>in 2007</u>.
> Right: Veronica TRAVELED all over the world <u>in 2007</u>.

Whether it indicates continued action or continued effect, the Present Perfect tense makes a statement about the present time.

Note that it is fine to write *Veronica has traveled all over the world* and omit any specific, completed time reference. In this case, you are making a statement about Veronica <u>today</u> (the kind of person she is, her experience and qualities, etc.). Because of this emphasis on the present time, the Present Perfect is actually more often found in sentences with Simple Present than with Simple Past.

Finally, the idea of completed action can be used simply to place a Present Perfect action earlier than another action in *-Ing* forms, infinitives or subordinate clauses.

> Right: She WILL PAY you when you ASK her.
> (the time of *will pay* = the time of *[will] ask*; note that the future *will* is often dropped in subordinate clauses)
> Right: She WILL PAY you when you HAVE TAKEN out the garbage.
> (the time of *will pay* is LATER than the future time of *have taken*)

If you use <i>Since</i> with a time phrase, such as <i>Since 1987</i>, use the Present Perfect.

Past Perfect: The Earlier Action

If two actions in a sentence occurred at different times in the past, we often use the <u>Past Perfect</u> tense for the earlier action and Simple Past for the later action. The Past Perfect is the "Past of the Past," or the "Past Twice Removed" from the present time.

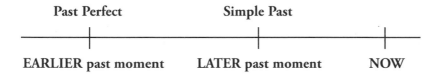

The Past Perfect tense is formed as follows:

> **Past Perfect = HAD + Past Participle**

Here are some examples of sentences using the Past Perfect tense:

> Right: The film HAD STARTED by the time we ARRIVED at the theater.
> Right: The teacher THOUGHT that Jimmy HAD CHEATED on the exam.

The earlier past action (*had started, had cheated*) is in the Past Perfect tense, while the later past action is in the Simple Past tense (*arrived, thought*). Do not use Past Perfect simply for "long ago" without a later past moment. Even a long-ago moment can be referred to with Simple Past: *An asteroid STRUCK the earth millions of years ago.*

Note that we <u>do not always</u> use the Past Perfect for earlier actions. In general, you should use Past Perfect only to clarify or emphasize a sequence of past events. The earlier event should somehow have a bearing on the context of the later event. Moreover, if the sequence is already obvious, we often do not need Past Perfect.

> Right: Antonio DROVE to the store and BOUGHT some ice cream.

We already know that *drove* happened before *bought*. A sequence of verbs with the same subject does not require Past Perfect. Rather, use the Simple Past for all the verbs.

> Right: Antonio DROVE to the store, and Cristina BOUGHT some ice cream.

In the sentence above, which has two main clauses linked by *and,* we are not emphasizing the order of events (although *drove* probably happened before *bought*). Clauses linked by *and* or *but* do not require the Past Perfect as a general rule.

> Right: Laura LOCKED the deadbolt <u>before</u> she LEFT for work.

Likewise, we already know that *locked* happens before *left* because of the word *before*. The words *before* and *after* indicate the sequence of events clearly and emphatically enough to make the use of the Past Perfect unnecessary.

Also note that the later past event does not need to be expressed with a Simple Past tense verb. You could just use a date or another time reference.

> Right: <u>By 1945</u>, the United States HAD BEEN at war for several years.

Using this construction, you can even make a tricky sentence in which the first clause expresses an early action in Simple Past. Then, a second clause expresses a <u>later</u> action in Past Perfect to indicate continued effect (by a still later past time).

> Right: The band U2 WAS just one of many new groups on the rock music scene in the early 1980's, but less than ten years later, U2 HAD fully ECLIPSED its early rivals in the pantheon of popular music.

Perfect Tenses: Only When Necessary

Do not use the perfect tenses when the simple tenses will do. The GMAT prefers simplicity.

> Wrong: Joe LEARNED about an epoch in which dinosaurs HAD WALKED the earth.
>
> Right: Joe LEARNED about an epoch in which dinosaurs WALKED the earth.

In the first example, the Past Perfect *had walked* is unnecessary. Although the action *had walked* does take place earlier than the action *learned*, the earlier action does not have a direct bearing on the context of the later action. The sequence of time does not need to be clarified or emphasized. Thus, the Past Perfect is considered wrong in this context.
You should use the perfect tenses only when you can justify them with the rules described in these sections. If an action began in the past and continues into the present (or its effect does), use the Present Perfect tense. If one action in the past precedes another, and you need to clarify or emphasize the time sequence, then use the Past Perfect tense. Otherwise, stick to the simpler tenses.

Use the Past Perfect tense if you need to clarify or emphasize a sequence of actions in the past.

Tense Sequence

Consider the following quotation:

> Scientist: "The <u>supercollider IS ready</u>, <u>it DID not COST too much</u>, and <u>it WILL PRO-VIDE new insights</u> into the workings of the universe."

How do we report this scientist's speech, if we use a past tense reporting verb such as *announced?* Typically, we move the tenses back in time one step.

> Report: The scientist ANNOUNCED that the <u>supercollider WAS ready</u>, that <u>it HAD not COST too much</u>, and that <u>it WOULD PROVIDE new insights</u> into the workings of the universe.

Compare the corresponding underlined clauses in the quotation and the report.

> (1) *The supercollider IS ready*   becomes   *...that the supercollider WAS ready.*

The Simple Present tense (*is*) becomes the Simple Past (*was*).

> (2) *It DID not COST too much*   becomes   *...that it HAD not COST too much.*

The Simple Past tense (*did... cost*) becomes Past Perfect (*had... cost*). The action becomes one step further removed from the present.

> (3) *It WILL PROVIDE insights*   becomes   *...that it WOULD PROVIDE insights.*

Finally, the Simple Future tense (*will provide*) becomes the <u>Conditional Tense</u>, which is formed by combining *would* with the base form of the verb: *would provide*. The helping verb *would* expresses the future from the past's point of view.

With a past tense reporting verb, move Present to Past, Past to Past Perfect, and Future to Conditional (that is, *will* to *would*).

The Subjunctive Mood

Again, verb mood expresses what the writer believes about, or wants to do with, the action expressed by the verb. In English, most sentences express facts with the <u>Indicative Mood</u> or commands with the <u>Imperative Mood</u>. You can expect to see the <u>Subjunctive Mood</u> in two special situations:

> (1) Unlikely or unreal conditions (usually after *if* or a similar word).
> (2) Proposals, desires, and requests formed with certain verbs and the word *that.*

These two uses correspond to two forms of the subjunctive mood: the Hypothetical Subjunctive and the Command Subjunctive.

The Hypothetical Subjunctive

We use the <u>Hypothetical Subjunctive</u> form in a few circumstances to indicate unlikely or unreal conditions. Principally, this form occurs after *if*, *as if*, or *as though*.

> Right: To overcome my fear of germs, I will think about disease <u>as though it WERE harmless</u>.

The speaker does not believe that disease actually <u>is</u> harmless. By using the Hypothetical Subjunctive *were*, the speaker reveals that he or she thinks that disease is <u>not</u> harmless.

The basic form of the Hypothetical Subjunctive is equivalent to the Simple Past of every verb, with one exception. For the verb *to be*, the form *were* is <u>always</u> used. (The Simple Past of *be* is both *were* and *was*: *I was, you were, he/she/it was, we/you/they were*.) Just remember the song "If I WERE a Rich Man" (not *If I WAS a Rich Man*) and you will remember to use *were*. However, the GMAT tests this usage rarely, if at all. Because of its similarity in form to the Simple Past, the Hypothetical Subjunctive is sometimes called the "Past Subjunctive." However, its use has to do with unlikely or unreal conditions, not with past time.

If . . . Then Constructions

Sentences that use the word *if* do not always use the Hypothetical Subjunctive. Sentences with an *if* condition and a *then* outcome can follow any of several tense/mood patterns.

> Right: IF you study diligently, [THEN] you will score highly.
> Right: You will score highly IF you study diligently.

Note that the actual word *then* is frequently omitted. Also, the *if* clause does not have to appear first in the sentence. Here are the five common patterns of *if...then* sentences.

(1) <u>General Rule with no uncertainty</u>
>   IF Sophie EATS pizza, THEN she BECOMES ill.
>   IF Present, THEN Present.

This pattern is equivalent to *whenever: WHENEVER Sophie EATS pizza, she BECOMES ill.*

(2) <u>General Rule with some uncertainty</u>
>   IF Sophie EATS pizza, THEN she MAY BECOME ill.
>   IF Present, THEN *Can* or *May*.

Here, the helping verbs *can* or *may* can be used to allow for a somewhat uncertain outcome.

(3) <u>Particular Case (in the future) with no uncertainty</u>
>   IF Sophie EATS pizza tomorrow, THEN she WILL BECOME ill.
>   IF Present, THEN Future.

Another possibility for the Particular Case (in the present) is Present Perfect: *If Sophie HAS EATEN pizza, then she WILL BECOME ill.*

Learn the five *If...Then* constructions. If a choice does not fit one of these five constructions, then it is almost certainly incorrect.

(4) Unlikely Case (in the future)
      IF Sophie ATE pizza tomorrow, THEN she WOULD BECOME ill.
      IF Hypothetical Subjunctive, THEN Conditional.

Here, the writer thinks that Sophie is <u>unlikely</u> to eat pizza tomorrow. In place of *would*, the form *could* can be used to indicate improbability as well.

(5) Case that Never Happened (in the past)
      IF Sophie HAD EATEN pizza yesterday, THEN she WOULD HAVE BECOME ill.
      IF Past Perfect, THEN Conditional Perfect.

Other patterns are possible, but *if... then* sentences that you encounter on the GMAT should conform to one of these five patterns.

Notice that *would* and *should* should NEVER go in the *if* part of the sentence!

The Command Subjunctive

The other form of the subjunctive mood is the <u>Command Subjunctive</u>, which is much more important on the GMAT than the Hypothetical Subjunctive.

The Command Subjunctive is used with certain <u>Bossy Verbs</u>, such as *require* or *propose*. Bossy Verbs tell people to do things.

      The agency REQUIRED that Gary BE ready before noon.
      We PROPOSE that the school board DISBAND.

In these examples, the verbs *Be* and *Disband* are in the Command Subjunctive mood. The form of the Command Subjunctive is the form you would use to command Gary or the school board directly:

      BE ready before noon, Gary!
      DISBAND, school board!

This form is also known as the <u>Bare Form</u> of the verb: the infinitive (*to be, to disband*) without the *to*. The bare form is like the Simple Present, with two important exceptions: (1) there is no *-S* on the end for third person singular (*that the school board DISBAND*, not *DISBANDS*), and (2) the form of the verb *to be* is always just *be*, not *is, are,* or *am*.

The subjunctive construction with a Bossy Verb is always as follows:

      Bossy Verb + *THAT* + subject + Command Subjunctive
      We PROPOSE THAT the school board DISBAND.

Stick to the five *If... Then* constructions. Do not use *Would* in the *If* clause. Do not use *Should* anywhere in an *If... Then* sentence.

Take note of the following **incorrect** constructions, all commonly tested on the GMAT:

Wrong:　We PROPOSE the school board DISBAND. (*That* is not optional.)
Wrong:　We PROPOSE THAT the school board DISBANDS.
Wrong:　We PROPOSE THAT the school board IS TO DISBAND.
Wrong:　We PROPOSE THAT the school board WILL DISBAND.
Wrong:　We PROPOSE THAT the school board SHOULD DISBAND.

Speakers of British (Commonwealth) English should pay particular attention to the last example above. In British English, you can often use *should* in place of a Command Subjunctive. Never do so on the GMAT, which is based on American English.

What makes the Command Subjunctive complicated is that not every Bossy Verb uses the Command Subjunctive. In fact, with some of the most common Bossy Verbs, such as *want*, you <u>cannot</u> use the Command Subjunctive:

Right:　The vice-president WANTS her TO GO to the retreat.
Wrong:　The vice-president WANTS THAT she GO to the retreat.

With *want*, you must use an infinitive (*to* + the bare form), as above.

Which Bossy Verbs take which construction: subjunctive or infinitive? Unfortunately, this issue is idiomatic. In other words, there is no rule. You simply have to memorize which verbs take which. If you are a native speaker, your ear will guide you. See the Idiom List in the next chapter for more details on each verb.

<u>Common Verbs that take ONLY the Command Subjunctive:</u>
demand, dictate, insist, mandate, propose, recommend, request, stipulate, suggest

　　We <u>demand</u> THAT HE BE here.

<u>Verbs that take ONLY the Infinitive:</u>
advise, allow, forbid, persuade, want

　　We <u>allow</u> HIM TO BE here.

<u>Verbs that take EITHER the Command Subjunctive OR the Infinitive</u>
ask, beg, intend, order, prefer, urge, require (pay particular attention to *require*)

　　We <u>require</u> THAT HE BE here.　　OR　　We <u>require</u> HIM TO BE here.

A few Bossy Verbs, most notably *prohibit,* take other constructions altogether:

　　Right:　The agency PROHIBITED Gary FROM WORKING on weekends.

Never use Should in place of a Command Subjunctive.

Manhattan **GMAT** Prep
the new standard

The Command Subjunctive can also be used with nouns derived from Bossy Verbs, such as *a demand* or *a request*.

>   Right: His <u>demand</u> THAT he BE paid full severance was not met.

Also, the Command Subjunctive is possible with *It is X*, in which *X* is an adjective, such as *essential*, that conveys urgency. *It is X* is not commonly tested on the GMAT.

>   Right: <u>It is essential</u> THAT Gary BE ready before noon.

Other adjectives conveying urgency include *advisable, crucial, desirable, fitting, imperative, important, mandatory, necessary, preferable, urgent,* and *vital*. Note also that you can use an infinitive in these constructions: *it is essential for Gary <u>to be</u> ready before noon.*

Avoid the use of the Command Subjunctive after *whether*. This usage is old-fashioned.

>   Right: I like ice cream, WHETHER it <u>BE</u> chocolate, vanilla, or any other flavor.
>   Right: I like ice cream, WHETHER it <u>IS</u> chocolate, vanilla, or any other flavor.

In summary, you should be familiar with the Subjunctive Mood, particularly the Command Subjunctive. When someone demands something in a sentence, pay attention to the verb and the *that* construction. Generally, for native speakers, memorizing verbs will be unnecessary, as your ear will allow you to determine which form or forms are possible.

> If a sentence includes a demand, look either for an infinitive or for *that* followed by Command Subjunctive.

Active vs. Passive Voice

Verbs are written in either <u>Active Voice</u> or <u>Passive Voice</u>. In the active voice, the subject of the sentence performs the action. In the passive voice, the subject of the sentence has an action performed on it by someone or something else.

>   Active: The hungry students ATE the pizza.
>   Passive: The pizza WAS EATEN by the hungry students.

The passive voice is formed with a form of the verb *to be* (in this case, *was*), followed by the past participle (*eaten*). Do not use other verbs besides *be*, such as *get*, to form the passive voice.

>   Wrong: The pizza GOT EATEN by the hungry students.
>   Wrong: The pizza must GET EATEN today.

Whoever actually performs the action in the sentence may follow the verb in a phrase headed by the preposition *by* (*by the hungry students*). Use *by* only for the actual doers of the action. Use *through* or *because of* when you want to describe any instrument or means, which might be an awkward subject in active voice:

>   Wrong: The pizza WAS accidentally EATEN BY a quirk of fate.
>   Wrong: A quirk of fate accidentally ate the pizza.
>   Right: THROUGH a quirk of fate, the pizza WAS accidentally EATEN.

Although the passive voice is not grammatically incorrect, it often makes sentences longer and more confusing. Also, it often makes it difficult to ascertain who performed the action. Since the GMAT prefers brevity and simplicity whenever possible, you should avoid answer choices written in the passive voice when the passive voice contributes to unnecessary wordiness or confusion.

> Passive: It HAS BEEN DECIDED by Jason that he will not attend college.
> Active: Jason HAS DECIDED not to attend college.

Notice that the corrected sentence is clearer and simpler.

Only <u>Transitive Verbs</u> (verbs that take direct objects) can be written in the passive voice. Verbs that do not take direct objects should never be written in the passive voice.

> Wrong: The aliens WERE ARRIVED on Neptune in the 20th century.
> Right: The aliens ARRIVED on Neptune in the 20th century.

Is Passive Voice Ever the Correct Answer?

Passive voice is sometimes used in correct answer choices on the GMAT.

> During this operation, new blood vessels are inserted, bypassing blockages.

This sentence includes the passive voice verb formation *are inserted*. However, the sentence is neither confusing nor wordy. The person performing the action, the unmentioned surgeon, is not important. The focus of the sentence is on the blood vessels inserted during the operation, rather than on the person who inserts them. The passive voice is actually ideal here, as the writer intends to de-emphasize the surgeon and to emphasize the action performed on the blood vessels.

The passive voice is also required when the non-underlined portion of the sentence contains the person or agent performing the action preceded by the word *by*.

> Wrong: The shuttle launch <u>seen around the world</u> by people of all ages, all races, and all religions.

The sentence above is missing a verb, and it is therefore a fragment. Because the *people* who are seeing the launch are mentioned at the end of the sentence, preceded by the word *by*, we must use the passive voice to complete this sentence:

> Right: The shuttle launch <u>WAS seen around the world</u> by people of all ages, all races, and all religions.

Note that you do not have to make active or passive voice parallel throughout a sentence. However, if all other issues are solved equally well in two sentences, choose the sentence that maintains parallelism of voice rather than the sentence that does not.

Passive voice is not grammatically incorrect, and it is sometimes even preferred. Do not automatically dismiss choices in passive voice.

Helping Verbs

The three <u>Primary Helping Verbs</u> are *BE, DO* and *HAVE*. As we have seen, *be* generates the progressive tenses & the passive voice, while *have* generates the perfect tenses. *Do* is used with Simple Present or Past to negate verbs (*I DO not like eggs*), emphasize verbs (*He DOES like eggs*), or ask questions (*DO you like eggs?*).

You can use helping verbs to stand for longer verbs or verb phrases.

Wordy:	I have never seen an aardvark, but my father <u>has seen an aardvark</u>.
Better:	I <u>have</u> never <u>seen</u> an aardvark, but my father <u>HAS</u>.

The first instance of the verb should usually match the helping verb in tense. If you need to change tenses, repeat the whole verb in the new tense.

Pay attention to every Helping Verb that you see. They play critical roles in the sentence.

Wrong:	I <u>have</u> never <u>seen</u> an aardvark, but last year my father <u>DID</u>.
Right:	I <u>have</u> never <u>seen</u> an aardvark, but last year my father <u>saw</u> one.

In the rare cases in which the tenses do not need to match, the exact verb form missing after the helping verb should be present elsewhere in the sentence.

Wrong:	Our cars were designed to <u>inspire</u> envy, and they <u>ARE</u>.
Right:	Our cars were designed to <u>inspire</u> envy, and they <u>DO</u>.

They DO inspire is fine, but *they ARE inspire* is not grammatical. For *they ARE* to work, the form *inspiring* would need to be present in the sentence.

Note that the helping verbs *be, do* and *have* stand for the <u>positive</u> form of a verb phrase, even if the full verb phrase expressed elsewhere in the sentence is <u>negative</u>.

Right:	Some people <u>do not eat soup</u>, but others <u>DO.</u> (= *do eat soup*)
Right:	Some people <u>do not eat soup</u> as others <u>DO.</u> (= *do eat soup*)

Use *be, do* and *have* in this way only if you mean the positive form of the verb.

In addition to these three primary helping verbs, there are several <u>Modal Helping Verbs</u>. The principal modal helping verbs are *can, could, may, might, must, shall, should, will* and *would*. As noted in Chapter 2, these verbs should not be used interchangeably.

Sometimes the GMAT uses modal verbs (or their substitutes, such as *have to* for *must*) in a redundant or awkward manner. The idea of obligation or advisability may already be expressed elsewhere, or the modal verb may be placed in the wrong part of the sentence.

Wrong:	This plan <u>ensures</u> that action MUST be taken.
Right:	This plan <u>ensures</u> that action WILL be taken.

Wrong:	Our division spent significant funds on HAVING TO build facilities.
Right:	Our division HAD TO spend significant funds on building facilities.

*Manhattan*GMAT*Prep

Some sentences include the construction *be to* in order to indicate obligation or future time. Since the form is ambiguous, the GMAT avoids it. Use *will* or *should* instead, depending on the intended meaning.

>   Wrong: We <u>ARE TO receive</u> an invitation.
>   Right: We <u>WILL receive</u> an invitation. OR   We <u>SHOULD receive</u> an invitation.

Finally, express a condition by using the word *if*, not by inverting the subject and adding a modal verb such as *should*. This inverted construction is considered awkward by the GMAT.

>   Awkward: SHOULD he PASS the test, he will graduate.
>   Right: IF he PASSES the test, he will graduate.

Verbals: An Overview

<u>Verbals</u> are verb forms used as adjectives, adverbs, or nouns. There is nothing strange or uncommon about verbals; we use them frequently in speech and in writing.

Verbals come in a few varieties. We have already encountered them in Chapter 4: Parallelism and in Chapter 6: Modifiers.

(1) Infinitives: *to watch, to throw, to see*
(2) Gerunds: *watching, throwing, seeing* (used as nouns)
(3) Participles:
>   (a) Present Participles: *watching, throwing, seeing* (used as adjectives or adverbs)
>   (b) Past Participles: *watched, thrown, seen* (used as adjectives)

Remember, you will never need to prove that you know the terms on the GMAT. However, you do need to know how the words themselves behave.

Infinitives

Infinitives, such as *to watch, to throw,* or *to see*, are considered the "dictionary" form of the verb: the most basic version. Infinitives may serve as nouns, adjectives, or adverbs.

>   Noun: I love <u>TO SWIM</u>.   *To swim* is the object of the verb *love*.
>   Adjective: The person <u>TO MEET</u> is here.   *To meet* modifies the noun *person*.
>   Adverb: Sue paused <u>TO EAT</u> lunch.   *To eat* modifies the verb *paused*.

In the last example, the infinitive expresses purpose: <u>why *she paused*</u> or <u>for what end</u>. You can also write *Sue paused <u>in order to eat</u> lunch*. The *in order to* construction is not automatically too wordy, as some people mistakenly think; you should feel free to use *in order to*.

Whether you use *in order to* or not, you should pay attention to infinitives of purpose.

>   Right: The contractors <u>demolished</u> the building <u>TO KEEP</u> it from falling down accidentally.

Infinitives can play many different roles. When you see an infinitive, identify its role: noun, adjective, or adverb.

The subject of the main verb *demolished* is the noun *contractors*, which is also the implied subject of the infinitive *to keep*, which expresses the purpose of the demolition. The object *it* refers to *the building*.

> Wrong: The building <u>was demolished</u> <u>TO AVOID</u> falling down accidentally.

The subject of the main verb *was demolished* is the noun *building*, which is also the implied subject of the infinitive *to avoid*. However, a building cannot avoid something intentionally. The sentence above is nonsensical.

> Right: The building <u>was demolished</u> <u>TO KEEP IT</u> from falling down accidentally.

The subject *building* would normally be the implied subject of the infinitive *to keep*. However, *it* refers to *building*. Since *building* is the <u>object</u> of the infinitive, the version above is fine as written. (We assume that the same unnamed people who demolished the building wanted to keep it from falling down accidentally.)

Note that infinitives can be used as nouns, but they are not very noun-like structures. Infinitives <u>can</u> be used as subjects of verbs, but in general you should postpone an infinitive subject using an Placeholder *It* (see Chapter 4, Pronouns).

> Awkward: TO ERR is human.
> Right: IT is human TO ERR.

Gerunds are used much more often than infinitives as subjects of verbs. Gerunds can be used after prepositions.

Infinitives are often used as objects of verbs, but they cannot be used as objects of prepositions, as normal nouns can. Moreover, you never modify an infinitive as you would modify a noun (that is, with adjectives or articles). You would never say *the quick to run*. Rather, you use adverbs: *to run quickly*.

Gerunds

Gerunds are *-Ing* forms used as nouns. *-Ing* forms are much more noun-like than infinitives. You can easily use them not only as objects of verbs, but also as subjects of verbs and objects of prepositions:

> Subject of verb: <u>SWIMMING</u> is fun.   *Swimming* is the subject of *is*.
> Object of verb: I love <u>SWIMMING</u>.   *Swimming* is the object of *love*.
> Object of preposition: I dream of <u>SWIMMING</u>.   *Swimming* is the object of *of*.

As we saw in Chapter 4, Parallelism, you can classify gerund phrases as Simple or Complex, depending on whether you internally treat the gerund like a verb or like a noun:

> Simple Gerund: EATING apples quickly.   (verb-like)
> Complex Gerund: The quick EATING of apples. (noun-like)

Remember that you should not make a simple gerund and a complex gerund parallel to each other. Also, do not create a complex gerund if a more familiar action noun already exists: *the quick consumption of apples* is better than *the quick eating of apples*.

A noun preceding a gerund must be in the possessive case if the noun is the doer of the action described by the gerund.

> Wrong: <u>Mike</u> SWIMMING is the product of new coaching techniques.
> Right: Mike's <u>SWIMMING</u> is the product of new coaching techniques.

Mike himself might be *the product of new coaching techniques* in some way, but if you want to talk about his behavior, you must say *Mike's swimming,* not *Mike swimming.*

Before applying this rule, make sure that the *-Ing* form does indeed function as a noun rather than as a noun modifier. Sometimes either interpretation may be possible.

> Suspect: I like <u>Mike</u> SWIMMING. (= I like *Mike* only as he swims, not as he runs? OR I like for him to be swimming rather than lifting weights?)
> Right: I like Mike's <u>SWIMMING</u>. (= I like his *swimming* itself.)
> Right: <u>Mike</u> SWIMMING is a sight to behold. (*Mike* himself can be the *sight*.)
> Right: Mike's <u>SWIMMING</u> is a sight to behold. (The *swimming* can be the *sight*.)

All the same, try to avoid possessing a gerund at all. In many cases, a less awkward phrasing is possible. For instance, it is generally much better to possess an action noun that already exists. If you must possess a gerund, use a personal pronoun such as *Its, Their, His* or *Her.*

Participles

As we saw in Chapter 6, Modifiers, both present participles and past participles may be used as modifiers.

Present participles are *-Ing* forms used to modify nouns, verbs, or even whole clauses. By now, you should note that the *-Ing* form can be used in many grammatical ways. In fact, there are four members of the "*-Ing* Dynasty," representing four key uses of the *-Ing* form:

Verb (Progressive Tense)	She is <u>FIXING the faucet</u>.
Noun (Gerund)	<u>FIXING the faucet</u> is not fun.
Adjective (Present Participle)	The person <u>FIXING the faucet</u> is tired.
Adverb (Present Participle)	She crouched under the sink, <u>FIXING the faucet</u>.

In contrast, the past participle is typically used as part of a perfect-tense verb or as an adjective:

Verb (Perfect Tense)	She has <u>BROKEN</u> the lamp.
Adjective (Present Participle)	The <u>BROKEN</u> lamp is on the stairs.

An *-Ing* form may be combined with a past participle: *<u>Having broken</u> the lamp, she has <u>been</u> <u>worrying</u> all night.*

When you see an *-Ing* form in a sentence, identify its role: verb, noun, adjective, or adverb.

When To Use Which Verbal or Verb

You should note the differences between using a present participle and using an infinitive at the end of a sentence.

Present Participle:	Investors sold the stock rapidly, CAUSING panic.
Infinitive:	Investors sold the stock rapidly TO CAUSE panic.

The present participle expresses a **result**: the rapid sale of the stock caused panic. However, with the present participle, we know nothing about <u>intention</u>. The investors may have intended to cause panic, or panic may simply have occurred as an unintentional byproduct of their actions.

In contrast, the infinitive expresses **intention**: the investors wanted to cause panic. However, with the infinitive, we know nothing about <u>result</u>. Panic may or may not have actually occurred. If the subject cannot <u>intend</u> anything (e.g., the subject is an inanimate object), then you should generally avoid using the infinitive.

You should also recognize the subtle differences between using a present participle (or a relative clause) and using an infinitive to modify a noun. Consider the following correct examples and their meaning:

Present Participle:	A technique ALLEVIATING pain is growing popular.
Relative Clause:	A technique THAT ALLEVIATES pain is growing popular.

Both of these examples indicate that the technique itself alleviates pain. In other words, *technique* is meant to be the subject of the action *alleviate*. Now consider the following example, which is also correct but slightly different.

Infinitive:	A technique TO ALLEVIATE pain is growing popular.

This sentence means that <u>you</u> (or someone else) can alleviate pain by means of this technique. In other words, *technique* is <u>not</u> meant to be the subject of the action *alleviate*. Often, when you modify a noun with an infinitive, that noun is not the implied subject of the infinitive. For instance, in the sentence *There is <u>a book to read</u>*, the modified noun (*book*) is the intended <u>object</u> of the reading. The book will not read; someone will read the book.

This subtlety is immaterial in the examples above, but in other circumstances, the difference is substantial:

Unlikely:	A plan CONQUERING the world is in his files.
Unlikely:	A plan THAT WILL CONQUER the world is in his files.
Probable:	A plan TO CONQUER the world is in his files.

In the examples above, the author probably intends to say that the plan is a <u>means</u> by which someone can conquer or will try to conquer the world. It is unlikely that the plan <u>itself</u> is actually conquering the world or will conquer the world. Thus, we should use the infinitive.

Pay attention to the subtle differences among the verbals. In some cases, the meaning is nearly the same; in other cases, it is not.

Manhattan **GMAT** Prep
the new standard

Problem Set

Each of the following sentences contains one or more underlined sections. If an underlined section contains no errors, mark it as CORRECT. Otherwise, write down a correct version of the underlined section. For extra credit, explain your decisions with respect to the tense, mood, and voice of the relevant verbs, and with respect to the nature of the relevant verbals.

1. Although Bernard normally <u>is eating</u>① inexpensive foods, and indeed <u>is eating</u>② a hot dog right now, he <u>is eating</u>③ lobster and steak at tomorrow's party.

2. Because Cole <u>wears</u>① a helmet when he <u>struck</u>② on the head by a falling coconut ten years ago, he <u>has escaped</u>③ serious injury in that episode.

3. Mozart, who died in 1791, <u>has lived</u>① in Salzburg for most of his life.

4. The local government <u>has built</u>① the school that was destroyed by the earthquake.

5. The editor of our local newspaper, who has earned much acclaim in her long career, <u>has been awarded</u>① a Pulitzer Prize yesterday.

6. She already <u>woke up</u>① when the phone rang.

7. <u>Having been shown</u>① into the office, Julia waited for the dentist to arrive.

8. Last Monday Mary realized that she <u>will have</u>① to spend all of that night rewriting her application because she <u>did not back up</u>② her files.

9. When he <u>swam</u>① across the lake, he struggled to keep his head above the water.

10. When he <u>swam</u>① across the lake, he lay down on the far shore and relaxed in the sunshine until he was thoroughly dry.

11. By the end of the Apollo program, twelve Americans <u>have walked</u>① on the moon.

12. Water freezes if it <u>were</u>① cooled to zero degrees Celsius.

13. Helen would feel better if she <u>was</u>① my daughter.

14. Helen would feel better if she <u>swallowed</u>① this pill.

15. Helen will feel better if she <u>swallows</u>① this pill.

16. Helen may feel better if she <u>would swallow</u>① this pill.

17. If the supplier <u>has signed</u>① a binding contract, he will deliver the goods.

18. If the supplier <u>has signed</u> a binding contract, he would have delivered the goods.

19. If Abraham Lincoln <u>were born</u> in Livonia, he <u>cannot become</u> the President of the United States.

20. Ethan is unsure what to do tonight: his boss wants <u>that he stay</u> at the office, but his wife insists <u>that he come</u> home for dinner.

21. <u>Brokered</u> by the President of Silonia, the ceasefire agreement mandates <u>Carpathian forces will cease</u> their advance into Zapadnia, but allows <u>them to engage</u> in limited operations in areas already captured.

22. Because epidemiological evidence suggests that some tomatoes <u>are</u> contaminated with bacteria, Rachel suggested that Patrick <u>make</u> a salad without tomatoes.

23. It is necessary that our condominium association <u>must comply</u> with the new ordinance, which requires homeowners <u>clear</u> the snow from the sidewalks in front of their property.

24. A <u>frightening</u> storm <u>has been lashing</u> South Padre Island, <u>forcing</u> Natalie and Todd to postpone their wedding.

25. In the Fischer-Tropsch process, which <u>developed</u> in Germany by Franz Fischer and Hans Tropsch, coal <u>is converted</u> into a liquid fuel similar to petroleum.

26. <u>The dealer was asked to sell a painting by Picasso.</u>

27. Sitting at the kitchen table, <u>a decision to bake a cake got made by Eric.</u>

28. Airline A does not charge passengers for in-flight snacks, although most other airlines <u>are</u>.

29. New regulations require that every cyclist in the Tour de France <u>has to be tested</u> for performance-enhancing substances.

30. Louise wanted <u>to buy</u> something <u>to eat</u>, so she stopped at the ATM <u>to withdraw</u> some cash.

31. The <u>athlete's wearing</u> the Brand X logo is a famous Olympian; <u>his swimming</u> has led to a lucrative endorsement contract.

1.   Although Bernard normally <u>is eating</u> inexpensive foods, and indeed <u>is eating</u> a hot dog right now, he <u>is eating</u> lobster and steak at tomorrow's party.

Is eating is in the present progressive tense. The first *is eating* should be *eats* (simple present tense). The word *normally* makes clear that this is a habitual action. We use the simple present for habitual actions. The second *is eating* is CORRECT. We use the present progressive for an action that is happening right now. The third *is eating* should be *will eat* (simple future tense). The simple future tense is preferred for a future action. We know the action is future because the party is tomorrow.

Correction: **Although Bernard normally <u>eats</u> inexpensive foods, and indeed <u>is eating</u> a hot dog right now, he <u>will eat</u> lobster and steak at tomorrow's party.**

2.   Because Cole <u>wears</u> a helmet when he <u>struck</u> on the head by a falling coconut ten years ago, he <u>has escaped</u> serious injury in that episode.

Wears (present tense) should be *was wearing* (past progressive tense). The verb needs to be in the past progressive because the action of wearing the helmet is a background state of affairs that was happening when the foreground event (the fall of the coconut) occurred.
Struck (active voice) should be *was struck* (passive voice). The verb has to be in the passive voice because the phrase *by a falling coconut* tells us that the coconut hit Cole.
Has escaped (present perfect tense) should be *escaped* (simple past tense). The verb has to be in the simple past because we are told that the escape occurred at a specific time in the past (*ten years ago*, in *that episode*).

Correction: **Because Cole <u>was wearing</u> a helmet when he <u>was struck</u> on the head by a falling coconut ten years ago, he <u>escaped</u> serious injury in that episode.**

3.   Mozart, who died in 1791, <u>has lived</u> in Salzburg for most of his life.

Has lived (present perfect tense) should be *lived* (simple past tense) or possibly *had lived* (past perfect). One possible reason to use the present perfect (*has lived*) is to indicate that an action or state of affairs is <u>still in progress</u>. Mozart is dead, so this reason does not apply here.
The other possible reason to use the present perfect is to indicate that an action, though completed in the past, still has some <u>continuing effect on the subject</u> of the verb. Since Mozart is dead, this reason does not apply either.
Since neither reason for using the present perfect applies to this sentence, we should use the simple past. There is no real need to use the past perfect (*had lived*), because the sequence of past events (Mozart's life and death) is obvious. Moreover, the actions are not contrasted (for instance, if he *lived* one place but *died* somewhere else). That said, to emphasize the sequence of events, you could choose to use the past perfect in this sentence.

Correction: **Mozart, who died in 1791, <u>lived</u> in Salzburg for most of his life.**
    OR   **Mozart, who died in 1791, <u>had lived</u> in Salzburg for most of his life.**

4.   The local government <u>has built</u> the school that was destroyed by the earthquake.

Has built (present perfect tense) should be *built* (simple past tense) OR *had built* (past perfect). Sometimes we use the present perfect to indicate that an action or state of affairs is still in progress.

However, the original process of building the school cannot be continuing now, because the school was destroyed by the earthquake. The government might be rebuilding the school now, but that is not the same as building the school. The other possible reason to use the present perfect is to indicate that an action, though completed in the past, still has some continuing effect on the subject and object of the verb. The effects of the action of building were essentially wiped out by the earthquake, because the earthquake destroyed the school. Since neither possible reason for using the present perfect applies to this sentence, we cannot use the present perfect.

Either the simple past or the past perfect is possible. In the simple past version, the writer's mental time-frame is concurrent with *built*. The following clause (*that was destroyed by the earthquake*) just serves to identify the school, and the writer might go on to discuss the building process. On the other hand, the past perfect emphasizes the sequence of events more than the simple past does. In the past perfect version, the writer's mental timeframe is concurrent with *was destroyed*. The use of *had built* indicates that the writer is dipping back in time only for a moment to the building process. In fact, the writer might proceed to write more about the destruction (perhaps the consequences of shoddy construction methods).

Correction: **The local government <u>built</u> the school that was destroyed by the earthquake.**
OR   **The local government <u>had built</u> the school that was destroyed by the earthquake.**

5.   The editor of our local newspaper, who has earned much acclaim in her long career, <u>has been awarded</u> a Pulitzer Prize yesterday.

Has been awarded (present perfect tense) should be *was awarded* (simple past tense). The verb has to be in the simple past because we are told that the action occurred at a specific time in the past (*yesterday*).

Correction: **The editor of our local newspaper, who has earned much acclaim in her long career, <u>was awarded</u> a Pulitzer Prize yesterday.**

6.   She already <u>woke up</u> when the phone rang.

Already woke up (simple past) should be *had already woken up* (past perfect). We need to use the past perfect here because the word *already* requires this use for a momentary action such as *wake up*, when placed prior to another past action. It would be fine to say *She was already awake when the phone rang*, because *was awake* is a state and thus takes up time. In that case, *already* would indicate that this state was in effect before the phone rang. However, when you use *already* with the simple past of a momentary action, you convey a present perfect meaning. As your spouse shakes you out of bed, you might say *I already woke up*, but in proper English you should say *I HAVE already woken up*. In other words, the action is complete, AND the effect (your wakefulness) continues to the present. In the sample sentence, since we want the subject's wakefulness to continue up through some point <u>in the past</u> (*when the phone rang*), we must use the past perfect of *wake up*.

Correction: **She <u>had</u> already <u>woken up</u> when the phone rang.**

7.   **<u>Having been shown</u> into the office, Julia waited for the dentist to arrive.**

CORRECT. The words *having been shown* are considered a participle, not a working verb. The whole phrase that precedes the comma (*Having been shown into the office*) functions as a participial phrase modifying the verb *waited*.

Nonetheless, the words *having been shown* have verb-like features, and they are strongly analogous to a verb in the <u>past perfect tense</u> and in the <u>passive voice</u>.

The presence of the helping verb *to be*, here in the form *been*, puts this in the <u>passive</u> voice. The use of the verb *to have*, here in the form *having*, indicates that the action of being shown into the office occurred <u>before</u> Julia waited for the dentist. Since this meaning is perfectly logical, the participle *having been shown* is correct.

8.   Last Monday Mary realized that she <u>will have</u> to spend all of that night rewriting her application because she <u>did not back up</u> her files.

Will have (simple future tense) should be *would have* (conditional tense). Mary made her realization on Monday. At that time, her sleepless night spent rewriting the application was in the <u>future</u>. However, last Monday night is now in the <u>past</u>. An action that was in the future (relative to the time of the main verb, *realized*), but is now in the past, must be rendered in <u>the conditional tense</u>. This tense is formed by replacing *will* with *would*.

Did not back up (simple past tense) should be *had not backed up* (past perfect tense). The past perfect tense is required here because Mary's failure to back up her files must logically have occurred <u>before</u> Mary became aware of (*realized*) this failure.

Correction: **Last Monday Mary realized that she <u>would have</u> to spend all of that night rewriting her application because she <u>had not backed up</u> her files.**

9.   **When he <u>swam</u> across the lake, he struggled to keep his head above the water.**

CORRECT. *Swam* and *struggled* are both in the simple past tense. This is appropriate because the swimming and the struggling must have happened at the same time.

10.   When he <u>swam</u> across the lake, he lay down on the far shore and relaxed in the sunshine until he was thoroughly dry.

Swam (simple past tense) should be *had swum* (past perfect tense). The verbs *lay* and *relaxed* are in the simple past tense. Because the swimming must have happened before the lying and relaxing *on the far shore*, the past perfect *had swum* is more appropriate than the simple past *swam*.

Correction: **When he <u>had swum</u> across the lake, he lay down on the far shore and relaxed in the sunshine until he was thoroughly dry.**

11.   By the end of the Apollo program, twelve Americans <u>have walked</u> on the moon.

Have walked (present perfect tense) should be *had walked* (past perfect tense). The past perfect is required because the twelve Americans did their walking before the end of the Apollo program. Here the phrase *end of the Apollo program* functions much like a specific date in the past.

Correction: **By the end of the Apollo program, twelve Americans <u>had walked</u> on the moon.**

12.   Water freezes if it <u>were</u> cooled to zero degrees Celsius.

Were (present tense of the hypothetical <u>subjunctive</u> mood) should be *is* (present tense of the <u>indicative</u> mood). This sentence is stating a general rule that admits of no uncertainty, so the *if*-clause must be in the indicative mood. You can also omit a tensed verb altogether from the *if*-clause: *Water freezes if cooled to zero degrees Celsius.*

Correction: **Water freezes if it <u>is</u> cooled to zero degrees Celsius.**

13.   Helen would feel better if she <u>was</u> my daughter.

Was (<u>past</u> tense of the <u>indicative</u> mood) should be *were* (<u>present</u> tense of the hypothetical <u>subjunctive</u> mood). The presence of *would* in the clause *Helen would feel better* requires the *if*-clause to be in the hypothetical subjunctive mood. In other words, the verb in the *if*-clause takes the hypothetical subjunctive mood because *would* indicates that Helen is not, or is unlikely to be, my daughter.

Correction: **Helen would feel better if she <u>were</u> my daughter.**

14.   **Helen would feel better if she <u>swallowed</u> this pill.**

CORRECT. *Swallowed* is in the <u>present</u> tense of the hypothetical <u>subjunctive</u> mood. The presence of *would* in the clause *Helen would feel better* requires that the *if*-clause be in the hypothetical subjunctive mood. In other words, the verb in the *if*-clause takes the hypothetical subjunctive mood because *would* indicates that Helen is unlikely to take the pill.

15.   **Helen will feel better if she <u>swallows</u> this pill.**

CORRECT. *Swallows* is in the <u>present</u> tense of the <u>indicative</u> mood. The presence of *will* in the clause *She will feel better* requires that the *if*-clause be in the indicative mood. In other words, the verb in the *if*-clause takes the indicative mood because, as the use of *will* demonstrates, the author is at least neutral in his or her beliefs about Helen's chances of swallowing the pill. Notice that in this example, as in the previous one, we use the present tense for a future action (taking the pill) in an *if*-clause.

16.   Helen may feel better if she <u>would swallow</u> this pill.

Would swallow should be *swallows*. *Would swallow* is incorrect because it uses *would* in an *if*-clause. Never use *would* in an *if*-clause! *Swallows* is in the <u>present</u> tense of the <u>indicative</u> mood. The presence of *may* in the clause *She may feel better* requires that the *if*-clause be in the indicative mood. In other words, the verb in the *if*-clause takes the indicative mood because, as the use of *may* demonstrates, the author is at least neutral in his or her beliefs about Helen's chances of swallowing the pill.

Correction: **Helen may feel better if she <u>swallows</u> this pill.**

17.   **If the supplier <u>has signed</u> a binding contract, he will deliver the goods.**

CORRECT. *Has signed* is in the <u>present perfect</u> tense of the <u>indicative</u> mood. The presence of *will* in the clause *he will deliver the goods* requires the *if*-clause to be in the indicative mood. In other words, the author is at least neutral in his or her beliefs about the supplier's likelihood of having signed the contract.

Notice that the use of the <u>present perfect</u> tense here indicates that the author is referring to a possible signing at an unspecified time in the <u>past</u>. This is equivalent to saying *If it is NOW true that the supplier has signed…* In contrast, the sentence *If the supplier signs a binding contract, he will deliver the goods* is also correct, but it refers to a possible signing in the <u>future</u>.

18.   If the supplier <u>has signed</u> a binding contract, he would have delivered the goods.

Has signed (present perfect tense of the indicative mood) should be *had signed* (past tense of the hypothetical subjunctive mood).

The presence of *would* in the clause *he would have delivered the goods* requires the *if*-clause to be in the hypothetical <u>subjunctive</u> mood. In other words, the supplier did not actually sign, or is unlikely to have signed, a binding contract. We need to use the <u>past</u> tense of the hypothetical subjunctive here because the presence of *have* in *would have delivered* makes clear that the delivery of the goods would have happened in the past.

Correction: **If the supplier <u>had signed</u> a binding contract, he would have delivered the goods.**

19.   If Abraham Lincoln <u>were born</u> in Livonia, he <u>cannot become</u> the President of the United States.

Was born (simple past tense of the indicative mood) should be *had been born* (past tense of the hypothetical subjunctive mood). The birth of Abraham Lincoln in Livonia is an unreal past event. Therefore, it must be rendered in the past hypothetical subjunctive.

Cannot become should be *could not have become*. The second clause of this sentence is the *then*-clause of an *if…then* sentence. Since the *if*-clause describes something that never happened, the *then*-clause must contain a helping verb such as *would, could,* or *might*. *Could* is closest in meaning to *can*, so *could* is the best option here. The reason we must say *could not HAVE become*, rather than simply *could not become*, is that Abraham Lincoln actually became President of the United States in the past.

Correction: **If Abraham Lincoln <u>had been born</u> in Livonia, he <u>could not have become</u> the President of the United States.**

20.   Ethan is unsure what to do tonight: his boss wants <u>that he stay</u> at the office, but his wife insists <u>that he come</u> home for dinner.

That he stay (command subjunctive) should be *him to stay* (infinitive), because *want* is a verb that requires the infinitive. *That he come* (command subjunctive) is correct because *insist* is a verb that requires the command subjunctive.

Correction: **Ethan is unsure what to do tonight: his boss wants <u>him to stay</u> at the office, but his wife insists <u>that he come</u> home for dinner.**

21.   <u>Brokered</u> by the President of Silonia, the ceasefire agreement mandates <u>Carpathian forces will cease</u> their advance into Zapadnia, but allows <u>them to engage</u> in limited operations in areas already captured.

Brokered is correct. In this sentence it functions as a modifier, not a working verb. The participial phrase *Brokered by the President of Silonia* modifies *the ceasefire agreement*. *Carpathian forces will cease* should be

that Carpathian forces cease, because *mandate* is a verb that must be followed by *that* and by a verb in the command subjunctive (*cease*, not *will cease*).

Them to engage is correct, because *allow* is a verb that takes only the infinitive.

Correction: **Brokered by the President of Silonia, the ceasefire agreement mandates <u>that Carpathian forces cease</u> their advance into Zapadnia, but allows <u>them to engage</u> in limited operations in areas already captured.**

22.   **Because epidemiological evidence suggests that some tomatoes <u>are</u> contaminated with bacteria, Rachel suggested that Patrick <u>make</u> a salad without tomatoes.**

CORRECT. We use *are* (indicative mood), not *be* (command subjunctive mood), even though the verb is in a *that*-clause following the verb *suggests*. This usage is correct because *suggests* in the first clause of this sentence is <u>not</u> being used as a Bossy Verb. The *epidemiological evidence* is not really telling anybody what to do, so *epidemiological evidence suggests* is not a signal for us to use the command subjunctive. In contrast, *suggested* in the second clause does count as a Bossy Verb, because Rachel is definitely telling Patrick what to do. When *suggest* is used as a Bossy Verb, it must be followed by the command subjunctive (*make*).

23.   It is necessary that our condominium association <u>must comply</u> with the new ordinance, which requires homeowners <u>clear</u> the snow from the sidewalks in front of their property.

Must comply should be *comply* (command subjunctive). *It is necessary* is an expression that functions like a Bossy Verb. In general, it can be followed by either an infinitive or a command subjunctive. In this sentence, however, we have to choose the command subjunctive because *it is necessary* is followed by *that*.

Clear (command subjunctive) should be *to clear* (infinitive). *Require* is a verb that can take either the command subjunctive or the infinitive. In this sentence, however, we have to choose the infinitive because *requires* is not followed by *that*. Never use the command subjunctive without a *that* in front of the clause containing the command subjunctive.

Correction: **It is necessary that our condominium association <u>comply</u> with the new ordinance, which requires homeowners <u>to clear</u> the snow from the sidewalks in front of their property.**

24.   **A <u>frightening</u> storm <u>has been lashing</u> South Padre Island, <u>forcing</u> Natalie and Todd to postpone their <u>wedding</u>.**

CORRECT. This sentence correctly uses all four members of the *–Ing* Dynasty. The participle *frightening* is an adjective modifying *storm*. *Has been lashing* is a <u>working verb</u> in the present perfect progressive tense. It is <u>present perfect</u> because the first helping verb is *has*. It is the <u>progressive</u> version of the present perfect tense because it also includes *to be* as a helping verb (*been*). Remember that an *–ing* word is never a working verb <u>unless</u> it is immediately preceded by a form of *to be*. The participle *forcing* works as an <u>adverb</u> modifying the verb in the first clause (*has been lashing*). The full adverb here is actually the <u>whole</u> participial phrase *forcing Natalie and Todd to postpone their wedding*. Like many participial adverbs, it tells us a <u>consequence</u> of the action in the clause that it modifies. Finally, *wedding* is a gerund. In other words, it is an *–ing* noun derived from a verb (*to wed*).

25.   In the Fischer-Tropsch process, which <u>developed</u> in Germany by Franz Fischer and Hans Tropsch, coal <u>is converted</u> into a liquid fuel similar to petroleum.

Developed (active voice) should be *was developed* (passive voice). The passive voice is required because the people who developed the process appear in the non-underlined phrase *by Franz Fischer and Hans Tropsch*.

Is converted (passive voice) is correct. The passive voice is required because unnamed agent(s), rather than the coal itself, cause the conversion of the coal into a liquid fuel. Supposing that the whole sentence were underlined and that you were therefore free to rewrite it completely, should you change it into the active voice? No, because the passive voice is ideally suited to the purposes of this sentence. The author wants to tell us about the Fischer-Tropsch process, not to list the various parties who happen to use that process. It is therefore fitting for the words *Fischer-Tropsch process* to be in the subject position. To put *Fischer-Tropsch* in the subject position, the verb *to develop* must be in the passive voice.

Correction: **In the Fischer-Tropsch process, which <u>was developed</u> in Germany by Franz Fischer and Hans Tropsch, coal <u>is converted</u> into a liquid fuel similar to petroleum.**

26.   <u>The dealer was asked to sell a painting by Picasso.</u>

The words *by Picasso* are ambiguous. Because *was asked* is in the passive voice, *by Picasso* could be meant to tell us <u>who</u> asked the dealer to sell the painting—in which case the sentence should read *Picasso asked the dealer to sell the painting*. Alternatively, *by Picasso* could simply be meant to identify the painting as a work by Picasso, in which case the sentence should read *The dealer was asked to sell a Picasso painting*.

Corrections: **Picasso asked the dealer to sell a painting.**
    OR   **The dealer was asked to sell a Picasso painting.**

27.   Sitting at the kitchen table, <u>a decision to bake a cake got made by Eric</u>.

The underlined words are the main clause of this sentence. There are a number of reasons to reject and restructure the original version of the clause:
    (1) the active voice makes the sentence more direct and concise;
    (2) the use of the passive voice, which results in *a decision* being at the start of the clause, makes it seem as if *a decision* had been *sitting at the kitchen table;*
    (3) the original version uses the wrong helping verb (*got*) in the verb *got made*. Always use *to be* as the helping verb in the passive voice.

Correction: **Sitting at the kitchen table, <u>Eric decided to bake a cake</u>.**

28.   Airline A does not charge passengers for in-flight snacks, although most other airlines <u>are</u>.

Are should be *do*. The full verb phrase in the first clause is *does not charge passengers for in-flight snacks*. Here *are* is a shortened version of *are charge passengers for in-flight snacks*. Since this latter phrase is grammatically incorrect, *are* is also incorrect. *Do*, on the other hand, is correct because it stands for *do charge passengers for in-flight snacks*. Notice, by the way, that *do* is preferable to *do charge passengers for in-flight snacks*, because *do* is more concise than the full phrase that it replaces.

Correction: **Airline A does not charge passengers for in-flight snacks, although most other airlines do.**

29.   New regulations require that every cyclist in the Tour de France <u>has to be tested</u> for performance-enhancing substances.

Has to be tested should be *be tested* (command subjunctive). *Has to be tested* is redundant because *has to* unnecessarily repeats the idea, already expressed by the verb *require*, that the testing is obligatory. *Be tested* is correct because *require*, when followed immediately by the conjunction *that*, takes the command subjunctive.

Correction: **New regulations require that every cyclist in the Tour de France <u>be tested</u> for performance-enhancing substances.**

30.   **Louise wanted <u>to buy</u> something <u>to eat</u>, so she stopped at the ATM <u>to withdraw</u> some cash.**

CORRECT. Infinitives can function as nouns, adjectives, and adverbs. Each of the three infinitives in this sentence correctly fulfills one of these roles. *To buy* serves as a noun. More precisely, the full phrase *to buy something to eat* serves as a noun. The phrase acts as a noun because it is the object of the verb *wanted*, much as *a snack* is the object of *wanted* in the sentence *Louise wanted a snack*. *To eat* serves as an adjective. It modifies the pronoun *something*, much as *edible* modifies *something* in the phrase *something edible*. Finally, *to withdraw* serves as an adverb. More precisely, the full phrase *to withdraw some cash* modifies the verb *stopped*, telling us the purpose for which Louise stopped.

31.   **The <u>athlete's wearing</u> the Brand X logo is a famous Olympian; <u>his swimming</u> has led to a lucrative endorsement contract.**

Athlete's wearing should be *athlete wearing*. In *athlete's wearing the…logo*, the word athlete's is an adjective modifying the gerund phrase *wearing the…logo*. In *athlete wearing the…logo*, however, *wearing the…logo* is a participial phrase that acts as an adjective modifying the noun *athlete*. To see which version is correct, we need to look at the rest of the clause. Who or what *is a famous Olympian*—the *wearing* or the *athlete*? Clearly it must be the *athlete*, so we must choose the version in which *athlete* is a noun. This means choosing *athlete wearing*, not *athlete's wearing*. In the second clause, *his swimming* is correct. Here *his* acts as an adjective, modifying the gerund *swimming*. Since the *swimming* itself has plausibly *led to a lucrative endorsement contract*, the second clause is correct.

Correction: **The <u>athlete wearing</u> the Brand X logo is a famous Olympian; <u>his swimming</u> has led to a lucrative endorsement contract.**

Sentence Correction

Now that you have completed your study of VERB TENSE, MOOD, & VOICE, it is time to test your skills on problems that have actually appeared on real GMAT exams over the past several years.

The problem set that follows is composed of past GMAT problems from two books published by GMAC (Graduate Management Admission Council):

The Official Guide for GMAT Review, 11th Edition (pages 39–43 & 638–660)
The Official Guide for GMAT Verbal Review (pages 234–253)

The problems in the set below are primarily focused on VERB TENSE, MOOD, & VOICE issues. For each of these problems, identify all verb constructions. For each verb, identify the tense, and (if appropriate) the mood and voice. Eliminate answer choices that contain errors in verb tense, mood, or voice.

Verb Tense, Mood, & Voice

11th Edition: 15, 48, 53, 57, 58, 59, 62, 75, 79, 81, 82, 83, 126, 137 \
Verbal Review: 3, 21, 28, 30, 37, 39, 40, 55, 61, 78, 80, 86, 95, 103

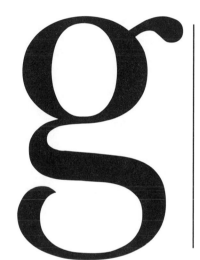

Chapter 8
of
SENTENCE CORRECTION

COMPARISONS

In This Chapter . . .

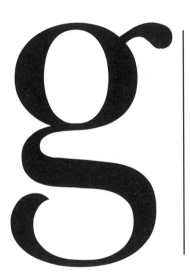

- *Like* vs. *As*
- More on *Like* and *As*
- Keeping Comparisons Parallel
- Omitted Words
- Comparative and Superlative Forms
- Numbers in Comparisons
- Other Comparison Constructions

COMPARISONS

Comparisons are a form of parallelism that deserves special attention. As the name indicates, comparisons compare two parts of the sentence (or occasionally more).

To spot GMAT comparisons, you must first learn certain signal words or phrases. Once you find a comparison, identify the two parts of the sentence that are being compared to each other. Finally, ensure that these two parts are truly parallel, both structurally and logically.

Comparison Signals	
like	as
unlike	as (adj.) as
more than	as much as
less than	as little as
faster than	as fast as
different from	the same as
in contrast to/with	

The most important comparison signals are **Like, Unlike, As**, and **Than**. Whenever you see one of these four words, stop and find the two items being compared. Other common comparison signals are shown in the chart above.

Like vs. As

Like and *as* are two very common comparison signals. You should learn to distinguish between them.

Like is a preposition. This means that **LIKE must be followed by nouns, pronouns, or noun phrases**. Never put a clause after *like!* (Remember, a clause contains a working verb, one that can be the main verb in a sentence.) You can correctly use *like* to compare two nouns.

Consider the following example:

> Right: LIKE <u>her brother</u>, <u>Ava</u> aced the test.

Here, *like* is followed by the noun phrase *her brother*. The whole phrase *Like her brother* indicates a comparison between *Ava* and *her brother* (two nouns). Note that *like* can be followed by gerunds (*-Ing* forms used as nouns): *LIKE <u>swimming</u>, <u>skiing</u> is great exercise*.

On the other hand, *as* can be either a preposition (appearing with a noun) or a conjunction (appearing with a clause). You can correctly use *as* to compare two clauses. Again, however, you cannot use *like* to compare clauses.

> Wrong: LIKE <u>her brother DID</u>, <u>Ava aced the test</u>.
> Right: AS <u>her brother DID</u>, <u>Ava aced the test</u>.

The words *her brother did* form a clause (*did* is a working verb). Therefore, you must use *as* to make the comparison between the two clauses *Ava aced the test* and *her brother did*. Using *like* to compare clauses is common in speech but always wrong in writing.

According to the GMAT, there is no difference in meaning between *Like her brother, Ava aced the test* and *As her brother did, Ava aced the test*. You can compare *Ava* and *her brother* directly, or you can compare what they did.

If you see the words *Like, Unlike, As*, or *Than*, you probably have a comparison. Look for what the sentence is comparing.

More on *Like* and *As*

Like means "similar to" or "in a manner similar to." A prepositional phrase with *like* can modify a noun <u>or</u> a verb, creating a comparison. Remember, only nouns can follow *like*.

<u>Example</u>	<u>Explanation</u>
A <u>person</u> LIKE <u>me</u> never wins.	What kind of person? One similar to me.
He <u>ran</u> LIKE <u>the wind</u>.	How did he run? In a manner similar to the wind.
LIKE <u>you</u>, I danced last night.	You danced last night. So did I.
I <u>danced</u> LIKE <u>you</u> last night.	You danced a certain way last night. I danced in a similar way.
I <u>danced the whole night away</u>, LIKE <u>someone possessed</u>.	I danced the whole night away. You can imagine someone possessed doing the same thing or something similar.

Notice that the position of the *like* phrase can change the meaning slightly, as in *LIKE you, I danced last night* and *I danced LIKE you last night.* Also, note that a *like* comparison might be metaphorical, not literal. *He ran like the wind* does not imply that the wind "runs"—only that the wind moves fast, and that he runs fast as well.

You have to be careful about ambiguity with a *like* phrase at the end of a sentence:

> (1) I want to coach divers LIKE Greg Louganis.
>   = I want to coach <u>divers</u> WHO ARE LIKE <u>Greg Louganis</u>.
> OR
>   = I want to <u>coach divers</u> IN THE SAME WAY AS Greg Louganis <u>does</u>.
>
> (2) I want to coach divers, LIKE Greg Louganis. (note the comma before *like*)
>   = LIKE <u>Greg Louganis</u>, <u>I</u> want to coach divers. (he coaches divers; I want to do so.)

Unlike is very common on the GMAT. Remember that you must ensure parallelism with *unlike*, even though *unlike* indicates that the two items are <u>not</u> like each other.

> Right: UNLIKE <u>you</u>, <u>I</u> danced last night. (You did not dance last night.)

Unlike can come at the end of a sentence (just as *like* can), as long as there is no ambiguity. In the latter situation, the noun following *unlike* will generally be compared to the subject.

> Right: <u>Most materials</u> under a wide range of conditions resist the flow of electric current to some degree, UNLIKE <u>superconductors</u>, which demonstrate zero electrical resistance.

Again, *as* is either a conjunction or a preposition, depending on the context. You should distinguish among several meanings.

Like can modify a noun or a verb, but *Like* must be followed by a noun, not a whole clause.

<u>Conjunction *As*</u> appears with a clause. It has three uses:

Duration *As*:   AS I strolled to the store, I smelled the air. (= while, during)
Causation *As*:   I will not tell you, AS you already know. (= since, because)
Comparison *As*: You should walk AS she wants you to. (= in the same way)

Comparison *As* is the most important conjunction use of *as* on the GMAT. It sometimes appears together with *just, so,* or even *so too.*

Right: JUST AS the trains were late yesterday, the buses are late today.
Right: JUST AS the trains were late yesterday, SO TOO are they late today.

Comparison *As* can also appear with a phrase, rather than a full clause.

Right: AS <u>in the previous case</u>, the judge took an early break.

<u>Preposition *As*</u> is used with a noun or noun phrase. It also has three uses:

Function *As*:   AS your leader, I am in charge. (= in the role of)
Equation *As*:   I think of you AS my friend. (= *you* are *my friend*)
Stage *As*:   AS a child, I thought I could fly. (= when I was)

In any of these prepositional senses, *As* does <u>not</u> mean "similar to."

Right: I will jump up LIKE a clown. (= in a clownish manner)
Right: I will jump up AS a clown. (= in a clown suit!)

To force the Comparison *As* meaning, use a clause. To make a clause, include a verb:

Right: I will jump up AS a clown MIGHT. (= like a hypothetical clown)
Right: I will jump up AS clowns DO. (= like actual clowns)

The structure *as...as...* creates a comparison. The first *as* is followed by an adjective or adverb. The second *as* is followed by a noun, a phrase, or even a whole clause.

Right: They are AS hungry AS you.
Right: They are AS hungry AS you are.
Right: They are AS hungry AS they were last night.

Note: In modern English, *like* is often misused to mean "for example." Even the *New York Times* endorses this faulty usage. But the GMAT is firm on the issue.

Wrong: I enjoy fast food LIKE hamburgers. (= *fast food* SIMILAR TO *hamburgers*)
Right: I enjoy fast food SUCH AS hamburgers.

Do not use *like* to introduce examples. Instead, use the phrase *such as*. See the Idiom List for more details.

> Do not use *like* to introduce examples. Instead, use *such as*.

Keeping Comparisons Parallel

Comparisons must be logically parallel. That is, they must compare similar things.

> Frank's build, LIKE his brother, is broad and muscular.

What two things are being compared? As written, the sentence is comparing *Frank's build* directly to *his brother*. This is not a logical comparison: someone's *build* is not in the same class of things as someone's *brother*. In order to correct this error, we need to change the comparison.

> Right: Frank's build, LIKE his brother's, is broad and muscular.

We do not need to repeat the word *build* after *brother's*—it is implied.

> Right: Frank's build, LIKE that of his brother, is broad and muscular.

We can also use the word *that* to stand for *build*. If the first noun were plural, we would use *those* instead: *Frank's toes, LIKE THOSE of his brother, are short and hairy.*

> Right: Frank, LIKE his brother, has a broad and muscular build.

Finally, we can change the first term and rephrase the sentence accordingly.

Take a look at a harder example:

> Beethoven's music, which broke a number of established rules with its structure and melodic form, is considered more revolutionary than Bach.

First, we find the comparison signal: *MORE revolutionary THAN...* Now we look for the two things being compared. It is often easier to find the second thing, which follows the comparison signal: *More revolutionary than Bach.* So, what is more revolutionary than Bach? The subject of the sentence: *Beethoven's music.* This comparison is not parallel.

We have to be careful, since sometimes we talk about the music of Bach as "Bach" (e.g., *I like to listen to Bach on the radio*). However, if the sentence has referred to Beethoven's music with the word *music*, then the sentence should do the same with Bach's music.

> Right: Beethoven's music, which broke a number of established rules with its structure and melodic form, is considered MORE revolutionary THAN BACH'S.

Note again that we do not have to repeat the word *music*, as long as we have written *Bach's*. We could also write *that of Bach* at the end of the sentence.

Comparisons must make sense. The two items being compared must be logically comparable.

Comparisons must be structurally parallel. That is, they must have a similar grammatical structure.

> I like to run through forests more than I enjoy walking through crowds.

Are the objects of comparison grammatically parallel? No, because *to run through forests* does not have the same structure as *walking through crowds. To run* is an infinitive, whereas *walking* is a gerund (*walking* is being used as a noun). To write a concise, parallel sentence, we should simply use one verb (*like*) and convert both objects to *-Ing* forms.

> Right: I like <u>running</u> through forests MORE THAN <u>walking</u> through crowds.

Omitted Words

As we have already seen, you can often omit words in the second part of a comparison. Possessive nouns provide one opportunity. All of the following sentences are correct.

My car is bigger than Brian's *[car]*.   My car is bigger than the Smiths' *[car]*.
My toes are longer than Brian's *[toes]*.   My toes are longer than the Smiths' *[toes]*.

Note that the <u>possessing</u> noun (*Brian, the Smiths*) can be singular or plural, regardless of whether the implied <u>possessed</u> noun (*car, toes*) is singular or plural. Any singular-plural combination is possible grammatically. You must simply make sure that the combination makes logical sense.

You can also omit units, verbs and even whole clauses from the second term, as long as there is no ambiguity.

> Right: Whereas I drink 2 quarts of milk a day, my friend drinks 3 *[quarts]*.
> Right: I walk faster than Brian *[walks]*.
> Right: I walk as fast now as *[I walked]* when I was younger.

In general, you should put in the omitted words or appropriate Helping Verbs (such as *be, do,* and *have*) only if you need to remove ambiguity.

> Right: Vishal eats more carrots than donuts. (*donuts* must be the object)
> Wordy: Vishal eats more carrots than HE DOES donuts.

The first example is not ambiguous (*donuts* cannot *eat carrots*), so if all else is the same, choose the first example over the slightly wordier second example.

> Ambiguous: I like cheese more than Yvette. (Yvette could be subject or object.)
> Right: I like cheese more than Yvette DOES. (= *than* Yvette *likes cheese*)
> Right: I like cheese more than I DO Yvette. (= *than I like* Yvette)

You need the helping verbs to resolve the role of Yvette in the second half of the comparison.

Feel free to omit unnecessary words in the second part of a comparison. However, it is also correct to include them.

*Manhattan***GMAT** Prep
the new standard

However, the GMAT occasionally allows unnecessary Helping Verbs.

Right: Apples are more healthy to eat than caramels.
Right: Apples are more healthy to eat than caramels ARE.

Do not throw out an answer choice simply because of an unnecessary Helping Verb in the second term of a comparison.

Comparative and Superlative Forms

When comparing two things, use the <u>Comparative Form</u> of an adjective or adverb. When comparing more than two things, use the <u>Superlative Form</u> of an adjective or adverb.

Do not say This car goes SLOWER than yours. Say This car goes MORE SLOWLY than yours.

<u>Regular Forms</u>
Comparative: She is SHORTER than her sister. (Add *-er*)
Superlative: She is the SHORTEST of her five siblings. (Add *-est*)
Comparative: You are MORE INTERESTING than he. (Add the word *more*)
Superlative: You are the MOST INTERESTING person here. (Add the word *most*)
Comparative: You are LESS INTERESTING than she. (Add the word *less*)
Superlative: You are the LEAST INTERESTING person here. (Add the word *least*)

For irregular forms, such as *good/better/best*, see the Glossary on "Comparative Forms" and "Superlative Forms."

 Do not compare an adverb that ends in *-ly* by changing the ending to *-er*. This error is common in speech. Instead, add *more*.

Wrong: Adrian runs QUICKLY. He runs QUICKER than Jacob.
Right: Adrian runs QUICKLY. He runs MORE QUICKLY than Jacob.

However, some adverbs that do not end in *-ly* are made into comparatives by adding *-er*.

Right: Adrian runs FAST. He runs FASTER than Jacob.

Do not use a comparative adjective unless you have a *than* in the sentence.

Wrong: With winter coming, I will have HIGHER energy bills.

The sentence <u>implies</u> the comparison *than now.* On the GMAT, however, you must make that comparison explicit.

Numbers in Comparisons

To indicate how much larger one quantity is than another, you have a few options.

If you want to relate the quantities by multiplication, use *times* and *as...as...* together.

> Right: The man is FIVE TIMES AS OLD AS his grandson.
> Wrong: The man is FIVE TIMES OLDER THAN his grandson.

The first sentence means that the man's age = 5 × his grandson's age. In the second example, the author is technically saying that the man is <u>six</u> times as old as his grandson. This meaning is unlikely; the author probably meant "five times as old."

In one GMAT problem (#72 in the Verbal Supplement), the correct answer says that certain numbers are "*5 times greater than...*" other numbers. In general, however, this usage should be avoided.

Use *times* without *as* or *than* to indicate direct multiplication. (*Twice* means *two times.*)

> Right: The cost of a ticket is $12, <u>SIX TIMES the cost ten years ago</u>.
> Right: The concert was attended by 300 people, <u>TWICE the previous attendance</u>.

If you want to relate two quantities by addition or subtraction, use *more than* or *less than*.

> Right: I am TEN years OLDER THAN you.
> Wrong: I am TEN years AS OLD AS you.

The first sentence means that my age = your age + 10 years. The second sentence is nonsensical.

The words *more* and *less* are rather flexible. They can be used as nouns (or pronouns), adjectives, or adverbs.

> Right: I own MORE THAN I should. (*more* = noun or pronoun)
> Right: I own MORE SHIRTS THAN I should. (*more* = adjective)
> Right: I sleep MORE THAN I should. (*more* = adverb)

In numerical comparisons, the words *high* and *low*, as well as *higher* and *lower*, should only be used as adjectives.

> Right: My bills are LOWER than they were last year.
> Wrong: I spend LOWER than I did last year.
> Right: I spend LESS than I did last year.

Write 3 Times As Old As, not 3 Times Older Than. On the other hand, write 3 Years Older Than, not 3 Years As Old As.

Other Comparison Constructions

Put *more* and *less* in the right positions. Watch out for ambiguity, especially when *more* comes before an adjective plus a noun.

> We have even MORE efficient engines than before.

Does this sentence mean that we have a <u>greater quantity</u> of efficient engines? Or do we have engines that are <u>more efficient</u>? The right answer will resolve the ambiguity.

> Right: We have even MORE engines that are efficient than before.
> Right: We have engines even MORE efficient than before.

Occasionally, a less common comparison signal appears in a GMAT sentence. For instance, some verbs, such as *exceed* or *surpass,* indicate comparisons. As always, make sure that the two items under comparison are parallel.

> Wrong: The incidence of the disease among men exceeds women.

An *incidence* cannot logically *exceed women.* In the construction *X exceeds Y,* the subject *X* and the object *Y* must be parallel. To fix the problem, you can repeat the noun *incidence* or use the pronoun *that.* In any case, you must repeat the preposition *among.*

> Right: <u>The incidence</u> of the disease among men EXCEEDS <u>the incidence</u> among women.
> Right: <u>The incidence</u> of the disease among men EXCEEDS <u>its incidence</u> among women.
> Right: <u>The incidence</u> of the disease among men EXCEEDS <u>that</u> among women.

The phrase *in addition to* is worth mentioning. At the beginning of a sentence, you can use this construction to add another example to the subject. You can also use it to add another example to a <u>different</u> noun in the sentence, such as the object of the verb or some other noun. This usage is endorsed by the GMAT.

> Right: IN ADDITION TO <u>taxes</u>, <u>death</u> is inevitable.
> Right: IN ADDITION TO <u>Munster cheese</u>, I like <u>Swiss</u>.

Pay attention to the position of More and Less. Make sure they are modifying the right noun, verb, adjective, or adverb.

Problem Set

A.   Like vs. As

Each of the following sentences contains a blank space. Fill the blank space with either "like" or "as," depending on which you think is appropriate. For extra credit, if you choose "as," write down one of the following letters to indicate the role played by "as":

(a) conjunction expressing duration (= while, during)
(b) conjunction expressing causation (= since, because)
(c) conjunction expressing comparison (= in the same way)
(d) preposition expressing function (= in the role of)
(e) preposition that equates two things
(f) preposition expressing a stage in life (= when this person was)

1.   The person in the recording sounds ___ a child.

2.   ___ a child has been injured, we must stop the party and call an ambulance.

3.   ___ a child, Rebecca lived in Bristol.

4.   My grandfather eats ___ a child, slurping loudly and helping himself to plenty of ketchup.

5.   Mrs. Jones watched ___ a child played with a stick.

6.   Frankie never went to law school, but he believes that years of watching *Law & Order* have taught him to think ___ a lawyer.

7.   Law students learn to think ___ a lawyer does.

8.   Eyewitnesses describe the missing passenger ___ a lawyer in his late forties.

9.   ___ lawyers, doctors are bound by a code of professional ethics.

10.   Having passed the state bar exam, she is licensed to work ___ a lawyer in Illinois.

B.   Comparison Signals, Comparatives, and Superlatives

In each of the following 15 sentences, underline all comparison signals and all comparative or superlative forms. If the sentence is fine, write CORRECT. If not, correct the errors in the sentence. For an ambiguous sentence, express each possible meaning of the sentence with a correct sentence of your own.

1.   Tatiana analyzes people like Oliver Sacks, the famous neurologist.

2.   A leopard cannot run as fast as a cheetah.   Correct

3.   A leopard cannot catch a wildebeest as fast as a cheetah.

4.   A leopard's skill in catching a wildebeest is as impressive as a cheetah.

5.   In contrast to the trapeze artists, who fumbled their routine, the antics of the circus clowns kept the audience entertained for hours.

6.   The clothes looked more appealing inside the store than on the racks outside.

7.   The clothes inside the store looked more appealing than on the racks outside.

8.   Thomas is more interested in video games than his girlfriend.

9.   Although the towers appear identical, the west tower is the tallest, standing 16 feet taller than the east tower.

10. Of all the cities in Australia, Sydney is the largest and the most well-known; Melbourne, however, can be equally as enjoyable to visit as its brasher, more frenetic rival.

11. Hugo is widely acknowledged to be our best employee, because he works harder and more creatively than anyone else in the company.

12. There are about the equivalent number of gym members in the boxing class as in the aerobics class.

13. The CEO earns twice higher than the average employee at this company.

14. Courtney's experiences at Haleford, a large research university with renowned professors, affluent students, and imposing buildings, were unlike her high school on the reservation.

A.   **Like vs. As**

1.   **The person in the recording sounds LIKE a child.**

We use *like*, not *as*, to make this comparison because *a child* is a noun, not a clause.

2.   **AS a child has been injured, we must stop the party and call an ambulance.**

     AS – (b) conjunction expressing causation (= since, because).

The logic of the sentence requires us to choose *as*, because the injury to the child is why *we must stop the party and call an ambulance.*

3.   **AS a child, Rebecca lived in Bristol.**

     AS – (f) preposition expressing a stage in life (= when this person was).

4.   **My grandfather eats LIKE a child, slurping loudly and helping himself to plenty of ketchup.**

We use *like*, not *as*, to make this comparison because *a child* is a noun, not a clause.

5.   **Mrs. Jones watched AS a child played with a stick.**

     AS – (a) conjunction expressing duration (= while, during).

6.   **Frankie never went to law school, but he believes that years of watching *Law & Order* have taught him to think LIKE a lawyer.**

We use *like*, not *as*, to make this comparison because *a lawyer* is a noun, not a clause. Moreover, *like* indicates similarity, but *as* would indicate an actual ability to function as a lawyer. Whoever can *think AS a lawyer* is probably a lawyer.

7.   **Law students learn to think AS a lawyer does.**

     AS – (c) conjunction expressing comparison (= in the same way).

We use *as*, not *like*, to make this comparison because *a lawyer does* is a clause, not a noun.

8.   **Eyewitnesses describe the missing passenger AS a lawyer in his late forties.**

     AS – (e) preposition that equates two things

The eyewitnesses are saying that the passenger is, or appears to be, *a lawyer in his late forties.*

9.   **LIKE lawyers, doctors are bound by a code of professional ethics.**

We use *like*, not *as*, to make this comparison because *a lawyer* is a noun, not a clause.

10.   **Having passed the state bar exam, she is licensed to work AS a lawyer in Illinois.**

     AS – (d) preposition expressing function (= in the role of)

B.   Comparison Signals, Comparatives, and Superlatives

1.   Tatiana analyzes people <u>like</u> Oliver Sacks, the famous neurologist.

The sentence is ambiguous, because the prepositional phrase *like Oliver Sacks, the famous neurologist* could have either of the following roles: (a) it could modify the noun *people*, telling us what kind of person Tatiana analyzes, or (b) it could modify the verb *analyzes*, telling us that Tatiana's way of analyzing people is similar Dr. Sacks' way of analyzing people.

Correction (a): **Tatiana analyzes people who are similar to Oliver Sacks, the famous neurologist.**

Correction (b): **Tatiana analyzes people in the same way as Oliver Sacks, the famous neurologist, does.**

Notice that the following sentence does not correctly express meaning (b): *Like Oliver Sacks, the famous neurologist, Tatiana analyzes people.* This last sentence means "Oliver Sacks analyzes people, and so does Tatiana." It tells us nothing of the manner in which Tatiana analyzes people.

2.   **A leopard cannot run <u>as fast as</u> a cheetah.**

     CORRECT.

The sentence is an abridgement of the longer sentence *<u>A leopard cannot run</u> as fast as <u>a cheetah can run</u>*. In the long version of the sentence, the clause *A leopard cannot run* is parallel to *a cheetah can run*. In the shortened version, which the GMAT would prefer for the sake of concision, the omitted words *can run* are understood.

Another acceptable version of this sentence is *A leopard cannot run as fast as a cheetah can*. Here the helping verb *can* stands for the full verb phrase *can run*.

3.   A leopard cannot catch a wildebeest <u>as fast as</u> a cheetah.

This sentence is ambiguous because we cannot be sure what is being compared to what. Is the phrase *as fast as a cheetah* meant to be an <u>adjective</u> that modifies *wildebeest*, in which case the comparison would be between *a wildebeest* and *a cheetah*? If so, then we can correct as follows:

Correction (a): **A leopard cannot catch a wildebeest that runs as fast as a cheetah.**

Or is the phrase *as fast as a cheetah* meant to be an adverb that modifies *catch*? If so, then we can correct as follows:

Correction (b): **A leopard cannot catch a wildebeest as fast as a cheetah can.**

In this latter version *can* stands for *can catch a wildebeest*, and the sentence compares the two clauses *A leopard cannot catch a wildebeest* and *a cheetah can (catch a wildebeest)*. For the sake of concision, it is better to say *can* rather than the full *can catch a wildebeest*.

4.   A leopard's skill in catching a wildebeest is <u>as impressive as</u> a cheetah.

This sentence makes an illogical comparison between a *skill* and a *cheetah*. A more logical comparison would be between a *skill* (that of the leopard) and another *skill* (that of the cheetah).

Correction: **A leopard's skill in catching a wildebeest is <u>as impressive as</u> a cheetah's.**
OR   **A leopard's skill in catching a wildebeest is <u>as impressive as</u> that of a cheetah.**

5.   <u>In contrast to</u> the trapeze artists, who fumbled their routine, the antics of the circus clowns kept the audience entertained for hours.

This sentence makes an illogical comparison between *trapeze artists* and *antics*. A more logical comparison would be between *trapeze artists* and *circus clowns*.

Correction: **<u>In contrast to</u> the trapeze artists, who fumbled their routine, the circus clowns kept the audience entertained for hours with their antics.**

6.   **The clothes looked <u>more appealing</u> inside the store <u>than</u> on the racks outside.**

      CORRECT.

This sentence compares how some clothes looked *inside the store* with how the same clothes looked *on the racks outside*. A less concise, but acceptable, version of this sentence would be *The clothes looked more appealing inside the store than **they did** on the racks outside*. There are no logical or grammatical problems with either version of this comparison.

7.   The clothes inside the store looked <u>more appealing than</u> on the racks outside.

This sentence seems to compare some <u>clothes</u> (*The clothes inside the store*) to a <u>location</u> (*on the racks outside*). It is hard to tell whether the author wants to compare two separate sets of clothes or one set of clothes in two display locations.

One way to correct the sentence would be to rewrite it as the sentence in problem 6.

Correction (a): **The clothes looked <u>more appealing</u> inside the store <u>than</u> on the racks outside.**

This version makes sense because it puts the phrase *inside the store* <u>after</u> the comparison signal *more appealing*, thus making that phrase available for a comparison with *on the racks outside*. In this version there is one set of clothes, and the comparison is between how these same clothes looked *inside the store* and how they looked *on the racks outside*. (Perhaps a customer brought the clothes into the store, and is describing the different appearance of the same clothes before and after the move.)

Correction (b): **The clothes inside the store looked <u>more appealing</u> <u>than</u> (did) those on the racks outside.**

This version compares <u>two</u> sets of clothes, *the clothes inside the store* and *those on the racks outside*, telling us that the former are more appealing than the latter. The word *did* is optional.

8.   Thomas is <u>more interested</u> in video games <u>than</u> his girlfriend.

This sentence is ambiguous.

Correction (a): **Thomas is <u>more interested</u> in video games <u>than</u> his girlfriend is.**

Correction (b): **Thomas is <u>more interested</u> in video games <u>than</u> (he is) in his girlfriend.**

In the latter version, the words *he is* are optional because the parallelism between *in video games* and *in his girlfriend* makes the meaning clear.

9.   Although the towers appear identical, the west tower is the <u>tallest</u>, standing 16 feet <u>taller than</u> the east tower.

Since this sentence compares only two items—the west tower and the east tower—we must use the <u>comparative</u> *taller* rather than the superlative *tallest*. We could make the sentence grammatical by simply changing *tallest* to *taller*. For the sake of concision, however, it would be better to avoid using the word *taller* twice.

Correction: **Although the towers appear identical, the west tower stands 16 feet <u>taller than</u> the east tower.**

10.   Of all the cities in Australia, Sydney is the <u>largest</u> and the <u>most well-known</u>; Melbourne, however, can be <u>equally as enjoyable</u> to visit <u>as</u> its <u>brasher, more frenetic</u> rival.

In the first clause, *Sydney* is being singled out from among a group (*all the cities in Australia*), so we must use superlative forms. *Largest* is a correct superlative. *Most well-known* may <u>look</u> correct insofar as *most* is a superlative. However, the correct way to say "most well" is "best," so *most well-known* should be *best-known*.

In the second clause, *equally as enjoyable...as* is incorrect because it is redundant. Never use *equally as* on the GMAT!

The second clause compares *Melbourne* with its *rival* (Sydney), so we must use <u>comparative</u>, rather than superlative, forms of the adjectives. (We <u>could</u> use superlatives (*brashest, most frenetic*), but doing so would change the <u>meaning</u> of the original sentence. We would be asserting that Melbourne has <u>many</u> rivals, of which Sydney is the *brashest* and *most frenetic*.)

Brasher is a correct comparative form. So is *more frenetic*. Why do we say *brasher* rather than *more brash*, but *more frenetic* rather than *freneticer*? The rule is simple: prefer the form that ends in –er (brasher), IF it exists. Otherwise, use the *more X* form (*more frenetic*). The word *freneticer* simply does not exist in English.

Correction: **Of all the cities in Australia, Sydney is the <u>largest</u> and the <u>best-known</u>; Melbourne, however, can be <u>as enjoyable</u> to visit <u>as</u> its <u>brasher, more frenetic</u> rival.**

11.   **Hugo is widely acknowledged to be our <u>best</u> employee, because he works <u>harder</u> and <u>more creatively</u> than anyone else in the company.**

         CORRECT.

In the first clause Hugo is being singled out from among a group (*our...employee(s)*), so we must use a <u>superlative</u> (*best*) to modify *employee*.

In the second clause there is a comparison between A and B, so we must use <u>comparative</u> rather than superlative forms. (The comparison is between how *he works* and *how anyone else in the company (works).*) The comparative form of the adverb *creatively* is *more creatively*. The comparative form of the adverb *harder* is simply *harder*, because *harder* is a short adverb that does not end in –*ly*.

12.   There are about <u>the equivalent number of</u> gym members in the boxing class <u>as</u> in the aerobics class.

The wordy phrase *the equivalent number of* should be replaced with *as many*. The phrase *in the aerobics class* is correct. It is short for **there are** *in the aerobics class*. For the sake of concision we can leave out the words *there are*.

Correction: **There are about <u>as many</u> gym members in the boxing class <u>as</u> in the aerobics class.**

13.   The CEO earns <u>twice higher than</u> the average employee at this company.

The words *twice higher than* are wrong for two reasons:

(a) *twice* can never modify *higher*, because the correct idiom is *twice as high as*.

(b) *higher*, like *lower*, can never function as an <u>adverb</u> in a numerical comparison. It thus cannot modify *earns*. To modify *earns* we need to say *as much as*, or in this sentence *twice as much as*.

Correction: **The CEO earns <u>twice as much as</u> the average employee at this company.**

14.   Courtney's experiences at Haleford, a large research university with renowned professors, affluent students, and imposing buildings, were <u>unlike</u> her high school on the reservation.

This sentence makes an illogical comparison between *experiences* and *high school*. A more logical comparison would be between one set of *experiences* (those at *Haleford*) and another set of *experiences* (those at *her high school*).

Correction: **Courtney's experiences at Haleford, a large research university with renowned professors, affluent students, and imposing buildings, were <u>unlike</u> her experiences in high school on the reservation.**

Sentence Correction

Now that you have completed your study of COMPARISONS, it is time to test your skills on problems that have actually appeared on real GMAT exams over the past several years.

The problem set that follows is composed of past GMAT problems from two books published by GMAC (Graduate Management Admission Council):

The Official Guide for GMAT Review, 11th Edition (pages 39–43 & 638–660)
The Official Guide for GMAT Verbal Review (pages 234–253)

The problems in the set below are primarily focused on COMPARISON issues. For each of these problems, identify the words, phrases, or clauses being compared. Eliminate answer choices that contain faulty comparisons, either logical or structural. Be sure to maintain parallelism and to use appropriate comparison words.

<u>Note</u>: Problem numbers preceded by "D" refer to questions in the Diagnostic Test chapter of *The Official Guide for GMAT Review, 11th Edition* (pages 39–43).

Comparisons

    11th Edition: 6, 10, 13, 16, 23, 26, 37, 66, 68, 73, 76, 85, 95, 96, 97, 99, 100, 104, 122,
        123, 125, 128, D35, D37, D47, D52
    Verbal Review: 10, 23, 31, 33, 36, 42, 45, 68, 92, 94, 98, 101, 105, 106

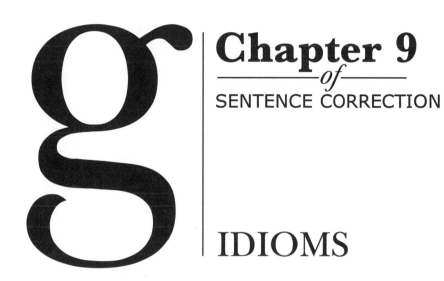

Chapter 9
of
SENTENCE CORRECTION

IDIOMS

In This Chapter . . .

- Using Your Ear: Spot – Extract – Replace
- Idiom List

IDIOMS

Idioms are expressions that have unique forms. There is no hard and fast rule for determining the form of an idiom. In fact, it is this very uniqueness that makes an expression an idiom. For example, we must say *They* <u>*tried to reach*</u> *the summit and* <u>*succeeded in doing*</u> so, not *They* <u>*tried in reaching*</u> *the summit and* <u>*succeeded to do*</u> so. The verb *to try* is followed by an infinitive, but the verb *to succeed* is followed by *in* and an *-Ing* form of the verb. Why? There is no reason. *Try to do* and *succeed in doing* are the accepted English conventions.

If you are a native English speaker, most idiomatic expressions are already wired into your brain from years of hearing and speaking English. For non-native speakers, the task is more difficult. However, the GMAT does tend to focus on certain common idioms. If you are not a native English speaker, you should memorize the expressions in the Idiom List that starts on the next page. Even if you are a native speaker, you should review the list.

The Spot – Extract – Replace Method will help you identify idiom errors.

Using Your Ear: Spot – Extract – Replace

Your ear is your most valuable weapon as you try to figure out the proper form of an idiom. This is the one time when you are allowed to justify your choice by saying "it sounds better!" However, you must understand how to use your ear wisely.

> (A) Some historians attribute the eventual development of accurate methods for measuring longitude as the monetary prizes offered by various governments.
> (B) Some historians attribute the eventual development of accurate methods for measuring longitude to the monetary prizes offered by various governments.

<u>(1) SPOT the suspect idiomatic expression.</u> Compare answer choices to find the core words and all variations. Include non-underlined words as necessary. In the choices above, the words that vary are *as* and *to*. The idiom revolves around the use of the verb *attribute*.

<u>(2) EXTRACT the various forms of the idiom</u> and put them into simpler sentences that you can easily compare. You can delete words, such as extraneous modifiers, or you can make up brand-new sentences. Either way, you should present the simplest possible versions to your ear.

> (A) Historians attribute the development AS the prizes.
> (B) Historians attribute the development TO the prizes.

Your ear should choose the second choice. *Attribute TO* is the correct idiom.

<u>(3) REPLACE the corrected idiom in the sentence</u> and confirm that it works.

> (B) Some historians <u>attribute</u> the eventual development of accurate methods for measuring longitude TO the monetary prizes offered by various governments.

The choice that your ear preferred should work in the entire GMAT sentence. If it does not work, check whether you spotted and extracted the idiom correctly.

Idiom List

Review the following GMAT-focused idioms. Almost every expression below has appeared at least once in a released GMAT problem. However, you should remember that the GMAT can make use of idioms not included below. To make the list memorable, we have put the expressions into real sentences. Non-native English speakers should spend extra time studying the list, but even native English speakers should review these idioms, since they cover many usage issues on the GMAT.

Label	Definition
RIGHT	Expressions that the GMAT considers correct.
SUSPECT	Expressions that the GMAT seems to avoid if possible. These expressions are sometimes grammatically correct, but they may be wordy, controversial, or simply less preferred than other forms.
WRONG	Expressions that the GMAT considers incorrect.

** Starred entries are the most important and prevalent on the GMAT.

** ABILITY

RIGHT: I value my ABILITY TO SING.

            (Note: I CAN SING is preferred to *I HAVE THE ABILITY TO SING.*)

WRONG: *I value my ABILITY OF SINGING.*

            I value my ABILITY FOR SINGING.

            I value the ABILITY FOR me TO SING.

ACT

RIGHT: The bay ACTED AS a funnel for the tide. (= functioned as)

            My friend ACTED LIKE a fool. (= behaved in a similar manner)

SUSPECT: *The bay ACTED LIKE a funnel for the tide.*

            Note: #56 in the 11th Edition of the Official Guide tests this idiom. The explanation claims that ACT LIKE must be used only with people. This claim is not true. In fact, #90 in the 11th Edition contains *peaks* that ACT LIKE *rocks* in the non-underlined section. The way to resolve this issue is to ask whether the author intends <u>metaphorical comparison</u> (= LIKE) or <u>actual function</u> (= AS). If "actual function" is possible, use AS.

AFFECT / EFFECT

RIGHT: The new rules will AFFECT our performance.

SUSPECT: *The new rules will HAVE AN EFFECT ON our performance.* (wordier)

WRONG: *The new rules will CAUSE AN EFFECT ON our performance.*

AFTER

RIGHT: AFTER the gold rush, the mining town collapsed.

SUSPECT: *FOLLOWING the gold rush, the mining town collapsed.* (ambiguous)

AGGRAVATE

RIGHT: His behavior AGGRAVATED the problem. (= made worse)

WRONG: *His behavior WAS AGGRAVATING TO the problem. (= was annoying to)*

AGREE

RIGHT: They AGREE THAT electrons exist.

SUSPECT: *There is AGREEMENT AMONG them THAT electrons exist.*
They AGREE electrons exist. (AGREE THAT is preferred)

WRONG: *There is AGREEMENT AMONG them TO THE FACT THAT electrons exist.*

AID

RIGHT: She AIDS her neighbor.
She provides AID TO victims. AID FOR victims is available.
Her AID IN WALKING the dog was appreciated.

WRONG: *Her AID TO WALK the dog was appreciated.*

AIM

RIGHT: We adopted new procedures AIMED AT REDUCING theft.
We adopted new procedures WITH THE AIM OF REDUCING theft.

SUSPECT: *We adopted new policies, THE AIM OF WHICH was TO REDUCE theft.*

WRONG: *We adopted new policies WITH THE AIM TO REDUCE theft.*

** ALLOW

RIGHT: The holiday ALLOWS Maria TO WATCH the movie today. (= permits)
Maria WAS ALLOWED TO WATCH the movie.
The demolition of the old building ALLOWS FOR new construction.
(= permits the existence of)

WRONG: *The holiday ALLOWED FOR Maria TO WATCH the movie.*
The holiday ALLOWED Maria the WATCHING OF the movie.
The holiday ALLOWS THAT homework BE done (or CAN BE done).
Homework is ALLOWED FOR DOING BY Maria.
The ALLOWING OF shopping TO DO (or TO BE DONE).

ALTHOUGH   See BUT.

AMONG   See BETWEEN.

** AND

RIGHT: We are concerned about the forests AND the oceans.
We are concerned about the forests, the oceans, AND the mountains.
We work all night, AND we sleep all day. (note the comma before AND)

SUSPECT: *We are concerned about the forests AND ALSO the oceans.*
We work all night AND we sleep all day. (link 2 clauses with comma + AND)

WRONG: *We are concerned about the forests, ALSO the oceans.*

ANXIETY

RIGHT: His ANXIETY ABOUT his company's future is ill-founded.
His ANXIETY THAT his company MAY BE SOLD is ill-founded.

WRONG: *His ANXIETY ABOUT his company MAY BE SOLD is ill-founded.*

APPLY

RIGHT: The rules APPLY TO all of us.

WRONG: *All of us ARE SUBJECT TO THE APPLICABILITY OF the rules.*

** AS

RIGHT: AS I walked, I became more nervous. (= during)
AS I had already paid, I was unconcerned. (= because, since)
AS we did last year, we will exceed our targets this year. (= in the same way)
AS the president of the company, she works hard. (= in the role of)
AS a child, I delivered newspapers. (= in the stage of being)
My first job was an apprenticeship AS a sketch artist.
AS PART OF the arrangement, he received severance.

SUSPECT: *AS A PART OF the arrangement, he received severance.*

WRONG: *My first job was an apprenticeship OF a sketch artist.*
They worked AS a sketch artist. (needs to agree in number.)
WHILE BEING a child, I delivered newspapers.
AS BEING a child, I delivered newspapers.
WHILE IN childhood, I delivered newspapers.

** AS... AS

RIGHT: Cheese is AS GREAT AS people say.
Cheese is NOT AS great AS people say.
We have AS MANY apples AS need to be cooked.
We have THREE TIMES AS MANY pears AS you.
We have AT LEAST AS MANY apples AS you.
We have ten apples, ABOUT AS MANY AS we picked yesterday.

SUSPECT: *Cheese is NOT SO great AS people say.*
We have AS MANY apples AS OR MORE apples THAN you.
We have AS MANY apples AS THERE need to be cooked.

WRONG: *Cheese is SO great AS people say.*
Cheese is SO great THAT people say.
Cheese is AS great THAT people say.
We have AS MANY apples THAN you.
We have SO MANY apples AS you.
We have AS MANY OR MORE apples THAN you.
We have THREE TIMES AS MANY MORE pears AS you.
We have ten apples, ABOUT EQUIVALENT TO what we picked yesterday.

AS LONG AS

RIGHT: I will leave, AS LONG AS it IS safe.
                    I will leave, SO LONG AS it IS safe.
                    I will leave, PROVIDED THAT it IS safe.

SUSPECT: *I will leave, BUT it HAS TO BE safe.*

WRONG: *I will leave, BUT it BE safe.*

AS... SO ⤴

RIGHT: AS you practice, SO shall you play. (= in the same way)
                    JUST AS you practice, SO shall you play.

WRONG: *You practice, SO shall you play.*
                    JUST LIKE you practice, SO shall you play.
                    JUST AS you practice, you play.

ASK

RIGHT: I ASKED FOR his AID.
                    He ASKED her TO GO to the store.
                    He ASKED THAT she GO to the store. (subjunctive)

WRONG: *He ASKED THAT she SHOULD GO to the store.* ⊣

ATTRIBUTE

RIGHT: We ATTRIBUTE the uprising TO popular discontent.

WRONG: *We ATTRIBUTE the uprising AS popular discontent.*

AVERAGE

RIGHT: Tech COMPANIES are as likely as the AVERAGE COMPANY to fail.

WRONG: *Tech COMPANIES are as likely as the INDUSTRY AVERAGE to fail.*

AWARE

RIGHT: AWARE OF the danger, he fled.
                    AWARE THAT danger was near, he fled.

WRONG: *WITH AN AWARENESS THAT danger was near, he fled.* ✳
                    WITH AN AWARENESS OF the danger, he fled.

BAN

RIGHT: They passed a BAN PROHIBITING us FROM CARRYING bottles.

WRONG: *They passed a BAN that we CANNOT CARRY bottles.* ✳

BASED ON

RIGHT: The verdict was BASED ON the evidence.
                    The jury reached a verdict BASED ON the evidence.

WRONG: *BASED ON the evidence, the jury reached a verdict.*
                    (The *jury* was not itself *BASED ON the evidence*.)

** BEING

RIGHT: BEING infected does not make you sick.
                The judges saw the horses BEING led to the stables.

SUSPECT: *BEING an advocate of reform, I would like to make a different proposal.*
                Note: The word BEING is <u>often</u> wordy or awkward. However, having caught on to the "BEING is wrong" shortcut, the GMAT problem writers have created a few problems that force you to choose BEING. BEING appears in many more wrong answers than right ones. But BEING <u>can</u> be used correctly as a gerund or as a participle. In the end, you should pick a BEING answer only if you are 100% sure that the other answer choices are wrong for clear grammatical reasons.

** BECAUSE

RIGHT: BECAUSE the sun SHINES, plants grow.
                Plants grow BECAUSE the sun SHINES.
                BECAUSE OF the sun, plants grow.
                BY SHINING, the sun makes plants grow.
                Plants grow, FOR the sun shines. (grammatically correct but very formal)

SUSPECT: Plants grow *BECAUSE OF the sun, WHICH SHINES.*
                Plants are amazing IN THAT they grow in the sun. (correct but wordy)

WRONG: *Plants grow BECAUSE OF the sun SHINING.*
                Plants grow AS A RESULT OF the sun SHINING.
                BECAUSE OF SHINING, the sun makes plants grow.
                ON ACCOUNT OF SHINING or ITS SHINING, the sun makes plants grow.
                BECAUSE the sun SHINES IS the REASON that plants grow.
                The ABILITY OF plants TO grow IS BECAUSE the sun shines.
                BEING THAT the sun shines, plants grow.

BEGIN

RIGHT: The movement BEGAN AS a protest. (= was born as)
                The movement BEGAN WITH a protest. (= protest was the first part)
                The protest BEGAN a movement. (= caused)

WRONG: *The movement WAS BEGUN FROM a protest.*

** BELIEVE

RIGHT: She BELIEVES THAT Gary IS right.
                She BELIEVES Gary TO BE right.
                IT IS BELIEVED THAT Gary IS right.
                Gary IS BELIEVED TO BE right.

SUSPECT: *Gary IS BELIEVED BY her TO BE right.*

BETWEEN

RIGHT: A battle ensued BETWEEN the reactionaries AND the radicals.
          A skirmish ensued AMONG the combatants. (more than 2 parties)

WRONG: *A battle ensued BETWEEN the reactionaries WITH the radicals.*
          A battle ensued AMONG the reactionaries AND the radicals.
          A battle ensued AMONG the reactionaries WITH the radicals.

BORDERS

RIGHT: WITHIN the BORDERS of a country.

WRONG: *IN the BORDERS of a country. INSIDE the BORDERS of a country.*

** BOTH... AND

RIGHT: She was interested BOTH in plants AND in animals.
          She was interested in BOTH plants AND animals.

WRONG: *She was interested BOTH in plants AND animals.*
          She was interested BOTH in plants AS WELL AS in animals.
          She was interested BOTH in plants BUT ALSO in animals.

** BUT

RIGHT: I STUDY hard BUT TAKE breaks.
          I STUDY hard, BUT I TAKE breaks.
          ALTHOUGH I TAKE frequent naps, I STUDY effectively.
          DESPITE TAKING frequent naps, I STUDY effectively.
          I TAKE frequent naps, YET I STUDY effectively.

SUSPECT: *DESPITE THE FACT THAT I TAKE frequent naps, I STUDY effectively.*
          ALTHOUGH a frequent napper, I STUDY effectively.
          (ALTHOUGH should generally be followed by a clause.)

WRONG: *I STUDY effectively ALTHOUGH TAKING frequent naps.*
          ALTHOUGH I TAKE frequent naps, YET I STUDY effectively.
          ALTHOUGH I TAKE frequent naps, AND I STUDY effectively.
          DESPITE TAKING frequent naps, YET I STUDY effectively.

** CAN

RIGHT: The manager CAN RUN the plant.
          The plant CAN CAUSE damage.

SUSPECT: *The manager IS ABLE TO RUN the plant.*
          The manager IS CAPABLE OF RUNNING the plant.
          The manager HAS THE ABILITY TO RUN the plant.
          The manager HAS THE CAPABILITY OF RUNNING the plant.
          It is POSSIBLE FOR the plant TO CAUSE damage.
          The plant POSSIBLY CAUSES damage.
          The plant HAS THE POSSIBILITY OF CAUSING damage.
          Note: ALL of these suspect forms are grammatically correct but wordier
          than CAN.

CHANCE
RIGHT: I have ONE CHANCE IN A THOUSAND OF WINNING tonight.

WRONG: *I have ONE CHANCE IN A THOUSAND FOR WINNING tonight.*
I have ONE IN A THOUSAND CHANCES TO WIN tonight.
I have ONE CHANCE IN A THOUSAND THAT I WILL WIN tonight.
I have ONE CHANCE IN A THOUSAND FOR ME TO WIN tonight.

CLAIM
RIGHT: They CLAIM THAT they CAN read minds.
They CLAIM TO BE ABLE to read minds.

SUSPECT: *They CLAIM the ABILITY to read minds.*
They CLAIM they CAN read minds.

WRONG: *They CLAIM BEING ABLE to read minds.*

COMPARABLE
RIGHT: Costs are rising, but incomes have not increased COMPARABLY.

SUSPECT: *Costs are rising, but incomes have not increased TO A COMPARABLE EXTENT.*

COMPARED / COMPARISON
RIGHT: IN COMPARISON WITH (or TO) horses, zebras are vicious.
A zebra can be COMPARED TO a horse in many ways.
COMPARED WITH a horse, however, a zebra is very hard to tame.
Note: The GMAT ignores the traditional distinction between COMPARED TO (emphasizing similarities) and COMPARED WITH (emphasizing differences).

SUSPECT: *AS COMPARED WITH (or TO) horses, zebras are vicious.*

WRONG: *WHEN COMPARED TO horses, zebras are vicious.*
Zebras are MORE vicious COMPARED TO horses.

CONFIDENCE
RIGHT: We have CONFIDENCE THAT the market WILL RECOVER.

SUSPECT: *We have CONFIDENCE IN the market's ABILITY TO RECOVER.*

WRONG: *We have CONFIDENCE IN the market TO RECOVER.*

CONNECTION
RIGHT: There is a strong CONNECTION BETWEEN his grades AND his effort.

WRONG: *There is a strong CONNECTION OF his grades AND his effort.*

** **CONSIDER**

RIGHT: I CONSIDER her a friend. I CONSIDER her intelligent.
        Note: You can switch the order of the two objects, if one is long.
        I CONSIDER illegal the law passed last week by the new regime.
        The law IS CONSIDERED illegal.

SUSPECT: *The judge CONSIDERS the law TO BE illegal.*

WRONG: *The judge CONSIDERS the law AS illegal (or AS BEING illegal).*
        The judge CONSIDERS the law SHOULD BE illegal.
        The judge CONSIDERS the law AS IF IT WERE illegal.

CONTEND

RIGHT: They CONTEND THAT they can decipher the code.

WRONG: *They CONTEND they can decipher the code.*
        They CONTEND the code TO BE decipherable.
        They CONTEND the ABILITY to decipher the code.

CONTINUE

RIGHT: The danger will CONTINUE TO GROW.

SUSPECT: *The danger will CONTINUE GROWING.* (correct but apparently not used)

WRONG: *The danger will CONTINUE ITS GROWTH.*
        The danger will CONTINUE GROWTH.
        The danger will CONTINUE ITS GROWING.

CONTRAST

RIGHT: IN CONTRAST WITH the zoo, the park charges no admission.
        IN CONTRAST TO the zoo, the park charges no admission.
        UNLIKE the zoo, the park charges no admission.

WRONG: *AS CONTRASTED WITH the zoo, the park charges no admission.*
        IN CONTRAST TO the zoo CHARGING admission, the park does not.

COST

RIGHT: Pollution COSTS us billions IN increased medical bills.

SUSPECT: *The COST OF pollution TO us is billions IN increased medical bills.*
WRONG: *Increased medical bills COST us billions BECAUSE OF pollution.*

COULD

RIGHT: You COULD DO anything you want.

SUSPECT: *You HAVE (or MAY HAVE) THE POSSIBILITY OF DOING anything you want.*

WRONG: *You COULD POSSIBLY DO anything you want.*

CREATE

RIGHT: We WILL CREATE a team TO LEAD the discussion.

WRONG: *We WILL CREATE a team FOR LEADING the discussion.*

CREDIT

RIGHT: Hugo CREDITS Sally WITH good taste.
Sally IS CREDITED WITH good taste.

WRONG: *Sally IS CREDITED FOR good taste (or FOR HAVING good taste).*
Sally IS CREDITED AS a person with good taste (or AS HAVING good taste).
Sally IS CREDITED TO BE a person with good taste.

DANGER

RIGHT: We ARE IN DANGER OF FORGETTING the past.

SUSPECT: *We ARE ENDANGERED BY FORGETTING the past.*

WRONG: *We ARE IN DANGER TO FORGET the past.*
We HAVE A DANGER OF FORGETTING (or TO FORGET) the past.

DECIDE

RIGHT: She DECIDED TO START a company.

SUSPECT: *Her DECISION WAS TO START a company.*

DECLARE

RIGHT: I DECLARED the election a fraud. I DECLARED the referendum invalid.
I DECLARED invalid the referendum that the new regime imposed.
They DECLARED THAT the election was a fraud.

SUSPECT: *They DECLARED the election was a fraud. (DECLARE THAT is preferred.)*
The judge DECLARED the election TO BE a fraud.

WRONG: *The judge DECLARED the election AS a fraud.*

DECLINE   See also NUMBER.

RIGHT: The price of oil DECLINED. Oil DECLINED in price.
The DECLINE IN the price of oil was unexpected.
My friend's reputation DECLINED.

WRONG: *My friend DECLINED in reputation.*
The DECLENSION IN the price of oil was unexpected. (obsolete meaning)

DEMAND

RIGHT: They DEMANDED THAT the store BE closed.
Their DEMAND THAT the store BE closed was not met.

WRONG: *They DEMANDED the store TO BE closed.*
They DEMANDED THAT the store SHOULD BE closed.

DEPEND

RIGHT: The outcome DEPENDS ON WHETHER he CAN make friends.

SUSPECT: *The outcome DEPENDS ON his ABILITY TO make friends.*

DESIGN

RIGHT: This window IS DESIGNED TO OPEN.

WRONG: *This window IS DESIGNED SO THAT IT OPENS.*
This window IS DESIGNED SO AS TO OPEN.

DETERMINE

RIGHT: The winner was DETERMINED <u>BY</u> a coin toss.

WRONG: *The winner was DETERMINED THROUGH (or BECAUSE OF) a coin toss.*
The winner was DETERMINED FROM (or AS A RESULT OF) a coin toss.

DEVELOP

RIGHT: The executive DEVELOPED her idea INTO a project.
The idea DEVELOPED INTO a project.

WRONG: *An idea DEVELOPED ITSELF INTO a project.*

DIFFER / DIFFERENT

RIGHT: My opinion DIFFERS FROM yours.
My opinion IS DIFFERENT FROM yours.

WRONG: *My opinion IS DIFFERENT IN COMPARISON TO yours.*
Note: The form *DIFFERENT THAN* does not appear in the 10th or the
11th Editions of the Official Guide. According to other style guides, you
should use DIFFERENT FROM, rather than *DIFFERENT THAN*, when
you are comparing nouns.

DIFFERENCE

RIGHT: There is a DIFFERENCE IN ability BETWEEN us.
There is a DIFFERENCE BETWEEN what you can do AND what I can
do.
There are DIFFERENCES IN what you and I can do.

WRONG: There are *DIFFERENCES BETWEEN what you and I can do.*

DIFFICULT

RIGHT: Quantum mechanics is DIFFICULT TO STUDY.

WRONG: *Quantum mechanics is DIFFICULT FOR STUDY.*

DISINCLINED

RIGHT: She IS DISINCLINED TO WRITE to her parents.

WRONG: *She HAS A DISINCLINATION TO WRITE to her parents.*
There IS A DISINCLINATION ON HER PART TO WRITE to her parents.
Her busy schedule BRINGS OUT A DISINCLINATION IN HER TO WRITE to her parents.

DISTINGUISH

RIGHT: The investor DISTINGUISHED BETWEEN trends AND fads.

SUSPECT: *The investor DISTINGUISHED trends FROM fads.*

WRONG: *The investor DISTINGUISHED trends AND fads.*
The investor DISTINGUISHED BETWEEN trends FROM fads.

DO

RIGHT: I did not eat the cheese, but my mother DID (or DID SO).

WRONG: *I did not eat the cheese, but my mother DID IT (or DID THIS).*

DOUBLE   See TWICE.

DOUBT

RIGHT: We DO NOT DOUBT <u>THAT</u> the apples are ripe.
We HAVE NO DOUBT <u>THAT</u> the apples are ripe.
She DOUBTS <u>WHETHER</u> Jan will arrive on time.

SUSPECT: *She DOUBTS THAT Jan will arrive on time.*
(The GMAT claims that DOUBT, used in a positive statement without NOT or NO, should be followed by WHETHER or IF, not THAT.)

WRONG: *We DO NOT DOUBT WHETHER the apples are ripe.*
We HAVE NO DOUBT WHETHER the apples are ripe.

DUE TO

RIGHT: The deficit IS DUE TO overspending. (= results from)
Our policy will not cover damage DUE TO fire. (= resulting from)
BECAUSE politicians SPEND money, we have a deficit.

WRONG: *DUE TO politicians SPENDING money, we have a deficit.*
DUE TO THE FACT THAT politicians SPEND money, we have a deficit.

ECONOMIC

RIGHT: The rise in gasoline prices has an ECONOMIC impact on consumers.
Our new car is more ECONOMICAL than our last. (= efficient)

WRONG   *The rise in gasoline prices has an ECONOMICAL impact on consumers.*

EFFECT   See AFFECT.

EITHER... OR

RIGHT: I will take EITHER the subway OR the bus.

WRONG: *I will take EITHER the subway AND the bus.*

ELECT

RIGHT: She ELECTED TO WITHDRAW her money early.

SUSPECT: *She ELECTED early WITHDRAWAL OF her money.*

WRONG: *She ELECTED WITHDRAWING her money early.*

** ENOUGH   See also SO / THAT

RIGHT: The book was SHORT ENOUGH TO READ in a night.
           The book was SHORT ENOUGH FOR me TO READ in a night.

WRONG: *The book was SHORT ENOUGH THAT I could read it in a night.*
           The book was SHORT ENOUGH FOR IT TO BE read in a night.
           The book was SHORT ENOUGH SO THAT I could read it in a night.
           The book was SHORT ENOUGH AS TO BE read in a night.

ENSURE

RIGHT: He ENSURES THAT deadlines ARE met (or WILL BE met).

WRONG: *He ENSURES THAT deadlines MUST BE met (or SHOULD BE met).*

ESTIMATE

RIGHT: She ESTIMATES the cost TO BE ten dollars.
           The cost IS ESTIMATED TO BE ten dollars.

WRONG: *She ESTIMATES the cost AT ten dollars.*

EVEN

RIGHT: I am EVEN RICHER THAN a prince.
           I earn AS MUCH money AS EVEN the wealthiest king.

WRONG: *I am RICHER EVEN THAN a prince.*
           I earn EVEN AS MUCH money AS the wealthiest king.

EVER

RIGHT: The economy is MORE fragile THAN EVER BEFORE.

WRONG: *The economy is MORE fragile THAN NEVER BEFORE.*
           The economy is MORE fragile AS NEVER BEFORE.
           The economy is MORE THAN EVER BEFORE fragile.

EVERY

RIGHT: FOR EVERY dollar SAVED, THREE dollars ARE WASTED.

SUSPECT: *FOR EVERY dollar SAVED, you WASTE THREE dollars.*

WRONG: *FOR EVERY dollar SAVED WASTES THREE dollars.*

EXCEPT

RIGHT: EXCEPT FOR a final skirmish, the war was over.

SUSPECT: *BESIDES a final skirmish, the war was over.*
            WITH THE EXCEPTION OF a final skirmish, the war was over.
            EXCEPTING a final skirmish, the war was over.

** EXPECT

RIGHT: We EXPECT the price TO FALL. The price IS EXPECTED TO FALL.
            We EXPECT THAT the price WILL FALL.
            IT IS EXPECTED THAT the price WILL FALL.
            Inflation rose more than we EXPECTED.

SUSPECT: *THERE IS AN EXPECTATION the price WILL FALL.*
            Inflation rose more than we EXPECTED IT TO.
            Inflation rose more than we EXPECTED IT WOULD.

WRONG: *The price IS EXPECTED FOR IT TO FALL.*
            IT IS EXPECTED THAT the price SHOULD FALL.

EXTENT

RIGHT: We enjoyed the film TO some EXTENT.
            "Thumbs part up" is the EXTENT TO WHICH we enjoyed the film.

WRONG: *"Thumbs part up" is the EXTENT THAT we enjoyed the film.*

FACT THAT

RIGHT: It is important to recognize THAT our strategy is working.
            We have succeeded BECAUSE we work hard.

SUSPECT: *It is important to recognize THE FACT THAT our strategy is working.*
            THE FACT THAT our strategy is working is important to recognize.

WRONG: *We have succeeded DUE TO THE FACT THAT we work hard.*

FAULT

RIGHT: The criminals ARE AT FAULT FOR BREAKING the law.

SUSPECT: *BREAKING the law IS THE FAULT OF the criminals.*

WRONG: *THAT the criminals BROKE the law IS AT FAULT.*
            IT IS THE FAULT OF the criminals WHO BROKE the law.

FIND

RIGHT: The scientist FOUND THAT the reaction WAS unusual.

SUSPECT: *The scientist FOUND the reaction TO BE unusual.*

WRONG: *The scientist FOUND the reaction WAS unusual.*

FOR (conjunction)   See BECAUSE.

FORBID
RIGHT: The law FORBIDS any citizen TO VOTE twice.

WRONG: *The law FORBIDS any citizen FROM VOTING twice.*

FROM... TO
RIGHT: The price fell FROM 10 euros TO 3 euros.
            The price fell TO 3 euros FROM 10 euros.

WRONG: *The price fell FROM 10 euros DOWN TO 3 euros.*
            The price rose FROM 3 euros UP TO 10 euros.

GOAL
RIGHT: The GOAL IS TO EXPAND the company.

SUSPECT: *The GOAL IS EXPANSION OF the company.*

WRONG: *The GOAL IS EXPANDING the company.*

HEAR
RIGHT: She HEARD THAT her investment HAD PAID off.

WRONG: *She HEARD OF her investment PAYING off.*

HELP
RIGHT: He HELPS RAKE the leaves.
            He HELPS TO RAKE the leaves.
            He HELPS me RAKE the leaves.
            He HELPS me TO RAKE the leaves.
            His HELP IN RAKING the leaves has been welcome.

WRONG: *He HELPS me IN RAKING the leaves.*
            I need him AS HELP TO RAKE the leaves.

IF   See also WHETHER.
RIGHT: Inflation can hurt profits IF costs increase. (IF = condition)
            I can eat ice cream, PROVIDED THAT my doctor approves. (= ONLY IF)

SUSPECT: *Inflation can hurt profits WHEN costs increase. (WHEN = time period)*

WRONG: *I can eat ice cream, PROVIDED my doctor approves. (requires THAT)*

** IN ORDER TO
RIGHT: She drank coffee IN ORDER TO STAY awake.
            She drank coffee TO STAY awake. (infinitive TO STAY indicates purpose.)

SUSPECT: *She drank coffee IN ORDER THAT or SO THAT she MIGHT stay awake.*
            She drank coffee SO AS TO STAY awake.

WRONG: *She drank coffee FOR STAYING awake.*
            Coffee was drunk by her IN ORDER TO STAY awake or TO STAY awake.
            Note: the subject COFFEE is not trying TO STAY awake.

*Manhattan*GMAT*Prep

** INDICATE

RIGHT: A report INDICATES THAT unique bacteria LIVE on our skin.

SUSPECT: *A report INDICATES the presence of unique bacteria on our skin.*
            (Note: this correct form seems to be avoided in right answers.)
            A report IS INDICATIVE OF the presence of unique bacteria on our skin.

WRONG: *A report INDICATES unique bacteria LIVE on our skin. (THAT is needed.)*
            A report IS INDICATIVE THAT unique bacteria LIVE on our skin.
            A report INDICATES unique bacteria AS present on our skin.
            A report INDICATES unique bacteria TO LIVE on our skin.

INFLUENCE

RIGHT: His example INFLUENCED me.

SUSPECT: *His example WAS INFLUENTIAL TO me (or AN INFLUENCE ON me).*

WRONG: *His example WAS INFLUENTIAL ON me.*

INSPIRE

RIGHT: His example INSPIRED me.

SUSPECT: *His example WAS INSPIRATIONAL TO me (or AN INSPIRATION TO me).*

INSTANCE

RIGHT: We eat out often; FOR INSTANCE, last week we ate out every night.

WRONG: *We eat out often; AS AN INSTANCE, last week we ate out every night.*

INSTEAD

RIGHT: They avoided the arcade and INSTEAD went to a movie.

WRONG: *They avoided the arcade and RATHER went to a movie.*
            They avoided the arcade, RATHER going to a movie.

INSTEAD OF   See RATHER THAN.

INTENT

RIGHT: I went with the INTENT (or INTENTION) OF LEAVING soon.
            I went with the INTENT TO LEAVE soon.

SUSPECT: *I went with the INTENT THAT I WOULD LEAVE soon.*

INTERACT

RIGHT: These groups often INTERACT WITH ONE ANOTHER (or EACH
            OTHER).

WRONG: *These groups often INTERACT AMONG ONE ANOTHER.*
            These groups often INTERACT WITH THEMSELVES.

INTERACTION

RIGHT:	The INTERACTION OF two nuclei COLLIDING releases energy.
SUSPECT:	*The INTERACTION BETWEEN two nuclei COLLIDING releases energy.*
WRONG:	*The INTERACTION WHERE two nuclei COLLIDE releases energy.*

INVEST

RIGHT:	She INVESTED funds IN research TO STUDY cancer.
WRONG:	*She INVESTED funds INTO or FOR research TO STUDY cancer.* *She INVESTED funds IN research FOR STUDYING cancer.*

ISOLATED

RIGHT:	The culture was ISOLATED FROM outside CONTACT.
SUSPECT:	*The culture was IN ISOLATION.*
WRONG:	*The culture was IN ISOLATION FROM outside CONTACT.*

JUST AS... SO

See AS / SO.

KNOW

RIGHT:	We KNOW her TO BE brilliant. She is KNOWN TO BE brilliant. We KNOW him AS "Reggie." He is KNOWN AS "Reggie."
WRONG:	*We KNOW her AS brilliant.* (KNOW AS = named)

LACK

RIGHT:	Old gadgets ARE LACKING IN features. Old gadgets LACK features. The LACK OF features is upsetting.
SUSPECT:	*There is A LACK OF engineers TO BUILD new gadgets.*
WRONG:	*Old gadgets LACK OF features.* *It is hard to build bridges LACKING engineers.*

LESS

See also THAN.

RIGHT:	Our utilities add up to LESS THAN 10% of our income.
WRONG:	*Our utilities add up to LOWER THAN 10% of our income.*

LET

RIGHT:	My doctor LETS me SWIM in the ocean.
WRONG:	*My doctor LEAVES me SWIM in the ocean.* *The surgery WILL LEAVE me TO SWIM in the ocean.*

** LIKE   See also SUCH AS.

RIGHT: LIKE his sister, Matt drives fast cars. (= both drive fast cars)
Matt drives fast cars LIKE his sister.
(= both drive fast cars, OR both drive fast cars in the same way)
Matt drives fast cars LIKE his sister's.
(= both drive <u>similar</u> cars; he does <u>not</u> drive his sister's car)

WRONG: *Matt drives fast cars LIKE his sister does.*
LIKE his sister, SO Matt drives fast cars.

** LIKELY

RIGHT: My friend IS LIKELY TO EAT worms.
IT IS LIKELY THAT my friend WILL EAT worms.
My friend is MORE LIKELY THAN my enemy [is] TO EAT worms.
My friend is TWICE AS LIKELY AS my enemy [is] TO EAT worms.
MORE THAN LIKELY, my friend WILL EAT worms.

WRONG: *My friend IS LIKELY THAT he WILL EAT worms.*

LOSS

RIGHT: I have suffered a LOSS OF strength. (= decline of a quality)
They have suffered a LOSS IN the euro. (= decline of an investment)

WRONG: *I have suffered a LOSS IN strength.*

MANDATE

RIGHT: The general MANDATED THAT a trench BE dug. (subjunctive)

SUSPECT: *We HAVE A MANDATE TO CALL an election soon.* (= have authority)

WRONG: *The general MANDATED a trench TO BE dug.*
The general MANDATES THAT a trench WILL BE dug.
We HAVE A MANDATE FOR an election in the near future.

MAKE

RIGHT: The leader MADE the resistance POSSIBLE.
The leader MADE IT POSSIBLE TO RESIST oppression.
The leader MADE IT POSSIBLE FOR us TO RESIST oppression.
(Note: The IT properly refers to the infinitive TO RESIST.)

SUSPECT: *The leader MADE POSSIBLE the resistance.*

WRONG: *The leader MADE POSSIBLE TO RESIST oppression.*

MASS

RIGHT: The truck HAS ten TIMES THE MASS of a small car.

WRONG: The truck IS ten TIMES THE MASS of a small car.

MAYBE   See PROBABLY.

MEANS
RIGHT: Music education is A MEANS TO improved cognition.

WRONG: *Music education is A MEANS OF improved cognition.*
              Music education is A MEANS FOR improved cognition.

MISTAKE
RIGHT: My spouse HAS MISTAKEN me FOR a wealthier person.

WRONG: *My spouse HAS MISTAKEN me AS a wealthier person.*
              My spouse HAS MISTAKEN me TO a wealthier person.

MORE   See THAN.
RIGHT: We observed A 10% INCREASE IN robberies last month.
              MORE AND MORE we have observed violent robberies on weekends.
              INCREASINGLY we have observed violent robberies on weekends.

SUSPECT: *We observed 10% MORE robberies last month.*

MOST
RIGHT: OF ALL the Greek gods, Zeus was THE MOST powerful. (superlative)
              He was THE SECOND MOST attractive AND THE MOST powerful.

WRONG: *OF ALL the Greek gods, Zeus was THE MORE powerful.*
              He was THE SECOND MOST attractive AND MOST powerful.

NATIVE
RIGHT: The kangaroo is NATIVE TO Australia. (said of animals, plants)
              My friend is A NATIVE OF Australia. (said of people)

WRONG: *The kangaroo is NATIVE IN Australia.*

** NOT... BUT
RIGHT: She DID NOT EAT mangoes BUT ATE other kinds of fruit.
              She DID NOT EAT mangoes BUT LIKED other kinds of fruit AND later
              BEGAN to like kiwis, too.
              A tomato is NOT a vegetable BUT a fruit.
              A tomato is NOT a vegetable BUT RATHER a fruit.
              The agency is NOT a fully independent entity BUT INSTEAD derives its
              authority from Congress. (note that the verbs *is* and *derives* are parallel)
              She DID NOT EAT mangoes; INSTEAD, she ate other kinds of fruit.

WRONG: *She DID NOT EAT mangoes BUT other kinds of fruit.*
              She DID NOT EAT mangoes; RATHER other kinds of fruit.

** NOT ONLY... BUT ALSO

RIGHT: We wore NOT ONLY boots BUT ALSO sandals.
                 We wore NOT ONLY boots, BUT ALSO sandals. (comma is optional)

SUSPECT: *We wore NOT ONLY boots BUT sandals.*
                 Note: The GMAT <u>has</u> used this construction in correct answers.
                 We wore NOT ONLY boots BUT sandals AS WELL.
                 We wore boots AND ALSO sandals.

WRONG: *We wore NOT ONLY boots AND ALSO sandals.*
                 We wore NOT ONLY boots BUT, AS WELL, sandals.

NUMBER

RIGHT: A NUMBER OF dogs ARE barking.
                 THE NUMBER OF dogs IS large.
                 THE NUMBER OF dogs HAS FALLEN, but THE NUMBER OF cats
                 HAS RISEN.
                 The grey oyster nearly vanished, but ITS NUMBERS have rebounded.

SUSPECT: *There HAS BEEN A DECLINE IN THE NUMBER OF dogs.*

WRONG: *THE NUMBERS OF dogs HAVE fallen.*
                 Dogs HAVE FALLEN IN NUMBER, but cats HAVE RISEN IN NUMBER.

OBJECT

RIGHT: We OBJECT TO these proceedings.

SUSPECT: *We HAVE AN OBJECTION TO these proceedings.*

ONCE ⟋

RIGHT: We might ONCE have seen that band.

WRONG: *We might AT ONE TIME have seen that band.*

** ONLY ⟋

RIGHT: Her performance is exceeded ONLY by theirs. (modifies *by theirs*)
WRONG: *Her performance is ONLY exceeded by theirs.* (technically modifies *exceeded*)
                 Note: ONLY should be placed just before the words it is meant to modify.
                 In both speech and writing, we often place ONLY before the verb, but this
                 placement is generally wrong, according to the GMAT, since we rarely mean
                 that the verb is the only action ever performed by the subject.

OR

RIGHT: I do NOT want water OR milk.

SUSPECT: *I do NOT want water AND milk.* (implies the combination)

** ORDER
RIGHT: The state ORDERS THAT the agency COLLECT taxes. (subjunctive)
            The state ORDERS the agency TO COLLECT taxes.

WRONG: *The state ORDERS THAT the agency SHOULD COLLECT taxes.*
            The state ORDERS the agency SHOULD (or WOULD) COLLECT taxes.
            The state ORDERS the agency COLLECTING taxes.
            The state ORDERS the agency the COLLECTION OF taxes.
            The state ORDERS the COLLECTION OF taxes BY the agency.
            The state ORDERS taxes collected.

OWE
RIGHT: He OWES money TO the government FOR back taxes.

SUSPECT: *He OWES money TO the government BECAUSE OF back taxes.*

PAY
RIGHT: The employer PAYS the same FOR this JOB as for that one.

WRONG: *The employer PAYS the same IN this JOB as in that one.*

PERHAPS   See PROBABLY.

PERSUADE
RIGHT: He PERSUADED her TO GO with him.

WRONG: *He PERSUADED her IN GOING with him.*
            He PERSUADED THAT she GO (or SHOULD GO) with him.

POTENTIALLY
RIGHT: A tornado IS POTENTIALLY overwhelming.

WRONG: *A tornado CAN POTENTIALLY BE overwhelming.* (redundant)

PRIVILEGE
RIGHT: The academy gave senior cadets DANCING PRIVILEGES.

SUSPECT: *The academy gave senior cadets THE PRIVILEGE OF DANCING.*

WRONG: *The academy gave senior cadets THE PRIVILEGE TO DANCE.*

PROBABLY
RIGHT: This situation IS PROBABLY as bad as it can get.
            This situation MAY BE as bad as it can get. (less certain than PROBABLY)
            PERHAPS (or MAYBE) this situation IS as bad as it can get.

SUSPECT: *IT MAY BE THAT this situation IS as bad as it can get.*

WRONG: *This situation IS MAYBE as bad as it can get.*

PROHIBIT

RIGHT: The law PROHIBITS any citizen FROM VOTING twice.

WRONG: *The law PROHIBITS any citizen TO VOTE twice.*
The law PROHIBITS THAT any person VOTE (or VOTES) twice.

PROPOSE

RIGHT: The attorneys PROPOSED THAT a settlement BE reached. (subjunctive)

WRONG: *The attorneys PROPOSED THAT a settlement IS reached.*
The attorneys PROPOSED a settlement BE (or TO BE) reached.
The attorneys PROPOSED a settlement IS TO BE reached.

PROVIDED THAT   See IF.

RAISE   See RISE.

RANGE

RIGHT: His emotions RANGED FROM anger TO joy.
His WIDELY RANGING emotions are hard to deal with. (= changing over time)
His WIDE RANGE of accomplishments is impressive. (= a variety)

WRONG: *His emotions RANGED FROM anger AND joy.*
FROM anger AND TO joy. FROM anger WITH joy.
FROM anger IN ADDITION TO joy.
His WIDELY RANGING accomplishments are impressive.

RANK

RIGHT: This problem RANKS AS one of the worst we have seen.

WRONG: *This problem HAS THE RANK OF one of the worst we have seen.*

RATE

RIGHT: The RATES FOR bus tickets are good for commuters. (= prices)
The RATE OF theft has fallen. (= frequency or speed)

WRONG: *The RATES OF bus tickets are good for commuters.*
The RATE FOR theft has fallen.

RATHER THAN

RIGHT: He wrote with pencils RATHER THAN with pens.

SUSPECT: *He wrote with pencils INSTEAD OF pens.*
Note: The GMAT seems to avoid INSTEAD OF even when it is correct.
He wrote with pencils, BUT NOT pens.

WRONG: *He wrote with pencils INSTEAD OF with pens.*

REASON
RIGHT: I have A REASON TO DO work today.
            She has A REASON FOR the lawsuit.
            This observation indicates a REASON THAT he is here.

SUSPECT: *This observation indicates a REASON WHY he is here.*

WRONG: *This observation indicates a REASON he is here.*
            The REASON he is here IS BECAUSE he wants to be.

REBEL
RIGHT: The colonists REBELLED AGAINST tyranny.

SUSPECT: *The colonists' REBELLION WAS AGAINST tyranny.*

RECOGNIZE
RIGHT: They RECOGNIZED THAT the entrance fee WAS a bargain.
            They RECOGNIZED the entrance fee TO BE a bargain.
            They RECOGNIZED the entrance fee AS a bargain.

WRONG: *They RECOGNIZED the entrance fee AS BEING a bargain.*

RECOMMEND
RIGHT: We RECOMMENDED THAT the shelter BE opened.

WRONG: *We RECOMMENDED THAT the shelter SHOULD BE opened.*

REDUCE
RIGHT: The coalition REDUCED prices.
            The coalition was considering A REDUCTION IN prices.

SUSPECT: *The coalition MADE (or CAUSED) A REDUCTION IN prices.*

WRONG: *The coalition MADE A REDUCTION OF prices.*

REFER
RIGHT: This term REFERS TO a kind of disease.
            REFERRING TO the controversy, the politican asked for calm.

SUSPECT: *This term IS USED TO REFER TO a kind of disease.*

WRONG: *This term IS IN REFERENCE TO a kind of disease.*
            IN REFERENCE TO the controversy, the politician asked for calm.

REGARD
RIGHT: He REGARDS the gold ring AS costly.
            The gold ring IS REGARDED AS costly.
            He IS REGARDED AS HAVING good taste.

WRONG: *The gold ring IS REGARDED THAT IT IS costly.*

RELUCTANT
RIGHT: They were RELUCTANT TO SAY anything.

WRONG: *They were RELUCTANT ABOUT SAYING anything.*

REPORT
RIGHT: A study HAS REPORTED THAT bees ARE DISAPPEARING rapidly.

WRONG: *A study HAS REPORTED bees AS DISAPPEARING rapidly.*

REQUEST
RIGHT: I REQUEST THAT he BE removed. (subjunctive)

WRONG: *I REQUEST him TO BE removed.*

** REQUIRE
RIGHT: She REQUIRES time TO WRITE (or IN ORDER TO WRITE).
She REQUIRES her friend TO DO work.
Her friend IS REQUIRED TO DO work.
She REQUIRES THAT her friend DO work. (subjunctive)
She REQUIRES OF her friend THAT work BE done. (subjunctive)

SUSPECT: *In this hostel, there is a REQUIREMENT OF work.*
There is a REQUIREMENT THAT work BE done.

WRONG: *She REQUIRES her friend DO work (or MUST DO) work.*
She REQUIRES her friend TO HAVE TO DO work.
She REQUIRES OF her friend TO DO work.
She REQUIRES THAT her friend DOES work (or SHOULD DO) work.
She REQUIRES THAT her friend IS TO DO work.
She REQUIRES DOING work (or THE DOING OF work).
She REQUIRES her friend DOING work.
In this hostel, there is a REQUIREMENT OF work BY guests.

RESEMBLE
RIGHT: A certain coffee mug RESEMBLES my father.

SUSPECT: *A certain coffee mug HAS A RESEMBLANCE TO my father.*

RESTRICTION
RIGHT: The government imposed RESTRICTIONS ON the price of gasoline.

WRONG: *The government imposed RESTRICTIONS FOR the price of gasoline.*

** RESULT

RIGHT: Wealth RESULTS FROM work.
Work RESULTS IN wealth.
Wealth IS A RESULT OF work.
Wealth grows AS A RESULT OF work.
AS A RESULT OF our work, our wealth grew.
The RESULT OF our work WAS THAT our wealth grew.

WRONG: *We worked WITH THE RESULT OF wealth.*
We worked WITH A RESULTING growth of wealth.
RESULTING FROM our work, our wealth grew.
BECAUSE OF THE RESULT OF our work, our wealth grew.
The RESULT OF our work WAS our wealth grew. (THAT is needed.)
The growth of wealth RESULTS.

REVEAL

RIGHT: The analysis REVEALED THAT the comet WAS mostly ice.

SUSPECT: *The analysis REVEALED the comet WAS mostly ice.*

WRONG: *The analysis REVEALED the comet TO HAVE BEEN mostly ice.*

RISE

RIGHT: Oil prices ROSE sharply last year.
A RISE IN oil prices has led to inflation.
RISING prices at the gas pump are hurting consumers.
The RISING OF the SUN always lifts my spirits.

SUSPECT: *Oil prices WERE RAISED sharply last year.* (implies intent and control)

WRONG: *A RAISE IN oil prices has led to inflation.* (RAISE = bet or pay increase)
A RISING OF PRICES at the gas pump is hurting consumers.

RULE

RIGHT: The judge RULED THAT the plaintiff WAS in contempt.

SUSPECT: *The judge RULED the plaintiff WAS in contempt.*

WRONG: *The judge RULED the plaintiff TO BE in contempt.*
The judge RULED ON the plaintiff WHO WAS in contempt.

SAME

RIGHT: The car looks THE SAME TO me AS TO you.
I drove to the store AT THE SAME TIME AS you [did].

WRONG: *The car looks THE SAME TO me AS you.* (ambiguous)
I drove to the store AT THE SAME TIME you did.

SECURE

RIGHT: Our authority IS SECURE.

WRONG: *We ARE SECURE ABOUT our authority.*

Manhattan **GMAT** *Prep*
the new standard

** SEEM

RIGHT: This result SEEMS TO DEMONSTRATE the new theory.
IT SEEMS THAT this result DEMONSTRATES the new theory.
IT SEEMS AS IF this result DEMONSTRATES the new theory.

SUSPECT: *This result SEEMS TO BE A DEMONSTRATION OF the new theory.*
This result SEEMS DEMONSTRATIVE OF the new theory.
This result SEEMS LIKE A DEMONSTRATION OF the new theory.

WRONG: *This result SEEMS AS IF IT DEMONSTRATES the new theory.*
This result SEEMS LIKE IT DEMONSTRATES the new theory.

SHOULD

RIGHT: A car SHOULD BE TAKEN to the mechanic frequently. (= obligation)

WRONG: *A car SHOULD PASS every two hours.* (= probability)
The owner REQUESTED THAT the car SHOULD BE TAKEN to the mechanic. (use the subjunctive BE TAKEN instead)

SHOW

RIGHT: A discovery SHOWS THAT an object IS strange.
A discovery SHOWS an object TO BE strange.

SUSPECT: *A discovery SHOWS an object IS strange.*

WRONG: *A discovery SHOWS an object AS strange (or AS BEING) strange.*

SIGNIFICANT ✶

RIGHT: Your edits HAVE SIGNIFICANTLY IMPROVED the book.

SUSPECT: *Your edits HAVE MADE A SIGNIFICANT IMPROVEMENT IN the book.*

WRONG: *Your edits HAVE BEEN SIGNIFICANT IN IMPROVING the book.*
Your edits HAVE BEEN SIGNIFICANT IN AN IMPROVEMENT OF the book.

SIMILAR ✶

RIGHT: ALL companies HAVE SIMILAR issues. (comparison requires plural)

WRONG: *EACH company HAS SIMILAR issues.*
EVERY company HAS SIMILAR issues.

SINCE

RIGHT: Xingo is THE MOST successful new product SINCE 1997. (= up to now)

WRONG: *Xingo is THE MOST successful new product AFTER 1997.*

SO... AS TO

SUSPECT: *The sauce was SO hot AS TO burn my mouth.*
            Note: The GMAT seems to have changed its mind on this idiom. In the 10th Edition of the Official Guide, problem #88 uses the construction in the correct answer. However, #33 in the 11th Edition says that this idiom is "incorrect" with no further explanation. Other authorities consider this idiom correct, and we agree. Nevertheless, you should be wary of its use.

WRONG: *The sauce had SUCH heat AS TO burn my mouth.*
            The sauce had SO MUCH heat AS TO burn my mouth.

** SO... THAT   See also ENOUGH.

RIGHT: The book was SO SHORT THAT I could read it in one night.
            The book was SHORT ENOUGH FOR me TO READ in one night.
            Note: These two expressions have slightly different emphases, but it is unlikely that you will need to choose an answer solely on this basis.

SUSPECT: *The book was SO SHORT I could read it. (THAT is preferred.)*
            The book was OF SUCH SHORTNESS THAT I could read it.
            The book had SO MUCH SHORTNESS THAT I could read it.
            SUCH was the SHORTNESS of the book THAT I could read it.

WRONG: *The book was OF SUCH SHORTNESS, I could read it.*
            The book was SHORT TO SUCH A DEGREE AS TO ALLOW me to read it.

SO LONG AS   See AS LONG AS.

** SO THAT

RIGHT: She gave money SO THAT the school could offer scholarships. (= purpose)

SUSPECT: *She gave money, SO the school was grateful. (= result)*

WRONG: *She gave money SO the school could offer scholarships.*

SO TOO

RIGHT: Bellbottoms ARE coming back in style, and SO TOO ARE vests.

SUSPECT: *Bellbottoms ARE coming back in style, and ALSO vests.*

WRONG: *Bellbottoms ARE coming back in style, and SO TOO vests.*

SUBSTITUTE

RIGHT: We SUBSTITUTED Parmesan cheese FOR mozzarella.

WRONG: *We SUBSTITUTED Parmesan cheese IN PLACE OF mozzarella.*

SUCCEED

RIGHT: She SUCCEEDED IN REACHING the summit.

WRONG: *She SUCCEEDED TO REACH the summit.*

SUCH

RIGHT: You may enjoy chemistry and physics, but I hate SUCH subjects.
You may enjoy chemistry and physics, but I hate THESE subjects.
Note: THESE means "these specifically." SUCH is more general.

WRONG: *You may enjoy chemistry and physics, but I hate subjects OF THIS KIND.*
You may enjoy chemistry and physics, but I hate subjects LIKE THESE.

**** SUCH AS**

RIGHT: Matt drives fast cars, SUCH AS Ferraris. (= example)
Matt enjoys driving SUCH cars AS Ferraris.
Matt enjoys intense activities, SUCH AS DRIVING fast cars.

WRONG: *Matt drives fast cars LIKE Ferraris. (= similar to, but "example" is implied)*
Matt drives Ferraris AND THE LIKE.
Matt drives Ferraris AND OTHER cars SUCH AS THESE.
Matt trains in many ways SUCH AS BY DRIVING on racetracks.
Matt enjoys intense activities, SUCH AS TO DRIVE fast cars.

SUGGEST

RIGHT: A study SUGGESTS THAT more work IS needed (or WILL BE) needed.
We SUGGEST THAT he BE promoted. (subjunctive)
This artwork SUGGESTS great talent.

SUSPECT: *This artwork IS SUGGESTIVE OF great talent.*

SURFACE

RIGHT: Craters have been seen ON THE SURFACE OF the moon.

SUSPECT: *Craters have been seen AT THE SURFACE OF the moon.*

TARGETED

RIGHT: This intervention is TARGETED AT a specific misbehavior.

WRONG: *This intervention is TARGETED TO a specific misbehavior.*

**** THAN**

RIGHT: His books are MORE impressive THAN those of other writers.
This paper is LESS impressive THAN that one.
This paper is NO LESS impressive THAN that one.
This newspaper cost 50 cents MORE THAN that one.
MORE THAN 250 newspapers are published here.

WRONG: *His books are MORE impressive AS those of other writers.*
This paper is MORE impressive RATHER THAN that one.
This paper is MORE impressive INSTEAD OF that one.
This paper is NO LESS impressive AS that one.
This paper is NONE THE LESS impressive THAN that one.
This newspaper cost 50 cents AS MUCH AS that one.
AS MANY AS OR MORE THAN 250 newspapers are published here.

THINK

RIGHT: She THINKS OF them AS heroes.
            She IS THOUGHT TO BE secretly wealthy.

WRONG: *They ARE THOUGHT OF BY her AS heroes.*
            She THINKS OF them TO BE heroes.
            She THINKS OF them BEING heroes.

** TO + verb   See IN ORDER TO.

TOOL

RIGHT: We have a TOOL FOR MAKING progress.
            We have a TOOL TO MAKE progress.
            Note: The GMAT does not seem to require WITH, although one makes
            progress WITH a tool.

TRAIN

RIGHT: She WAS TRAINED TO RUN a division.

WRONG: *She WAS TRAINED FOR RUNNING (or IN RUNNING) a division.*

TRY

RIGHT: They WILL TRY TO BUILD a company. (= intent or purpose)

SUSPECT: *We TRIED BREAKING the door down. (= experiment)*

WRONG: *They WILL TRY AND BUILD a company.*
            They WILL TRY THAT THEY BUILD a company.

TWICE

RIGHT: He is TWICE AS tall AS Alex [is].
            Leaves fall TWICE AS quickly AS they grow.
            Naomi wrote TWICE AS MANY letters AS Sara [did].
            Naomi wrote ten letters, DOUBLE THE NUMBER THAT Sara wrote.
            Naomi's income DOUBLED in three years.

WRONG: *He is TWICE AS tall THAN Alex [is].*
            Leaves fall TWICE AS quickly AS their rate of growth.
            Naomi wrote DOUBLE THE LETTERS THAT Sara did.
            Naomi's income INCREASED BY TWICE in three years.

** UNLIKE   See also CONTRAST.
RIGHT: UNLIKE the spiny anteater, the aardvark is docile.

WRONG: *UNLIKE WITH the spiny anteater, the aardvark is docile.*

USE

RIGHT: He USES the hammer TO BREAK a board.

He BREAKS a board WITH the hammer.

His hammer BREAKS a board.

He USES the hammer AS a weapon.

WRONG: *He USES a hammer FOR BREAKING a board.*

He USES the hammer LIKE a weapon.

He USES the hammer TO BE a weapon.

VARIATION

RIGHT: There are VARIATIONS IN sunspot frequency and strength over time.

WRONG: *There are VARIATIONS OF sunspot frequency and strength over time.*

There are VARIATIONS AMONG sunspot frequency and strength over time.

VIEW

RIGHT: I VIEWED this process AS a mistake.

WRONG: *I VIEWED this process TO BE a mistake (or LIKE) a mistake.*

WAY

RIGHT: We proposed a WAY OF REACHING the goal.

The WAY IN WHICH we discussed the idea was positive.

The best WAY TO REACH the goal IS TO FOCUS one's energy.

This process was developed TO ACHIEVE the target.

SUSPECT: *This process was developed AS A WAY OF ACHIEVING the target.*

WRONG: *We proposed a WAY FOR REACHING the goal.*

The best WAY TO REACH the goal IS FOCUSING one's energy.

WEIGH

RIGHT: My laptop WEIGHS LESS THAN a suitcase.

My laptop IS LIGHTER THAN a suitcase.

WRONG: *My laptop WEIGHS LIGHTER THAN a suitcase.*

WHERE

RIGHT: Sussex is the only county WHERE pomegranates grow in this state.

Sussex is the only county IN WHICH pomegranates grow in this state.

This incident represents a case IN WHICH I would call the police.

WRONG: *This incident represents a case WHERE I would call the police.*

WHETHER

RIGHT: I do not know WHETHER I will go.

SUSPECT: *I do not know WHETHER OR NOT I will go.*

WRONG: *I do not know IF I will go.* (IF requires a consequence)

WHETHER... OR

RIGHT: I decided to eat the food, WHETHER it was tasty OR NOT.
          WHETHER trash OR treasure, the recyclables must be picked up.

WRONG: *WHETHER trash OR ALSO treasure, the recyclables must be picked up.*
          WHETHER THEY BE trash OR treasure, the recyclables must go.

WHOSE / WHOM

RIGHT: The officer WHOSE task was to be here did not show up.
          The company WHOSE growth leads the industry is XYZ, Inc.

SUSPECT: *The officer, THE task OF WHOM was to be here, did not show up.*

WITH

RIGHT: The lions growled, WITH their fur STANDING on end.

WRONG: *WITH only 25% of the student body, seniors get 50% of the resources.*

WORRY

RIGHT: The committee was WORRIED ABOUT increased prices.

SUSPECT: *The committee's WORRY CONCERNING increased prices was well-founded.*

WRONG: *The committee was WORRIED OVER increased prices.*

YET   See BUT.

Problem Set

In each of the following problems, there will be multiple versions of a sentence. These versions will differ by the form of an idiom. <u>Underline</u> the idiom in each version. For idioms that are split up, be sure to <u>underline</u> both parts. Then evaluate each idiom using the Spot-Extract-Replace method. Label each version as RIGHT, SUSPECT, or WRONG.

1. (a) The conflict started <u>both because of</u> ethnic tensions <u>as well as because</u> of economic   *wrong*
dislocations.
   (b) The conflict started <u>both because of</u> ethnic tensions and <u>because of</u> economic   *wrong*
dislocations.
   (c) The conflict started <u>both</u> because of ethnic tensions <u>but also</u> because of economic   *wrong*
dislocations.

2. (a) These results indicate a serious decline in the health of the marsh's ecosystem.   *suspect*
   (b) These results <u>indicate</u> the health of the marsh's ecosystem has seriously declined.   *wrong*
   (c) These results are indicative that the health of the marsh's ecosystem has seriously   *suspect*
declined.
   (d) These results indicate that the health of the marsh's ecosystem has seriously   *right*
declined.
   (e) These results indicate the health of the marsh's ecosystem to have seriously   *wrong*
declined.

3. (a) The new position required of Emma to master three difficult software packages.
   (b) The new position required that Emma should master three difficult software
packages.
   (c) The new position required Emma master three difficult software packages.
   (d) The new position required that Emma was to master three difficult software
packages.
   (e) The new position required Emma to master three difficult software packages.
   (f) The new position required that Emma master three difficult software packages.
   (g) The new position required Emma to have to master three difficult software
packages.

4. (a) The ring-tailed squirrel is more adept at surviving harsh winter conditions as its
cousin, the golden-mantled squirrel.
   (b) The ring-tailed squirrel is more adept at surviving harsh winter conditions rather
than its cousin, the golden-mantled squirrel.
   (c) The ring-tailed squirrel is more adept at surviving harsh winter conditions instead of
its cousin, the golden-mantled squirrel.
   (d) The ring-tailed squirrel is more adept at surviving harsh winter conditions than its
cousin, the golden-mantled squirrel.

5. (a) Unlike humans and guinea pigs, most mammals have the ability of synthesizing
Vitamin C from glucose, a simple sugar.
   (b) Unlike humans and guinea pigs, most mammals have the capability of synthesizing
Vitamin C from glucose, a simple sugar.

(c) Unlike humans and guinea pigs, most mammals are able to synthesize Vitamin C from glucose, a simple sugar.

(d) Unlike humans and guinea pigs, most mammals are capable of synthesizing Vitamin C from glucose, a simple sugar.

(e) Unlike humans and guinea pigs, most mammals can synthesize Vitamin C from glucose, a simple sugar.

(f) Unlike humans and guinea pigs, most mammals have the ability to synthesize Vitamin C from glucose, a simple sugar.

6. (a) Advances in the production of high-temperature superconductors are expected to increase the viability of so-called "maglev" trains that float on magnetic fields.

(b) It is expected that advances in the production of high-temperature superconductors should increase the viability of so-called "maglev" trains that float on magnetic fields.

(c) It is expected that advances in the production of high-temperature superconductors will increase the viability of so-called "maglev" trains that float on magnetic fields.

(d) Advances in the production of high-temperature superconductors are expected for them to increase the viability of so-called "maglev" trains that float on magnetic fields.

7. (a) Faced with the recurrence of natural disasters, such as floods and wildfires, many state governments have imposed significant taxes on their citizens in order to prepare for the next calamity.

(b) Faced with the recurrence of natural disasters, such as floods and wildfires, many state governments have imposed significant taxes on their citizens for preparing for the next calamity.

(c) Faced with the recurrence of natural disasters, such as floods and wildfires, many state governments have imposed significant taxes on their citizens so as to prepare for the next calamity.

(d) Faced with the recurrence of natural disasters, such as floods and wildfires, many state governments have imposed significant taxes on their citizens in order that the governments might prepare for the next calamity.

(e) Faced with the recurrence of natural disasters, such as floods and wildfires, many state governments have imposed significant taxes on their citizens to prepare for the next calamity.

8. (a) According to scientists, it is likely that the Earth will experience significant ecological changes within the next century.

(b) According to scientists, the Earth is likely to experience significant ecological changes within the next century.

(c) According to scientists, the Earth is likely that it will experience significant ecological changes within the next century.

9. (a) In the wake of the scandal, the CEO ordered all company executives and even middle managers should provide detailed reports to the outside investigators.

(b) In the wake of the scandal, the CEO ordered the provision of detailed reports to the outside investigators by all company executives and even middle managers.

(c) In the wake of the scandal, the CEO ordered all company executives and even middle managers to provide detailed reports to the outside investigators.

(d) In the wake of the scandal, the CEO ordered that all company executives and even middle managers provide detailed reports to the outside investigators.

(e) In the wake of the scandal, the CEO ordered all company executives and even middle managers providing detailed reports to the outside investigators.

(f) In the wake of the scandal, the CEO ordered that all company executives and even middle managers should provide detailed reports to the outside investigators.

10. (a) The chemical processes were so complex they required additional analysis.
   (b) The chemical processes were complex enough to require additional analysis.
   (c) The chemical processes were of such complexity that they required additional analysis.
   (d) The chemical processes were complex to such a degree as to require additional analysis.
   (e) The chemical processes were complex enough that they required additional analysis.
   (f) The chemical processes were complex enough as to require additional analysis.
   (g) The chemical processes were so complex that they required additional analysis.
   (h) The chemical processes were complex enough for them to require additional analysis.

11. (a) The moon's gravitational pull, not only on the ocean water closest to the moon but also on the Earth itself, results in the twice-daily cycle of the tides.
   (b) The twice-daily cycle of the tides is a result of the moon's gravitational pull, not only on the ocean water closest to the moon but also on the Earth itself.
   (c) Resulting from the moon's gravitational pull, not only on the ocean water closest to the moon but also on the Earth itself, the tides undergo twice-daily cycle.
   (d) The twice-daily cycle of the tides results from the moon's gravitational pull, not only on the ocean water closest to the moon but also on the Earth itself.
   (e) The tides undergo a twice-daily cycle as a result of the moon's gravitational pull, not only on the ocean water closest to the moon but also on the Earth itself.
   (f) The moon pulls gravitationally not only on the ocean water closest to the moon but also on the Earth itself, with the result of the twice-daily cycle of the tides.
   (g) The tides undergo a twice-daily cycle because of the result of the moon's gravitational pull, not only on the ocean water closest to the moon but also on the Earth itself.
   (h) The moon pulls gravitationally not only on the ocean water closest to the moon but also on the Earth itself, with the resulting twice-daily cycle of the tides.
   (i) The tides undergo a twice-daily cycle because of the moon, which pulls gravitationally not only on the ocean water closest to the moon but also on the Earth itself.
   (j) The tides undergo a twice-daily cycle because the moon pulls gravitationally not only on the ocean water closest to the moon but also on the Earth itself.
   (k) The twice-daily cycle of the tides is because the moon pulls gravitationally not only on the ocean water closest to the moon but also on the Earth itself.
   (l) The tides undergo a twice-daily cycle because of the moon pulling gravitationally not only on the ocean water closest to the moon but also on the Earth itself.

12. (a) The flag of the new republic seems to represent the old empire.
   (b) The flag of the new republic seems representative of the old empire.

(c) It seems as if the flag of the new republic represents the old empire.
(d) It seems that the flag of the new republic represents the old empire.
(e) The flag of the new republic seems like it represents the old empire.
(f) The flag of the new republic seems as if it represents the old empire.
(g) The flag of the new republic seems to be a representation of the old empire.

13. (a) Many places are called Naples—not only the cities in Italy and in Florida, and also a town in Clark County, South Dakota (population 25).
    (b) Many places are called Naples—not only the cities in Italy and in Florida, but a town in Clark County, South Dakota (population 25) as well.
    (c) Many places are called Naples—not only the cities in Italy and in Florida, but also a town in Clark County, South Dakota (population 25).
    (d) Many places are called Naples—the cities in Italy and in Florida, and also a town in Clark County, South Dakota (population 25).
    (e) Many places are called Naples—not only the cities in Italy and in Florida but a town in Clark County, South Dakota (population 25).
    (f) Many places are called Naples—not only the cities in Italy and in Florida but, as well, a town in Clark County, South Dakota (population 25).

14. (a) The Caucasus region has several times as many indigenous languages per square mile than most other areas of the world.
    (b) The Caucasus region has several times as many indigenous languages per square mile as most other areas of the world.
    (c) The Caucasus region has several times so many indigenous languages per square mile as most other areas of the world.
    (d) The Caucasus region has several times more indigenous languages per square mile that most other areas of the world.
    (e) The Caucasus region has several times as many more indigenous languages per square mile as most other areas of the world.

15. (a) The sign in front of the Baker residence prohibits anyone to trespass on the property.
    (b) The sign in front of the Baker residence prohibits that anyone trespass on the property.
    (c) The sign in front of the Baker residence forbids anyone from trespassing on the property.
    (d) The sign in front of the Baker residence forbids anyone to trespass on the property.
    (e) The sign in front of the Baker residence prohibits anyone from trespassing on the property.

1. (a) The conflict started <u>both</u> because of ethnic tensions <u>as well as</u> because of economic dislocations. (*both... as well as...*) **WRONG**

    (b) The conflict started <u>both</u> because of ethnic tensions <u>and</u> because of economic dislocations. (*both... and...*) **RIGHT**

    (c) The conflict started <u>both</u> because of ethnic tensions <u>but also</u> because of economic dislocations. (*both... but also...*) **WRONG**

2. (a) These results <u>indicate</u> a serious decline in the health of the marsh's ecosystem. (*indicate* + noun) **SUSPECT (although grammatically correct)**

    (b) These results <u>indicate</u> the health of the marsh's ecosystem has seriously declined. (*indicate* + clause) **WRONG**

    (c) These results <u>are indicative that</u> the health of the marsh's ecosystem has seriously declined. (*are indicative that* + clause) **WRONG**

    (d) These results <u>indicate that</u> the health of the marsh's ecosystem has seriously declined. (*indicate that* + clause) **RIGHT**

    (e) These results <u>indicate</u> the health of the marsh's ecosystem <u>to have</u> seriously declined. (*indicate* + noun + *to do*) **WRONG**

    Note: The use of <u>decline</u> is also idiomatic. Both forms in this problem are correct (*a decline in the health* OR *the health has declined*).

3. (a) The new position <u>required of</u> Emma <u>to master</u> three difficult software packages. (*require of* + noun + *to dp*) **WRONG**

    (b) The new position <u>required that</u> Emma <u>should master</u> three difficult software packages. (*require that* + *should*) **WRONG**

    (c) The new position <u>required</u> Emma <u>master</u> three difficult software packages. (*require* + subjunctive clause) **WRONG**

    (d) The new position <u>required that</u> Emma <u>was to master</u> three difficult software packages. (*require that* + *is to do*) **WRONG**

    (e) The new position <u>required</u> Emma <u>to master</u> three difficult software packages. (*require* + noun + *to do*) **RIGHT**

    (f) The new position <u>required that</u> Emma <u>master</u> three difficult software packages. (*require that* + subjunctive clause) **RIGHT**

    (g) The new position <u>required</u> Emma <u>to have to master</u> three difficult software packages. (*require* + noun + *to have to do*) **WRONG**

4. (a) The ring-tailed squirrel is <u>more</u> adept at surviving harsh winter conditions <u>as</u> its cousin, the golden-mantled squirrel. (*more... as...*) **WRONG**

    (b) The ring-tailed squirrel is <u>more</u> adept at surviving harsh winter conditions <u>rather than</u> its cousin, the golden-mantled squirrel. (*more... rather than...*) **WRONG**

    (c) The ring-tailed squirrel is <u>more</u> adept at surviving harsh winter conditions <u>instead of</u> its cousin, the golden-mantled squirrel. (*more... instead of...*) **WRONG**

    (d) The ring-tailed squirrel is <u>more</u> adept at surviving harsh winter conditions <u>than</u> its cousin, the golden-mantled squirrel. (*more... than...*) **RIGHT**

5. (a) Unlike humans and guinea pigs, most mammals <u>have the ability of synthesizing</u> Vitamin C from glucose, a simple sugar. (*have the ability of doing*) **WRONG**

(b) Unlike humans and guinea pigs, most mammals <u>have the capability of synthesizing</u> Vitamin C from glucose, a simple sugar. (*have the capability of doing*) **SUSPECT (although grammatically correct)**

(c) Unlike humans and guinea pigs, most mammals <u>are able to synthesize</u> Vitamin C from glucose, a simple sugar. (*are able to do*) **SUSPECT (although grammatically correct)**

(d) Unlike humans and guinea pigs, most mammals <u>are capable of synthesizing</u> Vitamin C from glucose, a simple sugar. (*are capable of doing*) **SUSPECT (although grammatically correct)**

(e) Unlike humans and guinea pigs, most mammals <u>can synthesize</u> Vitamin C from glucose, a simple sugar. (*can do*) **RIGHT**

(f) Unlike humans and guinea pigs, most mammals <u>have the ability to synthesize</u> Vitamin C from glucose, a simple sugar. (*have the ability to do*) **SUSPECT (although grammatically correct)**
Note: Sometimes the simple verb *can* is not available. In those cases, you must go with one of the suspect but grammatically correct versions.

6. (a) Advances in the production of high-temperature superconductors <u>are expected to increase</u> the viability of so-called "maglev" trains that float on magnetic fields. (*are expected to do*) **RIGHT**

(b) <u>It is expected that</u> advances in the production of high-temperature superconductors <u>should increase</u> the viability of so-called "maglev" trains that float on magnetic fields. (*it is expected that + should do*) **WRONG**

(c) <u>It is expected that</u> advances in the production of high-temperature superconductors <u>will increase</u> the viability of so-called "maglev" trains that float on magnetic fields. (*it is expected that + will do*) **RIGHT**

(d) Advances in the production of high-temperature superconductors <u>are expected for them to increase</u> the viability of so-called "maglev" trains that float on magnetic fields. (*are expected for them to do*) **WRONG**

7. (a) Faced with the recurrence of natural disasters, such as floods and wildfires, many state governments have imposed significant taxes on their citizens <u>in order to raise</u> "rainy day" funds. (*in order to do*) **RIGHT**

(b) Faced with the recurrence of natural disasters, such as floods and wildfires, many state governments have imposed significant taxes on their citizens <u>for raising</u> "rainy day" funds. (*for doing*) **WRONG**

(c) Faced with the recurrence of natural disasters, such as floods and wildfires, many state governments have imposed significant taxes on their citizens so as to raise "rainy day" funds. (*so as to do*) **WRONG**

(d) Faced with the recurrence of natural disasters, such as floods and wildfires, many state governments have imposed significant taxes on their citizens in order that the governments might raise "rainy day" funds. (*in order that + might do*) **SUSPECT**

(e) Faced with the recurrence of natural disasters, such as floods and wildfires, many state governments have imposed significant taxes on their citizens to raise "rainy day" funds. (*to do*) **RIGHT**

8. (a) According to scientists, <u>it is likely that</u> the Earth <u>will experience</u> significant ecological changes within the next century. (*it is likely that* + noun + *will do*) **RIGHT**

(b) According to scientists, the Earth <u>is likely to experience</u> significant ecological changes within the next century. (noun + *is likely to do*) **RIGHT**

(c) According to scientists, the Earth <u>is likely that it will experience</u> significant ecological changes within the next century. (noun + *is likely that it will do*) **WRONG**

9. (a) In the wake of the scandal, the CEO <u>ordered</u> all company executives and even middle managers <u>should provide</u> detailed reports to the outside investigators. (*order* + noun + *should do*) **WRONG**

   (b) In the wake of the scandal, the CEO <u>ordered</u> <u>the provision</u> of detailed reports to the outside investigators by all company executives and even middle managers. (*order* + action noun) **WRONG** (because of the awkward prepositional phrases that must be placed afterward)

   (c) In the wake of the scandal, the CEO <u>ordered</u> all company executives and even middle managers <u>to provide</u> detailed reports to the outside investigators. (*order* + noun + *to do*) **RIGHT**

   (d) In the wake of the scandal, the CEO <u>ordered that</u> all company executives and even middle managers <u>provide</u> detailed reports to the outside investigators. (*order that* + noun + subjunctive mood) **RIGHT**

   (e) In the wake of the scandal, the CEO <u>ordered</u> all company executives and even middle managers <u>providing</u> detailed reports to the outside investigators. (*order* + noun + *doing*) **WRONG**

   (f) In the wake of the scandal, the CEO <u>ordered that</u> all company executives and even middle managers <u>should provide</u> detailed reports to the outside investigators. (*order that* + noun + *should do*) **WRONG**

10. (a) The chemical processes were <u>so complex</u> they required additional analysis. (*so complex* + clause) **SUSPECT**

    (b) The chemical processes were <u>complex enough to require</u> additional analysis. (*complex enough to do*) **RIGHT**

    (c) The chemical processes were <u>of such complexity that</u> they required additional analysis. (*of such complexity that* + clause) **SUSPECT**

    (d) The chemical processes were <u>complex to such a degree as to require</u> additional analysis. (*complex to such a degree as to do*) **WRONG**

    (e) The chemical processes were <u>complex enough that</u> they required additional analysis. (*complex enough that* + clause) **WRONG**

    (f) The chemical processes were <u>complex enough as to require</u> additional analysis. (*complex enough as to do*) **WRONG**

    (g) The chemical processes were <u>so complex that</u> they required additional analysis. (*so complex that* + clause) **RIGHT**

    (h) The chemical processes were <u>complex enough for them to require</u> additional analysis. (*complex enough for them to do*) **WRONG**

11. (a) The moon's gravitational pull, not only on the ocean water closest to the moon but also on the Earth itself, <u>results in</u> the twice-daily cycle of the tides. (cause + *results in* + effect) **RIGHT**

    (b) The twice-daily cycle of the tides <u>is a result of</u> the moon's gravitational pull, not only on the ocean water closest to the moon but also on the Earth itself. (effect + *is a result of* + cause) **RIGHT**

    (c) <u>Resulting from</u> the moon's gravitational pull, not only on the ocean water closest to the moon but also on the Earth itself, the tides undergo twice-daily cycle. (*resulting from* + cause, effect) **WRONG**

    (d) The twice-daily cycle of the tides <u>results from</u> the moon's gravitational pull, not only on the ocean water closest to the moon but also on the Earth itself. (effect + *results from* + cause) **RIGHT**

(e) The tides undergo a twice-daily cycle <u>as a result of</u> the moon's gravitational pull, not only on the ocean water closest to the moon but also on the Earth itself. (effect + *as a result of* + cause) **RIGHT**

(f) The moon pulls gravitationally not only on the ocean water closest to the moon but also on the Earth itself, <u>with the result of</u> the twice-daily cycle of the tides. (cause + *with the result of* + effect) **WRONG**

(g) The tides undergo a twice-daily cycle <u>because of the result of</u> the moon's gravitational pull, not only on the ocean water closest to the moon but also on the Earth itself. (effect + *because of the result of* + cause) **WRONG**

(h) The moon pulls gravitationally not only on the ocean water closest to the moon but also on the Earth itself, <u>with the resulting</u> twice-daily cycle of the tides. (cause + *with the resulting* + effect) **WRONG**

(i) The tides undergo a twice-daily cycle <u>because of</u> the moon, <u>which pulls</u> gravitationally not only on the ocean water closest to the moon but also on the Earth itself. (effect + *because of* + cause, *which does*) **SUSPECT**

(j) The tides undergo a twice-daily cycle <u>because</u> the moon pulls gravitationally not only on the ocean water closest to the moon but also on the Earth itself. (effect + *because* + cause) **RIGHT**

(k) The twice-daily cycle of the tides <u>is because</u> the moon pulls gravitationally not only on the ocean water closest to the moon but also on the Earth itself. (effect + *is because* + cause) **WRONG**

(l) The tides undergo a twice-daily cycle <u>because of</u> the moon <u>pulling</u> gravitationally not only on the ocean water closest to the moon but also on the Earth itself. (effect + *because of* + cause + *doing*) **WRONG**

12. (a) The flag of the new republic <u>seems to represent</u> the old empire. (*seem to do*) **RIGHT**

(b) The flag of the new republic <u>seems representative</u> of the old empire. (*seem* + adjective) **SUPECT**

(c) <u>It seems as if</u> the flag of the new republic represents the old empire. (*it seems as if* + clause) **RIGHT**

(d) <u>It seems that</u> the flag of the new republic represents the old empire. (*it seems that* + clause) **RIGHT** with a slightly different meaning from that of version (c)

(e) The flag of the new republic <u>seems like it represents</u> the old empire. (*seem like it does*) **WRONG**

(f) The flag of the new republic <u>seems as if it represents</u> the old empire. (*seem as if it does*) **WRONG**

(g) The flag of the new republic <u>seems to be</u> a representation of the old empire. (*seem to be*) **SUSPECT**

13. (a) Many places are called Naples—<u>not only</u> the cities in Italy and in Florida, <u>and also</u> a town in Clark County, South Dakota (population 25). (*not only… and also…*) **WRONG**

(b) Many places are called Naples—<u>not only</u> the cities in Italy and in Florida, <u>but</u> a town in Clark County, South Dakota (population 25) <u>as well</u>. (*not only… but… as well*) **SUSPECT**

(c) Many places are called Naples—<u>not only</u> the cities in Italy and in Florida, <u>but also</u> a town in Clark County, South Dakota (population 25). (*not only… but also…*) **RIGHT**

(d) Many places are called Naples—the cities in Italy and in Florida, <u>and also</u> a town in Clark County, South Dakota (population 25). (*… and also…*) **WRONG**

(e) Many places are called Naples—<u>not only</u> the cities in Italy and in Florida <u>but</u> a town in Clark County, South Dakota (population 25). (*not only… but…*) **SUSPECT**

(f) Many places are called Naples—<u>not only</u> the cities in Italy and in Florida <u>but, as well,</u> a town in Clark County, South Dakota (population 25). (*not only… but, as well,…*) **WRONG**

14. (a) The Caucasus region has <u>several times as many</u> indigenous languages per square mile <u>than</u> most other areas of the world. (x *times as many... than*) **WRONG**

   (b) The Caucasus region has <u>several times so many</u> indigenous languages per square mile <u>as</u> most other areas of the world. (x *times so many... as*) **WRONG**

   (c) The Caucasus region has <u>several times as many</u> indigenous languages per square mile <u>as</u> most other areas of the world. (x *times as many... as*) **RIGHT**

   (d) The Caucasus region has <u>several times more</u> indigenous languages per square mile <u>that</u> most other areas of the world. (x *times more... that*) **WRONG**

   (e) The Caucasus region has <u>several times as many more</u> indigenous languages per square mile <u>as</u> most other areas of the world. (x *times as many more... as*) **WRONG**

15. (a) The sign in front of the Baker residence <u>prohibits</u> anyone <u>to trespass</u> on the property. (*prohibit + to do*) **WRONG**

   (b) The sign in front of the Baker residence <u>prohibits that</u> anyone <u>trespass</u> on the property. (*prohibit that* + subjunctive mood) **WRONG**

   (c) The sign in front of the Baker residence <u>forbids</u> anyone <u>from trespassing</u> on the property. (*forbid + from doing*) **WRONG**

   (d) The sign in front of the Baker residence <u>forbids</u> anyone <u>to trespass</u> on the property. (*forbid + to do*) **RIGHT**

   (e) The sign in front of the Baker residence <u>prohibits</u> anyone <u>from trespassing</u> on the property. (*prohibit + from doing*) **RIGHT**

Sentence Correction

Now that you have completed your study of IDIOMS, it is time to test your skills on problems that have actually appeared on real GMAT exams over the past several years.

The problem set that follows is composed of past GMAT problems from two books published by GMAC (Graduate Management Admission Council):

The Official Guide for GMAT Review, 11th Edition (pages 39–43 & 638–660)
The Official Guide for GMAT Verbal Review (pages 234–253)

The problems in the set below are primarily focused on IDIOM issues. For each of these problems, identify the idiom. Eliminate any answer choices that use an unidiomatic expression. Use your ear, your study of the Idiom List, and the Spot–Extract–Replace method to help you identify the correct form of the idiom.

Note: Problem numbers preceded by "D" refer to questions in the Diagnostic Test chapter of *The Official Guide for GMAT Review, 11th Edition* (pages 39–43).

Idioms

   11th Edition: 2, 25, 27, 28, 29, 30, 31, 32, 40, 45, 51, 55, 63, 70, 92, 94, 107, 115, 118,
         121, D38, D45
   Verbal Review: 5, 9, 14, 17, 20, 26, 43, 48, 50, 54, 58, 69, 75, 89, 90, 109, 113

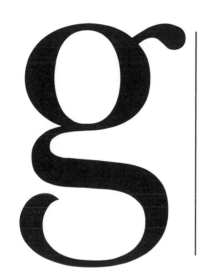

Chapter 10
of
SENTENCE CORRECTION

ODDS & ENDS

In This Chapter . . .

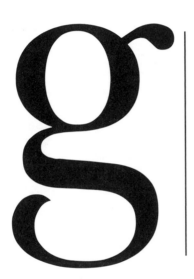

- Connecting Words
- Connecting Punctuation
- Quantity

ODDS & ENDS

You now have many issues to look for as you analyze a GMAT sentence. On a general level, remember GMC: Grammar, Meaning, and Concision. On a specific level, make sure to check each sentence for errors related to the following grammatical topics: (1) Subject–Verb Agreement, (2) Parallelism, (3) Pronouns, (4) Modifiers, (5) Verb Tense, Mood, & Voice, (6) Comparisons, and (7) Idioms.

Most GMAT errors fall into one of the preceding categories. There are, however, a few other types of errors which may be found in GMAT sentences. If you have checked for all the major types of errors and you are still undecided between two versions of the sentence, consider the following odds & ends—additional grammar topics that may help you identify the correct sentence:

> (1) Connecting Words
> (2) Connecting Punctuation
> (3) Quantity

Connecting Words

In order for phrases and clauses to combine into a complete, grammatical sentence, they must be linked together in the proper way with certain <u>Connecting Words</u>.

Remember that a correct sentence always contains at least one <u>main clause</u>. (A main clause is group of words that can stand on its own as a complete sentence. It contains both a subject and a verb, and it does not begin with a subordinating conjunction such as *because* or *if*.) As we saw in Chapter 3: Subject-Verb Agreement, a sentence that lacks a main clause is called a fragment.

A correct sentence can have more than one main clause; this very sentence has two. You must be careful, however, to use the right punctuation and/or connecting words to join two clauses. A comma is not enough to join two main clauses. A sentence that violates this rule is called a <u>Run-on Sentence</u>.

> Wrong: I need to relax, I have so many things to do!

This sentence is considered a run-on, because it connects two independent sentences with only a comma. You can correct the sentence by adding a logical connecting word, such as *but*:

> Right: I need to relax, BUT I have so many things to do!

The conjunctions *and, but,* and *or* are very common connecting words. These three words, along with *for, nor, yet,* and *so,* are also called <u>Coordinating Conjunctions</u>. Together with a comma, a coordinating conjunction can link two main clauses to form a grammatical sentence.

If you suspect that a sentence is a run-on, identify each main clause. Then make sure that the clauses are joined properly.

Consider a longer example:

> Wrong: New data from the Labor Department indicate that producer prices rose rapidly last month, some analysts contend that the economic slowdown in the euro zone and in Asia will stem the rise in commodity prices, lessening inflationary pressures in the United States.

The above sentence is a run-on because it uses only a comma to join two main clauses. The first main clause is *New data...rapidly last month*. The second main clause is the rest of the sentence: *some analysts contend...United States*. You can fix this sentence by adding a coordinating conjunction:

> Right: New data from the Labor Department indicate that producer prices rose rapidly last month, BUT some analysts contend that the economic slowdown in the euro zone and in Asia will stem the rise in commodity prices, lessening inflationary pressures in the United States.

And is the most important coordinating conjunction. Whenever you see an *and* after a comma, check for two possibilities: (1) a list (*apples, grapes, AND pears*), or (2) two main clauses (*I like apples, AND she likes grapes*). The GMAT will occasionally create a mixed-up sentence by linking a main clause to a fragment with *and* after a comma.

> Wrong: The term "Eureka," meaning "I have found it" in ancient Greek and famously uttered by Archimedes, AND ever since then, scientists have exclaimed the same word upon making important discoveries.

The capitalized *and* in the middle of the sentence links a fragment (*The term "Eureka,"* followed by two modifiers) to a main clause (*ever since then, scientists have exclaimed the same term...*). One way to fix the sentence is to make the fragment into a main clause as well:

> Right: The term "Eureka," meaning "I have found it" in ancient Greek, WAS famously uttered by Archimedes, AND ever since then, scientists have exclaimed the same word upon making important discoveries.

What comes before the *AND* is now a complete main clause, with its own subject and verb: *The <u>term</u> "Eureka,"... <u>was</u> famously <u>uttered</u> by Archimedes*.

<u>Subordinators</u> are another kind of connecting word. Subordinators, such as *because* and *although,* create subordinate clauses, which can in turn attach to a main clause with a comma. Previous examples of run-on sentences can be fixed with subordinators as well.

> Right: I need to relax, BECAUSE I have so many things to do!

> Right: ALTHOUGH new data from the Labor Department indicate that producer prices rose rapidly last month, some analysts contend that the economic slowdown in the euro zone and in Asia will stem the rise in commodity prices, lessening inflationary pressures in the United States.

Connecting words can help you avoid run-on sentences.

*Manhattan*GMAT*Prep
the new standard

You can think of a <u>comma</u> + <u>coordinating conjunction</u> as a neutral referee that allows two main clauses to coexist peacefully as equals. A <u>subordinator</u>, on the other hand, is decidedly partisan: it achieves harmony within a sentence by reducing one of the clauses to a subordinate clause.

Use only one connecting word at once.

Wrong:	ALTHOUGH I need to relax, YET I have so many things to do!
Right:	ALTHOUGH I need to relax, I have so many things to do!
Right:	I need to relax, YET I have so many things to do!

You should also make sure that clauses are connected by a <u>sensible</u> connecting word:

Wrong:	She is not interested in sports, AND she likes watching them on TV.

In the example above, the connecting word *and* is not sensible, because the two sentence parts are in opposition to each other. This meaning error can be corrected by choosing a different connecting word:

Right:	She is not interested in sports, BUT she likes watching them on TV.
Right:	ALTHOUGH she is not interested in sports, she likes watching them on TV.

The following is a list of common connecting words:

Coordinating Conjunctions: **For   And   Nor   But   Or   Yet   So**

Subordinators: **Although   Because   Before   After   Since   When   If   Unless That   Though   While**

Be sure to choose a connector that logically fits into a given sentence.

Finally, be on the lookout for sentences that join a main clause to something that should be a clause, but is not actually a clause.

Wrong:	Citizens of many countries are expressing concern about the environmental damage caused by the widespread release of greenhouse gases may be impossible to reverse.

The main clause in this sentence is *Citizens of many countries are expressing concern about the environmental damage caused by the widespread release of greenhouse gases*. There is nothing wrong with this main clause. But what are we to make of the rest of the sentence, which consists of the verb phrase *may be impossible to reverse?* This verb phrase has no subject. The GMAT wants you to think that *environmental damage* is the subject of *may be impossible to reverse*, but *environmental damage* cannot play two roles at once: object of the preposition *about* AND subject of the verb *may be*. We need to fix the sentence by bringing *may be impossible to reverse* inside a clause.

Subordinators always imply some relationship to the main clause.

One way to fix the sentence is to change the preposition *about* to the subordinator *that*.

> Right: Citizens of many countries are expressing concern THAT the environmental damage caused by the widespread release of greenhouse gases may be impossible to reverse.

In this correct version, the main clause is *Citizens... are expressing concern*. The subordinate clause begins with the word *that* and extends to the end of the sentence. Within that subordinate clause, *environmental damage* is the subject of *may be*.

Another way to fix the sentence is to put *may be impossible to reverse* inside a noun modifier.

> Right: Citizens of many countries are expressing concern about the environmental damage caused by the widespread release of greenhouse gases, <u>DAMAGE THAT may be impossible to reverse.</u>

In this correct version, the main clause ends right before the comma. The words *damage that may be impossible to reverse* constitute an absolute phrase (see Chapter 6: Modifiers). Inside that absolute phrase, the words *that may be impossible to reverse* are a noun modifier that modifies the word *damage*. Note that we had to add the word *damage* here.

Connecting Punctuation

There are four major punctuation marks that can connect sentence parts:

<u>Comma</u>	<u>Semicolon</u>	<u>Colon</u>	<u>Dash</u>
,	;	:	—

<u>Comma</u>

The comma (,) is the most common punctuation mark, as well as the most difficult to use correctly. Fortunately, you can rest assured that the GMAT does not make correct answers hinge solely on comma use. That is, the correct answer will never differ from an incorrect answer <u>only</u> by the placement of a comma.

However, you should certainly pay attention to commas, since they are important signals and separators of modifiers, items in a list, and other sentence elements. For instance, remember that non-essential modifiers are set off by commas, but essential modifiers are not separated by commas. *This car, purchased last year, is a Buick* contains a non-essential modifier, but *The car purchased last year is a Buick* contains an essential modifier.

Do not use a comma before *and* to separate two verbs that have the same subject. Either eliminate the comma or add a subject to the second verb, creating a second main clause.

> Wrong: Earl walked to school, AND later ate his lunch.
> Right: Earl walked to school AND later ate his lunch.
> Right: Earl walked to school, AND HE later ate his lunch.

And of course, a comma by itself cannot connect two complete sentences (main clauses).

> Wrong: Earl walked to school, he later ate his lunch.

Do not use a comma to connect two related main clauses; use a semicolon instead.

*Manhattan*GMAT*Prep
the new standard

Semicolon

The semicolon (;) connects two closely related statements. Each statement must be able to stand alone as an independent sentence. For instance, we can fix the previous example by using a semicolon.

Right: Earl walked to school; he later ate his lunch.

Consider another example:

Wrong: Andrew and Lisa are inseparable; doing everything together.

The second part of this sentence cannot stand on its own. Therefore, the two parts may not be connected by a semicolon.

Right: Andrew and Lisa are inseparable; they do everything together.

In the corrected example, the two sentence parts can each stand alone. Therefore, they may be connected by a semicolon. Moreover, when you use a semicolon, you should ensure that the two sentence parts are related in an independent, balanced way. If it seems that the author originally meant to subordinate one part to the other, you must preserve that intent.

Right: The dam has created dead zones, WHERE fish have disappeared.
Wrong: The dam has created dead zones; fish have disappeared.

In the second example above, the writer seems to be saying that *fish* all over the world *have disappeared.* The first example is appropriately limited to the *dead zones.*

The semicolon is often followed by a Conjunctive Adverb or other transition expression, such as *however, therefore,* or *in addition.* In this way, we can modify the equal relationship that a bare semicolon implies. Note that these transitional elements are not true conjunctions like *and.* As a result, you must use semicolons, not commas, to join the sentences.

Wrong: Andrew and Lisa are inseparable, THEREFORE, we never see them apart.
Right: Andrew and Lisa are inseparable; THEREFORE, we never see them apart.

A minor use of the semicolon is to separate items that themselves contain commas.

Wrong: I listen to *Earth, Wind & Fire, Wow, Owls,* and *Blood, Sweat & Tears.*
Right: I listen to *Earth, Wind & Fire; Wow, Owls;* and *Blood, Sweat & Tears.*

If you use a transition expression such as *therefore* in the second half of a sentence, make sure to use a semicolon.

Manhattan **GMAT** *Prep
the new standard

Colon

The colon (:) provides further explanation for what comes before it. For example, you can use a colon to equate a list with its components. You should be able to insert the word *namely* or the phrase *that is* after the colon.

What comes before the colon must be able to stand alone as a sentence. What comes after the colon does not have to be able to stand alone.

> Wrong: I love listening to: classical, rock, rap, and pop music.

In this example, the words preceding the colon (*I love listening to*) do not form a complete sentence.

> Right: I love listening to many kinds of music: classical, rock, rap, and pop.

In the corrected version, the words preceding the colon can stand alone as a sentence. Moreover, the words following the colon (*classical, rock, rap, and pop*) give further explanation of the *many kinds of music* mentioned. You can insert *namely* or *that is* after the colon, and the result would make sense.

> Right: I love listening to many kinds of music: namely, classical, rock, rap, and pop.

Whatever needs explanation should be placed as close to the colon as possible.

> Worse: <u>Three factors</u> affect the rate of a reaction: <u>concentration, surface area, and temperature.</u>
> Better: The rate of a reaction is affected by <u>three factors</u>: <u>concentration, surface area, and temperature.</u>

Notice that this principle helps justify the use of the passive voice in the second example.

You can put a main clause <u>after</u> a colon as well. The key is that this clause must explain what precedes the colon—perhaps the entire preceding clause.

> Right: On January 1, 2000, the national mood was completely different from what it would become just a few years later: at the turn of the century, given a seemingly unstoppable stock market and a seemingly peaceful world, the country was content.

The words after the colon, *at the turn of the century… was content,* can stand alone as a sentence. They serve to explain the entire clause that comes before the colon (a clause that asserts an upcoming change in the national mood, as of the first of the year 2000).

Do not confuse the semicolon (;) with the colon (:). The semicolon connects two related independent clauses, but the second does not necessarily explain the first. In contrast, the colon always connects a sentence with a further explanation.

Use a colon to explain something further. Make sure that the part in front of the colon can stand alone.

*Manhattan*GMAT*Prep
the new standard

<u>Dash</u>
The dash (—) is a flexible punctuation mark that the GMAT occasionally employs. You can use a dash as an emphatic comma, semicolon or colon.

Right: By January 2, 2000, the so-called "Y2K problem" was already widely considered a joke—although the reason for the non-event was the huge corporate and governmental investment in prior countermeasures.

In the case above, either a comma or a dash would be correct. Sometimes, a dash is preferred. For instance, you should use dashes to separate an appositive from an item in a list:

Right: My three best friends—Danny, Jimmy, and Joey—and I went skiing.

If you used commas in this sentence, you might think that <u>seven</u> people were going skiing.

You can also use the dash to restate or explain an earlier part of the sentence. Unlike the colon, the dash does not need to be immediately preceded by the part needing explanation.

Right: Post-MBA compensation for investment bankers tends to surge far ahead of that for management consultants—by tens, if not hundreds, of thousands of dollars a year.

The phrase after the dash (*by tens...a year*) explains the word *far* in the phrase *far ahead*. In comparison, a colon would not work so well here.

In short, you cannot really go wrong with a dash!

Quantity

In English, words and expressions of quantity are subject to strict grammatical rules. The GMAT tests your knowledge of these quantity rules.

<u>Rule #1: Words used for **countable** things vs. words used for **uncountable** things</u>
Some nouns in English are <u>Countable</u>. Examples include *hat(s)*, *feeling(s)*, and *person/people*. Other nouns are <u>Uncountable</u>. Examples include *patience, water,* and *furniture*. If you are unsure as to whether something is countable or not, perform the <u>counting test</u>:

For *hat*:   **One hat, two hats, three hats**. This works. *Hat* is countable.
For *patience*:   **One patience (?), two patiences (?), stop**. This does not work. *Patience* is not countable.

The table on the next page distinguishes between words and expressions that modify countable things and those that modify uncountable things:

Distinguish between countable things and uncountable things by trying to count them!

Countable Modifiers	Uncountable Modifiers
MANY hats	MUCH patience
NOT MANY hats	NOT MUCH patience
FEW hats	LITTLE patience
FEWER hats	LESS patience
FEWEST hats	LEAST patience
NUMBER of hats	AMOUNT of patience
FEWER THAN 10 hats	LESS THAN a certain AMOUNT of patience
NUMEROUS hats	GREAT patience
MORE NUMEROUS hats	GREATER patience

More, most, enough, and *all* work with both countable (plural) and uncountable (singular) nouns: *More hats; More patience; Most people; Most furniture; Enough hats; Enough patience; All people; All furniture.*

Do not use *less* with countable items. This error has become common in speech and in the signs above express lines in grocery stores: *10 items or <u>less</u>.* Since the noun *item* is countable, the sign should read *10 items or <u>fewer</u>.*

> Wrong: There were LESS Numidian <u>kings</u> than Roman <u>emperors</u>.
> Right: There were FEWER Numidian <u>kings</u> than Roman <u>emperors</u>.

Be careful with unit nouns, such as *dollars* or *gallons*. By their nature, unit nouns are countable: *one dollar, two dollars, three dollars.* Thus, they work with most of the countable modifiers. However, unit nouns represent uncountable quantities: *money, volume.* (You can count money, of course, but you cannot count the <u>noun</u> *money: one money (?), two moneys (?),* stop.) As a result, we use *less* with unit nouns, when we really want to indicate something about the underlying quantity.

> Right: We have LESS THAN twenty <u>dollars</u>.

This means that the amount of money we have, in whatever form, totals less than $20. If we write *We have FEWER THAN twenty dollars,* we mean the actual pieces of paper. (You would probably say *fewer than twenty dollar <u>bills</u>* to make the point even clearer.)

<u>Rule #2: Words used to relate **two** things vs. words used to relate **three or more** things</u>
To relate two things, you must use different words from the words you use to relate three or more things. Remember that you must use comparative forms of adjectives and adverbs (*better, worse, more, less*) to compare 2 things or people, but you must use superlative forms (*best, worst, most, least*) to compare 3 or more things or people.

The other distinction to remember is that you should use *between* only with 2 things or people. When you are talking about 3 or more things or people, use *among.*

> Wrong: I mediated a dispute BETWEEN Maya, Logan, and Kalen.
> Right: I mediated a dispute AMONG Maya, Logan, and Kalen.

Use Between to relate 2 things. Use Among to relate more than 2 things.

Rule #3: *__The Number__ or __Number Of__ versus __A Number__ or __The Numbers Of__*

As you may recall from the Subject–Verb Agreement section, the word *Number* is tricky. There are a few major points to remember.

(1) *The number of* is singular, and *A number of* is plural.

Right: THE NUMBER of dogs IS greater than the number of cats.
Right: A NUMBER of dogs ARE chasing away the cats.

(2) *The numbers of* is almost always incorrect. Stick to the expression *the number of.*

Wrong: THE NUMBERS of dogs in Montana ARE steadily increasing.
Right: THE NUMBER of dogs in Montana IS steadily increasing.

(3) However, *numbers* is possible in a few contexts. If you wish to make a comparison, use *greater than*, not *more than* (which might imply that the quantity of numbers is larger, not the numbers themselves). See the Idiom List for more details.

Wrong: The rare Montauk beaked griffin is not extinct; its NUMBERS are now suspected to be much MORE than before.
Right: The rare Montauk beaked griffin is not extinct; its NUMBERS are now suspected to be much GREATER than before.

Rule #4: *__Increase__ and __Decrease__ vs. __Greater__ and __Less__*

The words *increase* and *decrease* are not the same as the words *greater* and *less*. *Increase* and *decrease* express the change of one thing over time. *Greater* and *less* signal a comparison between two things.

Right: The price of silver INCREASED by ten dollars.
Right: The price of silver is five dollars GREATER than the price of copper.

Watch out for redundancy in sentences with the words *increase* and *decrease*.

Wrong: The price of silver FELL by a more than 35% DECREASE.
Right: The price of silver DECREASED by more than 35%.
Right: The price of silver FELL by more than 35%.

Decrease already includes the notion of falling or lowering, so *fell* is redundant. Similarly, *increase* includes the notion of rising or growing, so *rise* or *growth* would be redundant as well.

Pay attention to the specific meaning of quantity words. For instance, *increase* and *decrease* mean change over time.

Problem Set

Fix the following 10 sentences if necessary. Look for issues outlined in this chapter, including connecting words, connecting punctuation, and quantity words.

1. The music company was afraid of the accelerating decline of sales of compact disks would not be compensated by increased Internet revenue.

2. The petroleum distillates were so viscous, the engineers had to heat the pipe by nearly thirty degrees.

3. The invitees to the fundraiser include: corporate sponsors, major individual donors, and important local leaders.

4. The municipality's back-to-work program has had notable success, nevertheless, it is not suitable for a state-wide rollout for several reasons.

5. The negotiations between the company, the union, and the city government were initially contentious but ultimately amicable.

6. Though canals have experienced a severe decline in barge traffic over the past several decades, yet with the rise in fuel costs, "shipping" by actual ships may once again become an important means of transporting goods within the country.

7. Historically, the Isle of Man had an economy based primarily on agriculture and fishing; now, one based on banking, tourism, and film production.

8. The composer is regarded more for the quality than for the quantity of her work: in two decades, she has written less than twenty complete works, including just three symphonies.

9. Despite advancing in an absolute sense, the productivity of Zel-Tech's workforce has fallen significantly behind that of competitor workforces: by up to thousands of dollars per worker.

10. The Bentley trench, situated at more than a mile and a half below sea level and completely covered by Antarctic glaciers, and it is the lowest point on the planet not under the oceans.

The following 5 sentences contain circled sections. Use the rules in this chapter to correct any errors that you can find in the circled sections. Do not change anything that is not circled.

11. Harvey Dash, the remarkable sprinter, (broken) world records (in: two Olympic events,) the 100-meter(, and) 200-meter runs.

12.   Jim is trying to reduce the (number) of soda that he drinks (,) at last night's party, (although,) his resolve to drink (fewer) soda was sorely tested, he found himself quaffing (many) of sodas.

13.   Orinoco.com, a major internet retailer, announced mixed results for the second quarter (,) the (numbers) of people shopping at Orinoco.com grew (by a thirty-four percent rise) (but) profit per customer fell sharply (as) consumers shifted to lower-margin items in response to uncertain economic conditions.

14.   (Between) 1998 and 2003, there was heavy fighting in Parthia (between) numerous armed factions (yet) this conflict, so much more complicated than a conventional war (between) two states, involved no (less) than eight countries and twenty-five militias.

15.   Most legislators (—) including (much) in the governor's own party (—) realize that the governor's budget would imperil the state's finances (, nonetheless,) the budget is likely to be approved (, because) few legislators want to anger voters by cutting spending or raising taxes.

Manhattan **GMAT** Prep
the new standard

1.   **The music company was afraid THAT the accelerating decline of sales of compact disks would not be compensated by increased Internet revenue.**

The original sentence has a main clause (*The music company was afraid of the accelerating decline of sales of compact disks*) with another verb phrase—*would not be compensated by increased Internet revenue*—inappropriately tacked on. One way to fix the sentence is to replace the preposition *of* with the subordinator *that*.

2.   **The petroleum distillates were so viscous THAT the engineers had to heat the pipe by nearly thirty degrees.**

The original sentence is a run-on sentence. To fix the sentence, you need to insert the subordinator *that*.

3.   **The invitees to the fundraiser include corporate sponsors, major individual donors, and important local leaders.** (no colon after *include*)

The original sentence places a colon incorrectly after the word *include*. The words that come before a colon must constitute a complete sentence.

4.   **The municipality's back-to-work program has had notable success; nevertheless, it is not suitable for a state-wide rollout for several reasons.** (semicolon before *nevertheless*)

The word *nevertheless* is a conjunctive adverb, not a coordinating conjunction (such as *and*). As a result, you need to use a semicolon, not a comma, before *nevertheless*.

5.   **The negotiations AMONG the company, the union, and the city government were initially contentious but ultimately amicable.**

The word *between* can only be used with two things. You must use the word *among* to describe relationships of three or more things.

6.   **Canals have experienced a severe decline in barge traffic over the past several decades, yet with the rise in fuel costs, "shipping" by actual ships may once again become an important means of transporting goods within the country.** (no *Though* at the beginning of the sentence)

Using both *Though* and *yet* is redundant. It is preferable to keep *yet* in order to delineate the contrast clearly; otherwise, you might mistakenly consider the phrase *with the rise of fuel costs* as part of the first clause.

7.   **Historically, the Isle of Man had an economy based primarily on agriculture and fishing; now, IT HAS one based on banking, tourism, and film production.**

Just like the words that come before a semicolon, the words that come after a semicolon must constitute a complete sentence. In the original sentence, the second part of the sentence does not form a valid main clause.

8.   **The composer is regarded more for the quality than for the quantity of her work: in two decades, she has written FEWER than twenty complete works, including just three symphonies.**

Works is a countable noun, so the correct quantity word is *fewer*, not *less*.

Note that the colon is used correctly. The first part of the sentence is a complete main clause. Moreover, the second part of the sentence explains the assertion in the first part.

9.   **Despite advancing in an absolute sense, the productivity of Zel-Tech's workforce has fallen significantly behind that of competitor workforces—by up to thousands of dollars per worker.** (dash instead of colon)

The dash is a better choice than the colon if you need to explain a particular phrase, such as *significantly behind*, that cannot easily be moved closer to the explanation.

10.   **The Bentley trench, situated at more than a mile and a half below sea level and completely covered by Antarctic glaciers, IS the lowest point on the planet not under the oceans.**

The original sentence has a main clause linked to a sentence fragment by the use of *and*. In the corrected version, one main clause combines all the information given.

11.   **Harvey Dash, the remarkable sprinter, HAS BROKEN world records IN TWO OLYMPIC EVENTS: the 100-meter and 200-meter runs.**

Broken should be *has broken* (or *broke*). The original "sentence" is a fragment because it lacks a verb. To rectify this problem, we must change the past participle *broken* into a verb such as *has broken* or *broke*.

In: two Olympic events, should be changed to *in two Olympic events:* with a colon at the end. Recall that a colon cannot be placed anywhere but at the end of a main clause. The prepositional phrase *in two Olympic events* logically belongs to the main clause, so the colon should came at the end of that prepositional phrase. The colon then works to introduce the two examples.

The comma before *and* should be dropped. Here *and* is a parallelism signal joining two modifiers (*100-meter* and *200-meter*), not two main clauses. Thus, *and* should not be preceded by a comma.

12.   **Jim is trying to reduce the AMOUNT of soda that he drinks; at last night's party, HOWEVER, his resolve to drink LESS soda was sorely tested, AND he found himself quaffing A NUMBER of sodas.**

Number should be *amount* or *quantity*. Here we are thinking of *soda* as an uncountable substance—otherwise, *soda* would be *sodas*.

The comma after *drinks* should be a semicolon, which would appropriately separate two main clauses: *Jim is trying...that he drinks* and *at last night's party...sorely tested*.

Although should be *however*. *Although* is a subordinator; therefore, it must be placed at the start of a subordinate clause. In contrast, the conjunctive adverb *however* can be placed in the middle of a main clause.

Fewer should be *less*. Once again, we are regarding *soda* as an uncountable substance.

An *and* should be inserted after the comma after *tested*. This placement of *and* appropriately separates two main clauses: *at last night's party...sorely tested* and *he found...sodas*.

Many should be *a number*. Since there is an *-s* on the end of *sodas*, we know that *sodas* are now thought of as countable things—presumably servings of soda. *A number of* is an appropriate modifier for countable things.

13.   **Orinoco.com, a major Internet retailer, announced mixed results for the second quarter: the NUMBER of people shopping at Orinoco.com grew by THIRTY-FOUR PERCENT, but profit per customer fell sharply as consumers shifted to lower-margin items in response to uncertain economic conditions.**

Numbers should be *number*. The sentence is telling us that one particular figure (*number*) rose. It is not telling us that several different figures (*numbers*) rose.

By a thirty-four percent rise should be *by thirty-four percent*. The verb *grew* already conveys the idea of an increase, so there is no need to use the noun *rise*.

But should have a comma in front of it. *But* is a coordinating conjunction, and so it must be preceded by a comma in order to separate two main clauses. The two main clauses in question are *the number of people...percent* and *profit...fell sharply*.

As is correct. *As* is a subordinator in this context. Unlike a coordinating conjunction, a subordinator does not always have to be preceded by a comma when it links clauses.

14.   **Between 1998 and 2003, there was heavy fighting in Parthia AMONG numerous armed factions; this conflict, so much more complicated than a conventional war between two states, involved no FEWER than eight countries and twenty-five militias.**

The first *between* is correct, since only two dates are mentioned.

The second *between* should be *among*, since the fighting involved more than two factions.

Yet should be a semicolon. *Yet* is illogical because the action in the second clause (*this conflict...militias*) did not happen <u>despite</u> the action in the first clause (*Between...factions*), as a word such as *yet* suggests.

The third *between* is correct, since only two states are mentioned.

Less should be *fewer*, because countries and militias are countable entities.

15.   **Most legislators—including MANY in the governor's own party—realize that the governor's budget would imperil the state's finances; nonetheless, the budget is likely to be approved, because few legislators want to anger voters by cutting spending or raising taxes.**

Both dashes are correct here. These dashes serve the same role as commas or parentheses, except that the dashes add extra emphasis, drawing the reader's attention to the somewhat surprising information in the phrase *including...own party*.

Much should be *many*, because legislators are countable.

Nonetheless should be preceded by a semicolon. *Nonetheless* is a conjunctive adverb, like *however* and *therefore*. A conjunctive adverb needs to be preceded by a semicolon if it is to separate one main clause from another. The clauses in question are *Most legislators...state's finances* and *the budget is likely to be approved*.

The comma before *because* is correct. *Because* is a subordinating conjunction; therefore, it can be separated from a main clause by a comma.

Sentence Correction

Now that you have completed your study of ODDS & ENDS, it is time to test your skills on problems that have actually appeared on real GMAT exams over the past several years.

The problem set that follows is composed of past GMAT problems from two books published by GMAC (Graduate Management Admission Council):

The Official Guide for GMAT Review, 11th Edition (pages 638–660)
The Official Guide for GMAT Verbal Review (pages 234–253)

The problems in the set below are primarily focused on ODDS & ENDS issues. For each of these problems, identify any errors relating to the odds & ends topics. Eliminate any answer choices that misuse connecting words, connecting punctuation, or expressions of quantity.

Odds & Ends
> *11th Edition:* 4, 69
> *Verbal Review:* 88

Although there are only a few Official Guide problems focused on Odds & Ends issues, these issues show up in other Official Guide problems as well. Consult the Official Guide Matrix in the next chapter for more practice.

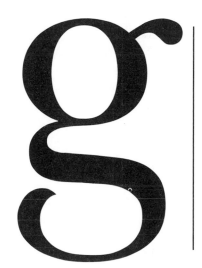

Chapter 11
of
SENTENCE CORRECTION

OFFICIAL GUIDE
PROBLEM SET &
PROBLEM MATRIX

Sentence Correction

from *The Official Guide for GMAT Review, 11th Edition* (pages 39–43 & 638–660) and *The Official Guide for GMAT Verbal Review* (pages 234–253).
The following is a REVIEW of all the Official Guide problem sets included in this guide.
Note: Problem numbers preceded by "D" refer to questions in the Diagnostic Test chapter of *The Official Guide for GMAT Review, 11th Edition* (pages 39–43).

Set 1: Complete after the GRAMMAR, MEANING, CONCISION chapter.
11th Edition: 8, 12, 14, 33, 36, 44, 50, 80, 103, 108, 120, 124, 135
Verbal Review: 2, 13, 57, 76, 83, 87

Set 2: Complete after the SUBJECT–VERB AGREEMENT chapter.
11th Edition: 1, 3, 21, 34, 41, 42, 52, 61, 74, 77, 90, 101, 116, 131, 138, D41, D43
Verbal Review: 8, 16, 24, 34, 35, 44, 59, 77, 104

Set 3: Complete after the PARALLELISM chapter.
11th Edition: 9, 11, 17, 18, 19, 22, 35, 39, 46, 47, 49, 54, 56, 60, 64, 65, 84, 86, 87, 88, 91, 106, 112, 113, 117, 119, 129, 130, 132, 134, 136, D36, D39, D46, D48, D50, D51
Verbal Review: 1, 4, 6, 11, 22, 25, 27, 46, 47, 51, 52, 56, 62, 64, 66, 70, 81, 82, 84, 93, 97, 99, 100, 108

Set 4: Complete after the PRONOUNS chapter.
11th Edition: 5, 43, 127, 133, D42
Verbal Review: 12, 15, 19, 29, 41, 44, 49, 53, 60, 65, 67, 71, 72, 74, 102, 107

Set 5: Complete after the MODIFIERS chapter.
11th Edition: 7, 20, 24, 38, 67, 71, 72, 78, 89, 93, 98, 102, 105, 109, 110, 111, 114, D40, D44, D49
Verbal Review: 7, 18, 32, 38, 63, 73, 78, 79, 91, 96, 110, 111, 112

Set 6: Complete after the VERB TENSE, MOOD, & VOICE chapter.
11th Edition: 15, 48, 53, 57, 58, 59, 62, 75, 79, 81, 82, 83, 126, 137
Verbal Review: 3, 21, 28, 30, 37, 39, 40, 55, 61, 78, 80, 86, 95, 103

Set 7: Complete after the COMPARISONS chapter.
11th Edition: 6, 10, 13, 16, 23, 26, 37, 66, 68, 73, 76, 85, 95, 96, 97, 99, 100, 104, 122, 123, 125, 128, D35, D37, D47, D52
Verbal Review: 10, 23, 31, 33, 36, 42, 45, 68, 92, 94, 98, 101, 105, 106

Set 8: Complete after the IDIOMS chapter.
11th Edition: 2, 25, 27, 28, 29, 30, 31, 32, 40, 45, 51, 55, 63, 70, 92, 94, 107, 115, 118, 121, D38, D45
Verbal Review: 5, 9, 14, 17, 20, 26, 43, 48, 50, 54, 58, 69, 75, 89, 90, 109, 113

Set 9: Complete after the ODDS & ENDS chapter.
11th Edition: 4, 69
Verbal Review: 88

*Manhattan*GMAT*Prep
the new standard

OFFICIAL GUIDE
PROBLEM MATRIX

The following pages contain a MATRIX that identifies the grammatical topics tested by each Sentence Correction question in *The Official Guide for GMAT Review, 11th Edition* (pages 39–43 & 638–660) and *The Official Guide for GMAT Verbal Review* (pages 234–253).

Use this MATRIX to complete the following exercise:

(1) Review each Sentence Correction question and find all of the grammatical problems in both the original sentence AND each of the answer choices.

(2) Use the MATRIX to check whether you have correctly identified all of the grammatical issues tested by each question.

The following matrix refers to Sentence Correction questions in *The Official Guide for GMAT Review, 11th Edition* (pages 39–43 & 638–660). <u>Note</u>: Problem numbers preceded by "D" refer to questions in the Diagnostic Test chapter (pages 39–43).

#	Concision & Clarity	Subj-Verb Agreement	Verb Tense/Voice/Mood	Pronouns
D35				
D36	wordiness	fragment		missing antecedents
D37	wordiness	fragment	verbal (gerund)	
D38	wordiness			
D39				
D40				ambiguous antecedents
D41		'discovery' is singular		missing antecedents
D42	wordiness		tense	ambiguous antecedents
D43	wordiness	'proportion' is singular		
D44		fragment		missing antecedent
D45		fragment	voice	
D46		fragment	tense	
D47				
D48				
D49			tense	
D50				ambiguous antecedents
D51	wordiness		voice	
D52	wordiness			
1	wordiness	'surge' is singular	tense	
2	wordiness		tense	
3	clarity; word placement	'Diabetes' is singular	tense	
4				
5	redundancy		voice	agreement in number
6	wordiness			
7			tense	
8	wordiness; word choice	'inventories' is plural		
9				
10				
11				
12	redundancy; word choice			
13				
14	double negative			
15		fragment		
16				
17			tense	
18			verbal (infinitive)	
19	redundancy, wordiness		verbal (gerund)	
20				missing antecedent
21		'fragments' is plural		
22				missing antecedent

#	Modifiers	Parallelism	Comparisons	Idioms / Diction	Odds & Ends
D35	misplaced modifiers	clauses	noun phrases	unlike	colon
D36		verb phrases		show; every	
D37		noun phrases	noun phrases	like; result	
D38		prep. phrases; infinitives		indicate; can / capable / ability	
D39		verb phrases		not / but; likely; begin	
D40	modifying phrases	modifying phrases			run-on sentence
D41		action noun phrases		indicate	
D42				object; so long as	
D43	modifying phrases				
D44	modifying phrases	modifying phrases			comma
D45	modifying phrases			declare	
D46	adverb vs. adjective	clauses		as / as; same	
D47			noun phrases	like; ability; develop	
D48		modifying phrases		more / than; tool	
D49	misplaced modifiers				
D50		verb phrases		way	
D51		nouns	clauses	can; because	
D52		clauses	clauses	as / so	
1				being	
2				more than; perhaps	
3				rank; only	
4			numbers	double	quantity: 'much' vs. 'many'
5					
6			noun phrases	like, as	
7	essential vs. non-essential				
8	adverb vs. adjective			if; can	
9	modifying phrases	verb phrases		but; surface	
10			noun phrases	reluctant	
11		verb phrases		create	
12	adverb vs. adjective			after; decline	
13			superlative form	most; since	
14	modifying clause			or	
15				although	
16			nouns	unlike	
17		verb phrases			
18	incorrect modifier	clauses		so too	run-on sentence
19		verbs of being		try	
20	modifier placement			based on	
21				estimate	
22		verb phrases			

#	Concision & Clarity	Subj-Verb Agreement	Verb Tense/Voice/Mood	Pronouns
23				
24				
25	wordiness			missing antecedent, agreement
26				
27	wordiness			
28				
29				agreement in number
30				
31				
32				
33	wordiness			
34	wordiness	'efforts' is plural		
35				
36	clarity of meaning			
37				
38				each
39			participles	
40				
41		'are' is plural		
42		fragment		
43	wordiness			missing antecedent
44	wordiness			
45	wordiness		tense, passive voice	
46	redundancy, wordiness			placeholder it
47				
48	redundancy, wordiness		subjunctive mood	
49	redundancy, wordiness	'programs' is plural		
50	wordiness			placeholder it
51	wordiness			ambiguous antecedent
52		fragment; agreement		agreement in number; each/all
53			subjunctive mood	
54	wordiness		passive voice	
55			tense	
56				
57	wordiness		conditional	ambiguous antecedents
58			tense	that of
59	redundancy, word placement		tense	
60				
61		'enrollments' is plural	tense	agreement in number
62	false concision		tense	

#	Modifiers	Parallelism	Comparisons	Idioms / Diction	Odds & Ends
23			comparative vs. superlative	most; difficult; probably	
24	participle modifier				
25				because	
26			prepositional phrases	same	semicolon; articles
27				danger	
28		verb phrases		whether; can	
29				seem; indicate	
30				as / as; even	
31				credit	
32				expect	
33				so / that; economic	
34				significant; reduce	
35		adjective phrases		find	
36				so that	
37			clauses	as many as	
38	adjective vs. adverb			targeted	
39		verb phrases			
40				between	
41		prepositions			
42				believe	
43	participle modifier				
44				require; from / to	
45	'that' modifier clause	verb phrases		confidence; instead	
46		clauses			
47		adverbial phrases, 'and'			
48		verb phrases		recommend	
49	essential vs. non-essential	verb phrases			
50				fault	
51				for (conjunction)	
52				similar	
53				require	
54		verb phrases		try; restriction	
55		verb phrases		not only / but also; aggravate	
56		participle phrases, mod. clauses		act	
57				secure	
58				doubt	
59	adjective vs. adverb				
60	adjective vs. adverb	verb phrases		means	
61		verb forms		number	
62				allow	

#	Concision & Clarity	Subj-Verb Agreement	Verb Tense/Voice/Mood	Pronouns
63			tense; verbals	ambiguous/illogical anteced.
64	wordiness			
65				agreement in number
66				
67	wordiness			
68	wordiness		tense	
69	wordiness	'dioxins' is plural		
70		'it' is singular		
71				
72			passive voice	
73				
74	clarity of meaning	fragment	verb tense	
75			tense	
76			tense	
77	redundancy	'costs' is plural		
78			tense	
79			tense	
80	wordiness, clarity of meaning			
81			tense	
82			subjunctive mood	
83			subjunctive mood	
84				missing antecedents
85				
86	clarity of meaning	fragment	passive voice	
87		fragment		missing antecedent
88			verbals	
89				relative pronouns
90		'pattern' is singular		
91				ambiguous antecedent
92			subjunctive mood	agreement in number
93				agreement in number
94			infinitive use	
95			tense	
96				
97	wordiness, redundancy			
98	wordiness			ambiguous antecedent
99				
100	wordiness			
101		fragment	tense; infinitive use	
102				ambiguous antecedent

#	Modifiers	Parallelism	Comparisons	Idioms / Diction	Odds & Ends
63				whether	
64	essential vs. non-essential	nouns, 'is' vs. 'refers to'		allow	
65		infinitives			
66		verb forms	noun phrases	unlike; require	
67	dangling modifier			attribute	
68			noun phrases; modifiers	unlike; disinclined	
69					much vs. many
70		infinitives; 'and'		enough	
71	use of 'which' modifier			know	
72	modifier placement				
73		verbs, prepositions	clauses	like, as	
74					
75				same	
76			clauses	as / as	
77			numbers	less	
78	misplaced modifier				
79				use	
80				require	
81					
82				require	
83				mandate	
84		infinitives		require	
85			clauses		
86		verbs, prepositional phrases			
87		noun phrases		not / but rather	semicolon
88		verb phrases		more	
89					
90					
91		verb phrases			
92		clauses		order	
93	unclear modifiers				
94				whether; can; train; help	
95	unclear modifiers		nouns	unlike	
96			noun phrases	more than	
97	misplaced modifier	clauses	nouns	like, as	
98	Incorrect relative pronouns				quantity words
99		clauses	clauses	as / so	
100			numbers		
101	Incorrect relative pronouns				
102	misplaced mod., relative clause				

#	Concision & Clarity	Subj-Verb Agreement	Verb Tense/Voice/Mood	Pronouns
103	clarity	logic		
104	wordiness			
105	wordiness			
106				
107			possessed gerund	
108	redundancy			
109				
110	clarity	logic		illogical antecedent
111	clarity	logic		ambiguous antecedent
112		'reduction' is singular	possessed gerund	
113	clarity			
114	wordiness			
115				unmodified these
116		'market' is singular	tense	
117				
118	wordiness			
119			verbals	
120	redundancy; concision; clarity			
121				
122				
123				agreement in number
124	wordiness; clarity		tense	
125				
126		'density' is singular	if / then constructions	
127				agreement in number
128	wordiness			
129			passive voice	
130	wordiness			
131	wordiness; clarity	'words' is plural	tense	
132	wordiness			
133				agreement, logic
134				
135	clarity		tense	
136	clarity; redundancy		tense	
137			tense	agreement
138		agreement errors		

#	Modifiers	Parallelism	Comparisons	Idioms / Diction	Odds & Ends
103	essential vs. non-essential		clauses		
104		participial phrases	clauses	like, as; rather than	
105	misplaced mod.; essential			can	
106		verb phrases		either / or; aid	
107	'which' modifier clause			distinguish	
108				being; whether	
109	dangling/misplaced modifiers				
110	need a comma for modifier				
111	illogical modifiers				semicolon
112		noun phrases with 'both'		both / and	
113		verb phrases			run-on sentence
114	proper modifier for 'hypothesis'				
115		infinitives		consider	
116					
117		action noun phrases			
118				lack; so / that; so / as to	
119		action noun phrases			
120				cost	
121	misplaced modifier			claim	
122			noun phrases	as / like	
123			clauses	than	
124					
125	misplaced modifier		noun phrases	like; view	
126					quantity words
127		verb phrases		so / that	
128			clauses	twice; as / as	
129		verb phrases		persuade	
130	relative pronouns	clauses			
131	relative clauses				
132		action noun phrases			
133				refer	
134		noun phrases			
135				as	
136		verb phrases		decline	
137		clauses		expect	
138				determine	

The following matrix refers to Sentence Correction questions in *The Official Guide for GMAT Verbal Review* (pages 234–253).

#	Concision & Clarity	Subj-Verb Agreement	Verb Tense/Voice/Mood	Pronouns
1				
2	clarity: known/unknown			
3	wordiness		tense	
4			tense	
5	redundancy		voice	
6				ambiguous or missing antecedents
7	wordiness		voice	
8		'cost' is singular; fragment		
9				
10		fragment		
11		compound subject is plural		
12				agreement in number
13	wordiness; clarity		tense	
14				
15				agreement in number
16	redundancy; wordiness	'values' is plural	passive voice	
17	clarity			
18				
19				ambiguous agreement; number
20			passive voice	agreement in number
21			tense	
22	wordiness, clarity		passive voice	
23	wordiness			
24		2 singular subjects		
25				
26	wordiness, clarity			
27	altered intent			
28			tense consistency	
29	clarity of meaning		tense	ambiguous antecedents
30		compound subject is plural	tense	agreement in number
31				
32			tense	agreement
33				
34	wordiness	'equipment' is singular		
35	clarity of meaning	'rise' is singular	tense	
36	wordiness			
37	redundancy		tense	
38	clarity of meaning		voice	
39			tense; if/then	
40			tense	

OFFICIAL GUIDE PROBLEM MATRIX (Verbal Review)   Chapter 11

#	Modifiers	Parallelism	Comparisons	Idioms / Diction	Odds & Ends
1		verb phrases			
2		clauses		agree	run-on sentence
3	rel. pronouns; misplaced mod.				
4		verb phrases		not / but; evolve	
5				number; raise	
6	illogical modifiers	noun phrases			
7	dangling modifier			decide	
8				rise	
9				range	
10	which		clauses	instance; such as; like	semicolon; run-on
11		noun clauses			
12				as; being	
13				except; being	
14				between	
15					
16					
17				mistake; rise	
18	illogical modifiers			with; being; although	
19				because; potentially	
20				think	
21	misplaced modifiers				
22		partly		because	
23				like; as	
24					
25		simple gerunds		aim	
26		verb phrases		significant; reduce; aid	
27	illogical modifiers	clauses			
28				refer; anxiety	
29	illogical modifiers		superlative form		
30					
31			nouns	like; as	
32	meaning; rel. clause vs. participle				
33	adjective vs. adverb		numbers	than	
34	misplaced modifiers				
35		independent clauses		continue	
36			action noun phrases	than	
37	misplaced modifiers				
38	dangling modifier				
39	adjective vs. adverb		clauses		
40				elect; rather than	

255

#	Concision & Clarity	Subj-Verb Agreement	Verb Tense/Voice/Mood	Pronouns
41	clarity		subjunctive mood	agreement
42				
43	wordiness			
44	clarity of meaning	'term' is singular	tense	agreement
45				
46	wordiness	fragment	voice	
47				
48				
49			tense	agreement in number
50				
51				
52				
53	wordiness			ambiguous antecedent
54	wordiness; clarity			
55	redundancy		subjunctive mood	relative pronouns
56	clarity			
57	wordiness		tense	
58	clarity	fragment		ambiguous antecedent
59		logic		agreement; ambiguity
60				missing antecedent
61	wordiness, clarity of meaning		verbal (infinitive)	missing pronoun
62				
63	clarity			
64				missing antecedent
65			tense	it vs. so
66				
67	wordiness			agreement in number
68		agreement errors		
69	wordiness; clarity			missing antecedent
70			tense	missing antecedent
71				ambiguous antecedents
72				agreement in number
73				
74	redundancy		voice	agreement in number
75	wordiness			
76	redundancy; wordiness			
77		singular pronouns		agreement in number
78	clarity		if / then constructions	
79				ambiguous/missing antec.
80		fragment	tense	

#	Modifiers	Parallelism	Comparisons	Idioms / Diction	Odds & Ends
41				require	
42			noun phrases	unlike	
43				as; being	
44				range	
45		verb phrases	noun phrases	contrast	
46		verb phrases		not only / but also	semicolon
47		subordinate clauses	position of more	ever	
48				ban; prohibit	
49	adjective vs. adverb				
50			noun phrases	invest; even	
51		action noun phrases		from / to	
52		verb phrases		not only / but also	
53				rule; owe	
54		adjectives; clauses		reveal; both / and	
55				demand	
56	adjective vs. adverb	noun phrases		rather than	
57	dangling modifier			lack	
58				so / that	
59					
60		noun phrases		not / but	semicolon
61				to + verb	
62		infinitives			
63	dangling & misplaced mod.			suggest; reason	semicolon
64		adjective phrases			
65				do so	
66		verb phrases		not only / but also	
67		noun phrases		rate	
68			noun phrases	unlike	
69				to + verb; than	
70		infinitives			
71		verb phrases		not only / but also	
72			numbers	number	semicolon
73	misplaced mod.; adj. vs. adverb			being	
74					
75			noun phrases	as /as	
76				rate	
77					
78	adj. vs. adverb; misplaced mod.				
79	illogical modifiers				
80				to + verb	

#	Concision & Clarity	Subj-Verb Agreement	Verb Tense/Voice/Mood	Pronouns
81	wordiness			
82				
83	redundancy		if / then constructions	
84	wordiness			
85	redundancy			missing antecedent
86			tense	missing antecedent
87	clarity: multiple meanings			
88		agreement		
89				agreement in number
90	wordiness			
91				
92				
93				
94				
95	wordiness		if / then constructions	
96			subjunctive mood	
97				
98			verbal (gerund)	
99				
100	wordiness			
101				
102			tense	agreement
103			tense	
104		'papers' is plural	tense	
105	wordiness, clarity		tense	missing antecedents
106				
107				ambiguous antecedents
108				
109	wordiness			missing antecedents
110	wordiness			
111	wordiness			
112				
113	redundancy			

#	Modifiers	Parallelism	Comparisons	Idioms / Diction	Odds & Ends
81		noun phrases		worry; and; in that; being	
82		action noun phrases		variation	
83					
84	illogical modifiers	verb phrases		either / or; result	
85					
86				allow	
87				with	
88					quantity words
89				than; such	
90				order	
91	misplaced modifier			substitute	
92			numbers	as / as	
93	misplaced modifier	verb phrases; noun phrases		and; both / and	
94			implied clauses	as / as; than	
95				connection	
96	misplaced modifiers			propose	
97		noun phrases			
98			subordinate clauses		
99		infinitives		rather than	
100	misplaced modifiers	simple gerunds	examples	such as; like	
101			independent clauses	but; unlike	
102					
103	possessives				
104		noun phrases			
105		noun phrases	examples	such as; like; more	
106			ambiguous comparison	isolated	
107	misplaced modifiers; essential				run-on sentence
108		prepositional phrases		not only / but also	
109	who vs. that			influence; inspire	
110	misplaced modifier				
111	misplaced/awkward mod.			being	semicolon
112	misplaced modifier				
113				result	

Appendix
of
SENTENCE CORRECTION

GLOSSARY

Glossary

The following is a list of grammatical terms used in this guide.

Absolute Phrase – A phrase that consists of a noun and a noun modifier and that modifies a whole clause or sentence. An absolute phrase cannot stand alone as a sentence, but it often expresses an additional thought. An absolute phrase is separated from the main clause by a comma; it may come before or after that main clause. See Modifier.
Examples:
The car fell into the lake, the cold water filling the compartment.
His arm in pain, Guillermo strode out of the building.

Action Noun – A noun that expresses an action. Action nouns are often derived fron verbs. In general, action nouns should be made parallel only to other action nouns or to complex gerunds.
Examples:
- TION: construction, pollution, redemption
- AL: arrival, reversal
- MENT: development, punishment
- Same as verb: change, rise

Active Voice – The form of a verb in which the subject is doing the action expressed by the verb. See Voice.
Examples: The driver swerved. The tires exploded. They broke the lamp.

Additive Phrase – Modifier phrases that "add" nouns onto another noun. However, additive phrases cannot change the number of the noun they modify.
Examples:
along with me   in addition to the memo   as well as a dog
accompanied by her   together with the others   including them.

Adjective – A word that modifies a noun.
Examples:
Descriptive: wonderful food, terrible sleep, green eyes, hungry minds
Demonstrative: this song, that moon, these costs, those sides
Noun used as adjective: forest fire, garage band
Present participle: the changing seasons
Past participle: the hidden ranch

Adverb – A word that modifies a verb, an adjective, another adverb, or even a whole clause. Most adverbs end in *-ly,* but not all.
Examples:
The stone fell slowly. A swiftly frozen lake. We ran very quickly.

*ManhattanGMAT*Prep

Antecedent – The noun that a pronoun refers to.
Example:
The <u>rowers</u> lifted the <u>boat</u> and flipped <u>it</u> over <u>their</u> heads.
Rowers is the antecedent of *their. Boat* is the antecedent of *it.*

Appositive – A noun or noun phrase that is placed next to another noun to identify it. Often separated from the rest of the sentence by commas.
Example:
The coach, <u>an old classmate of mine</u>, was not pleased.
An old classmate of mine is an appositive phrase to the noun *coach.*

Article – The words *a, an,* or *the.* An article must be followed by a noun (perhaps with modifiers in between). Articles can be considered special adjectives.

Bare Form – The dictionary form of a verb (what you would look up in a dictionary). A bare form has no endings added on, such as *-s, -ed,* or *-ing.* The bare form is the infinitive without the *to* in front.
Examples:
Assess bark command decide eavesdrop furnish gather

Bossy Verb – A verb that tells someone to do something. Bossy verbs take the Command Subjunctive or an infinitive (or either construction), depending on the verb.
Examples:
I <u>told</u> him to run. He <u>requested</u> that the bus wait another minute.
The verb *to tell (told)* takes the infinitive. *Request* takes the Command Subjunctive.

Case – The grammatical role that a noun or pronoun plays in a sentence.
Subject Case (subject role): I, you, she, he, it, we, they
Object Case (object role): me, you, her, him, it, us, them
Possessive Case (ownership role): my/mine, your(s), her(s), his, its, our(s), their(s)
Nouns show the possessive case by adding *'s* or *s'.*

Clause – A group of words that contains a subject and a working verb.
Examples:
Main or independent: <u>This is nice</u>. <u>Yesterday I ate a pizza in haste</u>.
Subordinate or dependent: Yesterday I ate a pizza <u>that I did not like</u>. <u>When I think about that pizza</u>, I feel ill.

Collective Noun – A noun that looks singular (it does not end in *-s*) but that refers to a group of people or things. Almost always considered singular on the GMAT.
Examples:
The <u>army</u> is recruiting again. This <u>team</u> was beaten.

Command Subjunctive – Subjunctive form used with certain Bossy Verbs and similar constructions. Same in form as a direct command. See Subjunctive Mood.
Examples:
The draft board required that he register for selective service.

Comparative Form – Form of adjectives and adverbs used to compare two things or people. Regular comparative forms are either the base word plus *-er* (if the base is short, e.g. *greener*) or the base word preceded by *more* (*more intelligent*). Irregulars are listed below:

Adjective or Adverb	Comparative
Good/Well	Better
Bad/Badly	Worse
Much, Many	More
Little	Less
Far	Farther, further

Comparisons – Structures by which we compare things or people in sentences. Usually marked with signal words such as *like, unlike, as,* or *than.* Comparisons can be between 2 things or people (comparative) or among 3 or more things or people (superlative).

Complex Gerund – A gerund (an *-Ing* form of a verb used as a noun) that is made even more "noun-like" by the form of the surrounding words:
(1) Articles (*a, an, the*)   I prefer a quick reading of the text.
(2) Adjectives   I prefer a quick reading of the text.
(3) *Of*-phrases for objects   I prefer a quick reading of the text.
The gerund phrase *a quick reading of the text* is the object of the verb *prefer.* Contrast *I prefer quickly reading the text.*
Complex gerund phrases can be put in parallel with action nouns, but simple gerund phrases cannot be. See Gerund.

Concrete Noun – A noun that does not represent an action. Concrete nouns refer to things, people, places, and even time periods or certain events. Generally, concrete nouns are not logically parallel to action nouns.
Examples:
volcano hole proton senator area month Halloween

Conditional Tense – A verb tense formed by combining the helping verb *would* with the base form of the verb. See Tense.
Examples:
Future as seen from the past: He said that he would write.
Hypothetical result of unlikely condition: If she liked pizza, she would like this restaurant.

Conjunction – A word that joins two parts of a sentence together. Coordinating and correlative conjunctions give the two parts equal weight. Subordinating conjunctions put one part in a logically junior role, in relation to the other part.
Examples:
Coordinating: and, but, or   (Less common) for, nor, so, yet
Correlative: either...or... neither...nor... not...but... not only...but also...
Subordinating: after, although, because, before, if, since, when, etc.

Conjunctive Adverb – A transition word or phrase that is used after a semicolon to help connect two main clauses. Conjunctive adverbs are not true conjunctions.
Examples:
therefore, thus, consequently, however, nevertheless, furthermore, etc.
The general was stuck in traffic; <u>therefore</u>, the ceremony started late.

Connecting Punctuation – The comma (,), the semicolon (;), the colon (:), and the dash (—). Used to link parts of the sentence.

Connecting Words – Conjunctions, conjunctive adverbs, and relative pronouns. Used to link parts of the sentence.

Countable Noun – A noun that can be counted in English. For instance, you can say *one hat, two hats, three hats.* Countable nouns can be made singular or plural.
Examples:
hat/hats   month/months   thought/thoughts   person/people

Dangling Modifier – A noun modifier that does not properly modify or describe any noun in the sentence. In fact, the noun that should be modified has been omitted from the sentence. Likewise, a verb modifier that requires a subject but lacks one in the sentence is considered dangling. Dangling modifiers are always incorrect. See <u>Modifier</u>.
Example:
<u>Walking along the river</u>, the new tower can be seen.
The modifier *walking along the river bank* has no subject. The sentence could be rewritten thus: *Walking along the river, one can see the new tower.*

Demonstrative Pronoun – The pronouns *this, that, these,* and *those.* Demonstrative pronouns can be used as adjectives (*these plants, that company*). They can also be used in place of nouns, but they must be modified in some way, according to the GMAT. See <u>Pronoun</u>.
Example:
The strategy taken by Livonia is preferable to <u>that</u> taken by Khazaria.
The demonstrative pronoun *that* properly stands for the noun *strategy.* The pronoun *that* is modified by the phrase *taken by Khazaria.*

Dependent Clause – A clause that cannot stand alone without a main or independent clause. A dependent clause is led by a subordinator. Also known as a Subordinate Clause. See <u>Clause</u>.

Manhattan **GMAT** Prep
the new standard

Direct Object – The noun that is acted upon by a verb in the active voice. Can be a pronoun, a noun phrase, or a noun clause.
  Examples:
  I broke <u>the lamp</u>. Who let <u>the big dogs</u> out? I believe <u>that you are right</u>.

Essential Modifier – A modifier that provides necessary information. Use an essential modifier to identify the particular noun out of many possibilities or to create a permanent description of the noun. Do not use commas to separate an essential modifier from the modified noun. See <u>Modifier</u>.
  Example:
  I want to sell the car <u>that my sister drove to the city</u>.

Fragment – A group of words that does not work as a stand-alone sentence, either because it is begun by a subordinator or because it lacks a subject or a verb.
  Examples:
  Although he bought a pretzel. The device developed by scientists.

Future Tense – The form of a verb that expresses action in the future. Also known as Simple Future. See <u>Tense</u>.
  Examples:
  The driver <u>will swerve</u>. The tires <u>will be punctured</u>. They <u>will break</u> the lamp.

Gerund – An *-Ing* form of a verb used as a noun.
  Examples:
  <u>Skiing</u> is fun. She enjoys <u>skiing</u>. She often thinks about <u>skiing</u>.

Gerund Phrase – A phrase centered on an *-Ing* form of a verb used as a noun.
  Examples:
  Simple: <u>Skiing difficult trails</u> is fun.
  Complex: We discussed <u>the grooming of the horses</u>.

Helping Verb – A verb used with another verb. Helping verbs create various grammatical structures or provide additional shades of meaning.
  Primary: Be Do Have
                   I <u>am</u> running. He <u>did</u> not run. She <u>has</u> run.
  Modal: Can Could May Might Must Shall Should Will Would
                   We <u>must</u> go to the bank. He <u>should</u> take his medicine.

Hypothetical Subjunctive – Subjunctive form that indicates unlikely or unreal conditions. This form is used in some cases after the words *if, as if,* or *as though,* or with the verb *to wish.* The Hypothetical Subjunctive is equivalent to the Simple Past tense of every verb, except the verb *to be:* the Hypothetical Subjunctive of *be* is *were* for every subject. See <u>Subjunctive Mood</u>.
  Examples:
  If he <u>were</u> in better shape, he would win the race.

Idiom – An expression that has a unique form. Idioms do not follow general rules; rather, they must simply be memorized.

If-Then Statement – A sentence that contains both a condition (marked by an *If*) and a result (possibly marked by a *Then*). Either the condition or the result may come first. The verbs in If-Then statements follow particular patterns of tense and mood.
Examples:
If he were in better shape, he would win the race.
They get sick if they eat dairy products. If she swims, then she will win.

Imperative Mood – The form of a verb that expresses direct commands. Identical to the bare form of the verb, as well as to the Command Subjunctive. See <u>Mood</u>.
Examples:
<u>Go</u> to the store and <u>buy</u> me an ice cream cone.

Indefinite Pronoun – A pronoun that does not refer to a specific noun. Most indefinite pronouns are singular:

Anyone, anybody, anything	No one, nobody, nothing
Each, every *(as pronouns)*	Someone, somebody, something
Everyone, everybody, everything	Whatever, whoever

Either, neither *(may require a plural verb if paired with or/nor)*
A few indefinite pronouns are always plural:
Both Few Many Several
The SANAM pronouns can be either singular or plural, depending on the noun in the *Of*-phrase that follows the pronoun.
Some Any None All More/Most

Independent Clause – A clause that can stand alone as a grammatical sentence. Contains its own subject and verb. Also known as a <u>Main Clause</u>.

Indicative Mood – The form of a verb that expresses facts or beliefs. Most verbs in most English sentences are in the indicative mood. See <u>Mood</u>.
Examples:
I <u>went</u> to the store and <u>bought</u> an ice cream cone. I <u>will do</u> so again.

Indirect Object – The noun that expresses the recipient or the beneficiary of some action. Can be a pronoun, a noun phrase, or a noun clause.
Examples:
I gave <u>him</u> the lamp. She found <u>the man</u> a good book.

Infinitive – The bare form of the verb plus the marker *to*. Used as a noun or as a modifier within a sentence.
Examples:
I prefer <u>to read</u> novels. The strategy <u>to execute</u> is Arnold's. She drove many miles <u>to see</u> her uncle.

-Ing Form – The bare form of the verb plus the ending *-Ing*. When used as a noun, the *-Ing* form is called a gerund. When used as a modifier or as part of the progressive tense, the *-Ing* form is called a present participle.

Present Participle (part of verb): I am <u>eating</u> an apple.

Gerund (noun): <u>Eating</u> an apple is good for you.

Present Participle (noun modifier): The man <u>eating</u> an apple is my friend.

Present Participle (verb modifier): I sat on the porch, <u>eating</u> an apple.

Intransitive Verb – A verb that does not take a direct object. Intransitive verbs cannot be put in the passive voice.

Examples:

The driver <u>swerved</u>. I <u>went</u> to the library.

Intransitive verb *-Ing* forms followed by nouns are usually adjectives: *The <u>swerving driver</u> wound up on the sidewalk.*

Linking Verb – A verb that expresses what a subject is, rather than what it does. The most important linking verb is *to be*.

Main Clause – A clause that can stand alone as a grammatical sentence. A main clause contains its own subject and verb and is not introduced by a subordinator. Also known as an <u>Independent Clause</u>.

Examples:

<u>I prefer to read novels</u>. <u>He was changing the tires</u>.

Middleman – Words that the GMAT inserts between the subject and the verb to hide the subject. Middlemen are usually modifiers of various types.

Misplaced Modifier – A noun modifier that is not positioned next to the noun it needs to describe in the sentence. Misplaced modifiers are incorrect. See <u>Modifier</u>.

Example:

I collapsed onto the sofa, <u>exhausted by a long day of work</u>.

The modifier *exhausted by a long day at work* is misplaced. The sentence should be rewritten thus: *Exhausted by a long day of work, I collapsed onto the sofa.*

Modal Helping Verb – See <u>Helping Verb</u>.

Modifier – Words, phrases or clauses that describe other parts of the sentence. <u>Noun modifiers</u> modify nouns. <u>Verb modifiers</u> modify verbs.

Mood – The form of the verb that indicates the attitude of the speaker toward the action.

Indicative: I <u>drive</u> fast cars. We <u>drove</u> to Las Vegas.

Imperative: <u>Drive</u> three blocks and <u>turn</u> left.

Command Subjunctive: I suggested that he <u>drive</u> three blocks.

Hypothetical Subjunctive: If he <u>drove</u> three blocks, he would see us.

Non-essential Modifier – A modifier that provides extra information. You do not need a non-essential modifier to identify the noun, since it is already identified in some other way. Use commas to separate a non-essential modifier from the modified noun. See Modifier.
Example:
I want to sell this beat-up old car, <u>which my sister drove to the city</u>.

Noun – A word that means a thing or a person. Nouns can be the subject of a verb, the direct or indirect object of a verb, or the object of a preposition. Nouns can be modified by an adjective or another noun modifier.

Noun Clause – A subordinate clause (with its own subject and verb) that acts as a noun in the sentence. That is, it is the subject of a verb, the object of a verb, or the object of a preposition. Led by relative pronouns *which, what, when, why, whether* or *that*.
Examples:
I care about <u>what he thinks</u>. <u>Whether I stay or go</u> is unimportant.
I believe <u>that you are right</u>.

Noun Modifier – A word, phrase or clause that describes a noun.
Examples:
Adjective: <u>This</u> <u>big</u> window needs replacing.
Past Participle: <u>Broken in the storm</u>, this window needs replacing.
Present Participle: The window <u>rattling against the sill</u> needs replacing.
Prepositional Phrase: The window <u>on the right</u> needs replacing.
Appositive: This window, <u>an original installation</u>, needs replacing.
Infinitive: The window <u>to replace</u> is on the second floor.
Relative Clause: The window <u>that needs replacing</u> has a missing pane.

Noun Phrase – A phrase that acts as a noun in the sentence. A noun phrase typically consists of a noun and its modifiers.
Examples:
<u>A new government survey of taxpayers</u> is planned.
The subject of the sentence is the noun phrase consisting of the noun *survey* and its modifiers (*a, new, government, of taxpayers*).

Noun-Adjective – A noun that is placed in front of another noun and that functions as an adjective.
Examples:
A <u>government</u> survey. The <u>stone</u> wall.
A *government survey* is a type of survey, and a *stone wall* is a type of wall.

Object Case – The form of a pronoun used as the object of a verb or of a preposition. Nouns do not change form in the object case. See Case.

Parallel Element – A part of a sentence made parallel to another part or parts of the sentence through the use of parallel markers.
Examples:
We will invite both <u>his friends</u> and <u>her family</u>.

Parallel Marker – The words that link or contrast parts of a sentence, forcing them to be parallel.
Examples:
We will invite <u>both</u> his friends <u>and</u> her family.

Parallelism Category – A type of word, phrase, or clause. Something in one parallelism category can be made parallel to something else of the same type, but it should not be made parallel to anything in another category.
Examples:
Concrete Nouns: I like to eat <u>peanut butter</u> and <u>ice cream</u>.
Action Nouns and Complex Gerunds: I like to watch <u>the release of the doves</u> and <u>the changing of the guard</u>.
Simple Gerunds: I like <u>eating ice cream</u> and <u>watching birds</u>.
Working Verbs: I <u>like</u> ice cream but <u>hate</u> sorbet.
Infinitives: I like <u>to eat</u> ice cream and <u>to watch</u> birds.
Adjectives and Participles: I like ice cream, either <u>frozen</u> or <u>warm</u>.
Clauses: She knows <u>that I like ice cream</u> and <u>that I hate sorbet</u>.

Parts of Speech – The basic kinds of words. A word's part of speech is determined both by what the word means and by what role or roles the word can play in a sentence.
Examples:
Noun: peanut   lake   vacuum   considerations   opportunity
Verb: swim   proceed   execute   went   should
Adjective: wonderful   blue   the   helpful
Adverb: slowly   very   graciously
Preposition: of   for   by   with   through   during   in   on
Conjunction: and   but   or   although   because

Participle – One of two kinds of words derived from verbs. Present Participles end in -*ing*. Past Participles usually end in -*ed*, but there are many irregular forms. Participles are used in complex verb tenses or as modifiers. Like other <u>Verbals</u>, participles do not indicate tense by themselves. See also <u>Past Participle</u> and <u>Present Participle</u>.
Examples:
Present Participle: hiking   growing   giving   being   doing
Past Participle: hiked   grown   given   been   done

Passive Voice – The form of a verb in which the subject is receiving the action expressed by the verb. See <u>Voice</u>.
Examples: The driver <u>was thrown</u> from the car. The crystal vases <u>have been broken</u> by the thieves.

Past Participle – The participle used in perfect tenses and passive voice. A past participle may also be used as an adjective. Past participles tend to indicate completed action, although not necessarily in the past (relative to now).
Examples:
The tires will be <u>punctured</u>. They have <u>broken</u> the lamp. A <u>frozen</u> lake.
Regular past participles are formed by adding *-d* or *-ed* to the base form of the verb. Many irregular past participles are listed below, together with irregular past-tense forms. Sometimes the past-tense form and the past participle are identical. Non-native English speakers should study this list. Native English speakers already know these forms intuitively.

Base form	Past tense	Past participle	Base form	Past tense	Past participle
be	was, were	been	lose	lost	lost
become	became	become	make	made	made
begin	began	begun	pay	paid	paid
break	broke	broken	put	put	put
bring	brought	brought	rise	rose	risen
build	built	built	say	said	said
buy	bought	bought	see	saw	seen
catch	caught	caught	seek	sought	sought
choose	chose	chosen	sell	sold	sold
come	came	come	send	sent	sent
cost	cost	cost	set	set	set
cut	cut	cut	show	showed	shown
do	did	done	shrink	shrank	shrunk
draw	drew	drawn	speak	spoke	spoken
drive	drove	driven	spend	spent	spent
eat	ate	eaten	spread	spread	spread
fall	fell	fallen	stand	stood	stood
fight	fought	fought	steal	stole	stolen
find	found	found	strike	struck	struck
forget	forgot	forgotten	sweep	swept	swept
freeze	froze	frozen	take	took	taken
give	gave	given	teach	taught	taught
go	went	gone	tell	told	told
grow	grew	grown	think	thought	thought
hold	held	held	throw	threw	thrown
keep	kept	kept	understand	understood	understood
know	knew	known	win	won	won
lead	led	led	write	wrote	written

Past Perfect Tense – The form of a verb that expresses action that takes place before another past action or time. The past perfect tense is formed with the verb *had* and the past participle. See <u>Tense</u>.
Examples:
The officer said that the driver <u>had swerved</u>. By the time we arrived, the tires <u>had</u> already <u>been punctured</u>.

Past Tense – The form of a verb that expresses action in the past. See <u>Tense</u>.
Examples:
The driver <u>swerved</u>. The tires <u>were punctured</u>. They <u>broke</u> the lamp.
Common irregular past-tense forms are listed under the entry for <u>Past Participles</u>.

Person – Indicates whether the word refers to the speaker or writer (first person), the listener or reader (second person), or someone/something else (third person). Personal pronouns are marked for person. Present tense verbs in the third person singular add an *-s*: *the doctor writes*.
Examples:
First person: I me my we us our
Second person: you your
Third person: she he it its they them their

Phrase – A group of words that has a particular grammatical role in the sentence. The type of phrase is often determined by one main word within the phrase. A phrase can contain other phrases. For instance, a noun phrase can contain a prepositional phrase.
Examples:
Noun phrase: <u>The short **chapter** at the end of the book</u> is important.
Verb phrase: The computer <u>must have been **broken**</u> in the move.
Adjective phrase: The employee <u>most **reluctant** to volunteer</u> was chosen.
Prepositional phrase: The wolf <u>**in** the cage</u> has woken up.

Plural – A category of number that indicates "more than one." Nouns, pronouns, and verbs can be made plural. See <u>Singular</u>.
Examples:
<u>Many</u> <u>dogs</u> <u>are</u> barking; <u>they</u> <u>are</u> keeping me awake.

Possessive Case – The form of a pronoun or a noun that "owns" another noun. In possessive case, nouns add *-'s* or *-s'*. See <u>Case</u>.

Preposition – A word that indicates a relationship between the object (usually a noun) and something else in the sentence. In some cases, prepositions can consist of more than one word.
Examples:
of in to for with on by at from as into about like after between through over against under out of next to upon

Prepositional Phrase – A phrase that contains both a preposition and its object. Prepositional phrases can modify either nouns or verbs.
Examples:
A drink <u>of water</u> would be nice. She was born <u>in 1981</u>.

Present Participle – The participle used in progressive tenses. A present participle may also be used as a noun, a noun modifier or a verb modifier. Present participles tend to indicate ongoing action, although not necessarily at the present moment. To form a present participle, add -*ing* to the base form of the verb, possibly doubling the last consonant.
Examples:
The tires were <u>rolling</u>. Jump in that <u>swimming</u> pool. <u>Hiking</u> is great.

Present Perfect Tense – The form of a verb that expresses action that begins in the past and continues to the present (or whose effect continues to the present). The present perfect tense is formed with the verb *has* or *have* and the past participle. See <u>Tense</u>.
Examples:
The driver <u>has swerved</u>. The tires <u>have been punctured</u>. They <u>have bro-ken</u> the lamp.

Present Tense – The form of a verb that expresses action in the present. The Simple Present (non-progressive) often indicates general truths. See <u>Tense</u>.
Examples:
The driver <u>swerves</u>. The tires <u>are</u> on the car. They <u>speak</u> English.

Primary Helping Verb – See <u>Helping Verb</u>.

Progressive Tenses – The form of a verb that expresses ongoing action in the past, present, or future. See <u>Tense</u>.
Examples:
The driver <u>is swerving</u>. The tires <u>were rolling</u>. They <u>will be running</u>.

Pronoun – A word that stands for a noun. The noun is called the antecedent.
Examples:
Personal: it its they them their I me my we us our you your
Demonstrative: this that these those
Indefinite: some more all any one none much few several everyone
Reciprocal: each other one another
Reflexive: itself themselves
Relative: which that who whose whom when where whether what

Relative Clause – A subordinate clause headed by a relative pronoun. Relative clauses may act as noun modifiers or, more infrequently, as nouns.
Examples:
The professor <u>who spoke</u> is my mother. <u>What you see</u> is <u>what you get</u>.

Relative Pronoun – A pronoun that connects a subordinate clause to a sentence. The relative pronoun plays a grammatical role in the subordinate clause (e.g., subject, verb object, or prepositional object). If the relative clause is a noun modifier, the relative pronoun also refers to the modified noun. If the relative clause is a noun clause, then the relative pronoun does not refer to a noun outside the relative clause.

Examples:

The professor <u>who spoke</u> is my mother.

The relative pronoun *who* is the subject of the clause *who spoke. Who* also refers to *professor,* the noun modified by the clause *who spoke.*

<u>What you see</u> is a disaster waiting to happen.

The relative pronoun *what* is the object of the clause *what you see. What* does not refer to a noun outside the clause. Rather, the clause *what you see* is the subject of the sentence.

Reporting Verb – A verb, such as *indicate, claim, announce,* or *report,* that in fact reports or otherwise includes a thought or belief. A reporting verb should be followed by *that* on the GMAT.

Example:

The survey <u>indicates</u> that CFOs are feeling pessimistic.

Run-on Sentence – A sentence incorrectly formed out of two main clauses joined without proper punctuation or a proper connecting word, such as a subordinator.

Example:

The film was great, I want to see it again.

This sentence could be fixed with a semicolon as follows: *The film was great; I want to see it again.* Or one of the clauses could be made into a subordinate clause: *Because the film was great, I want to see it again.*

SANAM Pronouns – An indefinite pronoun that can be either singular or plural, depending on the object of the *Of*-phrase that follows. The SANAM pronouns are *Some, Any, None, All, More/Most.*

Examples:

<u>Some</u> of the milk <u>has</u> gone bad. <u>Some</u> of the children <u>are</u> angry.

Sentence – A complete grammatical utterance. Sentences contain a subject and a verb in a main clause. Some sentences contain two main clauses linked by a coordinating conjunction, such as *and.* Other sentences contain subordinate clauses tied to the main clause in some way.

Examples:

My boss is angry.

This sentence contains one main clause. The subject is *boss;* the verb is *is.*

He read my blog, and he saw the photos that I posted.

This sentence contains two main clauses linked by *and.* In the first main clause, the subject is *he;* the verb is *read.* In the second main clause, the subject is *he;* the verb is *saw.* There is also a subordinate clause, *that I posted,* led by the relative pronoun *that.*

Simple Gerund – A gerund (an -*Ing* form of a verb used as a noun in the overall sentence) that acts like a verb in its immediate surroundings:
(1) Adverbs   I prefer <u>quickly</u> reading the text.
(2) Direct objects   I prefer quickly <u>reading</u> <u>the text</u>.
The gerund phrase *quickly reading the text* is the object of the verb *prefer*.
Contrast *I prefer <u>a quick reading of the text</u>.*
Simple gerund phrases cannot be put in parallel with action nouns, but complex gerund phrases cannot be. See <u>Gerund</u>.

Singular – A category of number that indicates "one." Nouns, pronouns, and verbs can be made singular. See <u>Plural</u>.
Examples:
<u>A</u> <u>dog</u> <u>is</u> barking; <u>it</u> <u>is</u> keeping <u>me</u> awake.

State Verb – A verb that expresses a condition of the subject, rather than an action that the subject performs. State verbs are rarely used in progressive tenses.
Examples:
Her assistant <u>knows</u> Russian. I <u>love</u> chocolate. This word <u>means</u> "hello."

Subgroup Modifier – A type of modifier that describes a smaller subset within the group expressed by the modified noun.
Example:
French wines, <u>many of which I have tasted</u>, are superb.

Subject – The noun or pronoun that "goes with" the verb and that is required in every sentence. The subject performs the action expressed by an active-voice verb; in contrast, the subject receives the action expressed by a passive-voice verb. The subject and the verb must agree in number and in person.
Examples:
The <u>market</u> closed. <u>She</u> is considering a new job. <u>They</u> have been seen.

Subjunctive Mood – One of two verb forms indicating desires, suggestions, or unreal or unlikely conditions.
Examples:
Command Subjunctive: She requested that he <u>stop</u> the car.
Hypothetical Subjunctive: If he <u>were</u> in charge, he would help us.

Subordinate Clause – A clause that cannot stand alone without a main or independent clause. A subordinate clause is led by a subordinator. Also known as a Dependent Clause. See <u>Clause</u>.

Subordinator – A word that creates a subordinate clause.
Examples:
Relative Pronoun: which   that   who   whose   whom   what
Subordinating Conjunction: although   because   while   whereas

Superlative Form – Form of adjectives and adverbs used to compare three or more things or people. The reference group may be implied. Regular superlative forms are either the base word plus *-est* (if the base is short, e.g. *greenest*) or the base word preceded by *most* (*most intelligent*). Irregulars are listed below:

Adjective or Adverb	Superlative
Good/Well	Best
Bad/Badly	Worst
Much, Many	Most
Little	Least
Far	Farthest, furthest

Tense – The form of the verb that indicates the time of the action (relative to the present time). The completed or ongoing nature of the action may also be indicated.
Examples:
Present: She <u>speaks</u> French.
Past: She <u>spoke</u> French.
Future: She <u>will speak</u> French.
Present Progressive: She <u>is speaking</u> French.
Past Progressive: She <u>was speaking</u> French.
Future Progressive: She <u>will be speaking</u> French.
Present Perfect: She <u>has spoken</u> French.
Past Perfect: She <u>had spoken</u> French.

***That*-Clause** – A clause that begins with the word *that*.
Examples:
Relative Clause: The suggestion <u>that he made</u> is bad.
The clause *that he made* modifies *suggestion*. *That* is the object of the clause (in other words, *he made that = the suggestion*).
Subordinate Clause: He suggested <u>that the world is flat</u>.
The clause *that the world is flat* is the object of the verb *suggested*.
Subordinate Clause: The suggestion <u>that the world is flat</u> is bad.
The clause *that the world is flat* modifies *suggestion*. However, *that* is not the object of the clause, nor is it the subject. Rather, *that* provides a way for the idea in the sentence *the world is flat* to be linked to *the suggestion*.

Transitive Verb – A verb that takes a direct object. Transitive verbs can usually be put in the passive voice, which turns the object into the subject.
Examples:
The agent <u>observed</u> the driver. The driver <u>was observed</u> by the agent.
Transitive verb *-Ing* forms followed by nouns are usually simple gerund phrases: *The agent was paid for <u>observing the driver</u>.*
Some verbs can be either transitive or intransitive. In particular, verbs that indicate changes of state can be either: *The lamp <u>broke</u>. I <u>broke</u> the lamp.*
This duality means that some *-Ing* forms in isolation can be ambiguous. The phrase *melting snow* could mean "the act of causing snow to melt" or "snow that is melting." Use context to resolve the ambiguity.

Uncountable Noun – A noun that cannot be counted in English. For instance, you cannot say *one patience, two patiences, three patiences.* Most uncountable nouns exist only in the singular form and cannot be made plural.
Examples:
patience furniture milk information rice chemistry

Verb – The word or words that express the action of the sentence. The verb indicates the time of the action (tense), the attitude of the speaker (mood), and the role of the subject (voice). The verb may also reflect the number and person of the subject. Every sentence must have a verb.

Verb Modifier – A word, phrase or clause that describes a verb.
Examples:
Adverb: He walked <u>quickly</u>.
Prepositional Phrase: He walked <u>toward the building</u>.
Subordinate Clause: He walked <u>because he was thirsty</u>.
Present Participle: He walked ahead, <u>swinging</u> his arms.
Infinitive: He walked <u>to buy</u> a drink.
Preposition + Simple Gerund: He walked <u>by putting</u> one foot in front of the other.

Verbal – A word or phrase that is derived from a verb and that functions as a different part of speech in the sentence: as a noun, as an adjective (noun modifier), or as an adverb (verb modifier).
Examples:
Infinitive: He likes <u>to walk</u> to the store.
Gerund: I enjoy <u>walking</u>.
Present Participle: She is on a <u>walking</u> tour.
Past Participle: The facts <u>given</u> in the case are clear.

Voice – The form of the verb that indicates the role of the subject as performer of the action (active voice) or recipient of the action (passive voice).
Examples:
Active Voice: She <u>threw</u> the ball.
Passive Voice: The ball <u>was thrown</u> by her.

Warmup – Words that the GMAT inserts at the beginning of the sentence to hide the subject in question. Warmups are either modifiers of various types or "frame sentences" (that is, you really care about the subject of a subordinate clause, not the subject of the main clause).

Working Verb – A verb that could be the main verb of a grammatical sentence. A working verb shows tense, mood, and voice, as well as number and person in some circumstances. The use of this term helps to distinguish working verbs from verbals, which cannot by themselves be the main verb of a sentence.